love, Amy

AN ACCIDENTAL MEMOIR TOLD IN NEWSLETTERS FROM CHINA

AMY YOUNG

Love, Amy: An Accidental Memoir Told in Newsletters from China
By Amy Young
© 2017 Amy Young

Edited by Deb Hall
Cover design by Vanessa Mendozzi
Book design by Andy Bruner

ISBN 978-1546743293

To my mom
Marsha Young

As the recipient of a lifetime of your
notes, cards, and letters,
this book would not exist without
your pen and love.

I love you.

Contents

Introduction

I, Paul, am writing these greetings with my own hand.
—Apostle Paul

Living abroad can be an adventure. Guess what? So can reading a book by someone who learned to kill mice with a frying pan, spent time in a coma in a Chinese hospital, and visited students in countryside schools—all the while seeing God at work in and around her. The best adventures come with choices; as you embark on your reading journey you will have choices too.

I wrote the introduction because I wanted to share how I grew to love writing newsletters. But you may not write newsletters and since we are going to be spending time together, let's shoot straight with each other. You might not care about the process and want to get to the adventure. Permission granted to skip the introduction and dive straight into Year One in China. However, if you write newsletters, I see you. I know this part of your life can be hard. I want to help.

"You're lucky you're still in your first year. Wait until your second year and you have told all your stories. You'll have nothing to say in your newsletters." I can't remember her name, but in my mind's eye, I see us in crisp detail.

It was, as she accurately said, my first year on the field as a cross-cultural worker. I had five months under my belt of teaching at Sichuan College of Education, located in Chengdu, the provincial capital of Sichuan, and had made it to semester break. I had plans to travel with friends during the holiday. After a forty-eight-hour train ride from Chengdu to Shanghai with three friends and spending several days of "freezing tourism"—what else do you call vacationing in a part of the country with temperatures in the forties and all the buildings unheated?—we boarded another long train down to Guangzhou, a city on the border between mainland China and Hong Kong. The trip continued with an overnight boat ride with bunk beds in a big open room. Using my backpack as a pillow, I can't say it was the most restful night, but hey, we were on an overnight boat going to Hong Kong! We had come south. South! We were going to thaw and I might finally be warm.

During my five months in China my only exposure to news and the West came in weekly manila envelopes. My mom mailed me copies of my subscription to *Newsweek,* my sister mailed me *Sports Illustrated,* and my dad was an avid newspaper article clipper. Walking up the ramp from the boat depot onto the streets of Hong Kong, even though it was early morning and the city was mostly asleep, I was Alice entering Wonderland. My friends and I joked we had gone from the land of *mei-you* (said may-yo, meaning "don't have") to the land-of-*you* (pronounced yo, meaning "have"). If you have lived overseas or speak another language, you probably have language jokes that never get old to you, but they might not translate well. Over and over we practically squealed, "We're not in the land of *mei-you* anymore! It's all *you!*"

Honestly, we thought we were comedians. Looking back, I think we were cold, tired, worn-, and starving—you can only eat uncooked ramen noodles so many meals in a row—yet well-intentioned cross-cultural servants. The joke held its own as we walked in the early morning light to a McDonald's for breakfast. Did you hear me?! *You*—"have"— McDonald's! Enjoying the most magical meal I'd had in weeks, we couldn't believe we were actually in a land where it was this easy to feed yourself. By far the most challenging part of visiting Shanghai had been finding food, which made no sense: we were in a city of millions yet couldn't figure out where they ate. But *mei-you* was in the past, and now we were in the land-of-*you*.

In addition to food, guess what else the land of *you* had? Advertisements. Of course it did! If you have McDonald's, you have other aspects of consumer societies. Stating that Hong Kong had advertisements feels a bit like saying, "The ocean has water." So obvious, one forgets how deep an ocean is. Walking the streets of Hong Kong that first day with my friend Cynthia, we finally had to find a quiet place to sit down and process the pornography and disgusting consumerism that assaulted us. So-called "normal" advertising looked anything but normal when you haven't seen any for months. Was it necessary to have a neckline that low? Keep in mind, I'd forgotten what my neckline looked like under my seven sweaters I wore just to stay warm. Alice may be in Wonderland, but it turns out Wonderland has a dark side.

After several days in Hong Kong, and several more meals at McDonald's, our organization's annual conference started, the primary reason behind our trek south. For security reasons we were at a campsite outside of the city center. In subsequent years that conference was referred to as Camp Snoopy.

Four of us who roomed together in a "cabin" knew each other well. Because as first-year teachers we had spent an intense month together preparing for our time in China. We were eager to catch up and swap stories from our first semester. However, the other four women occupying the remaining two rooms were seasoned second-year teachers. We first-year teachers were a bit in awe of them and how much time they had spent in China. During introductions one of the second-years said the infamous line, "You're lucky you're still in your first year. Wait until your second year and you have told all your stories. You'll have nothing to say in your newsletters."

Wait, what?

Could it be true? Would I run out of things to share with family, friends, and supporters? At that point, I knew that I would return for a second year, yet I had no clue that a couple of decades would pass and I would still be in full-time ministry. Was it the fate of every second-year-in-the-field person to pump from a dry well when it came to newsletter writing? She seemed a credible source, as she was upbeat, loved teaching the Chinese, and enjoyed living in China. This wasn't a doom-and-gloom message from a cynic. She seemed to be genuinely envious of our new status that came with a fresh material for newsletters.

The Sad Truth Followed by the Good News

Fast-forward a few years and I had maybe sixty or so monthly newsletters under my belt. I was now living in the country's capital and serving on the staff of my organization. For the first time I was not on a two-person team and lived in closer proximity to fellow workers. You could probably see this coming, but it was a shock to me: it turns out that most of my colleagues dreaded writing newsletters. Dread wasn't the only word used to describe the process. Loathsome. Hate. Shudder at the thought of. Fret. Worry. Stressful. Once again, my sensitive and tuned-in self said, "Wait, what? You don't like writing newsletters?" Nope, they didn't. Actually, I was the odd person out.

What type of letters will be produced when people dread writing newsletters? When they cringe at how quickly time passes and they "have to" write another letter? Permission to speak frankly? Boring letters. You know it because you've read them—or at least moved your eyeballs around in case if asked you could honestly answer, "Yes, I read it." Are we all fated to dread newsletters—both the writing and the reading?

Here is the simple good news of writing and reading newsletters: newsletters can be anticipated, savored, honest, heartbreaking, and hopeful.

I can already sense the eye rolling by some as well as the pushback. "Easy for you to say—you wrote a book, you blog, you love writing." Guess what turned me into a writer? Newsletter writing! Prior to moving to China, I was a junior high math teacher. Guess how much writing you do in seventh and eighth grade math classes? Thank the Lord, not much. Guess my absolute least favorite kind of math problems? So-called story problems. Nicknamed "so-called story problems" because they are anything but a good story. I get lost with one train going this way and another going the opposite direction with Person A arriving late to the station and Person B expecting a baby in 4,852 hours. What day will the baby be born? How would I know? I'm with Person A on the train riding away from this nonsense.

In full disclosure, I earned a masters of arts in Teaching English as a Second Language (TESL); and as a graduate teaching assistant at the University of Kansas, I was assigned to teach level-three writing (we had a five-level program). In level three, students transitioned from writing paragraphs to writing five-paragraph essays. Margaret, my supervisor, helped me fall in love with the teaching of both academic writing and a good topic sentence. But it turns out that five-paragraph essays and newsletter writing are distant cousins, at best.

My history of writing started with writing infrequent letters to my parents when I went to college, mostly in response to my mom's letters. Growing up I absorbed the discipline of letter writing by watching my mom type letters with carbon paper so that the two sets of grandparents and my aunt would be able to stay informed about the goings-on of our family. I knew letter writing was a value to her, and I knew she and Dad were paying for college, the least I could do was write a few letters back to them. My writing turned "public" the spring of 1992 in anticipation of a summer trip to China. I needed to raise funds and prayers and, in short, people who would support me.

The organization with which I first traveled to China for this brief summer trip had a communication department that helped long-term workers by formatting and mailing their newsletters; but for those of us going on summer trips, we were sent a list of newsletter-writing tips, a few sample letters, and best of all, clip art. Yes, my newsletter writing career started with me clipping out pictures of pandas munching on bamboo and taping them into a letter I had printed off with random spaces to break up the text. I no longer have that first letter, but I remember the follow-up letter I wrote to supporters at the end of the summer. After updating a bit on the activities of the summer I wrote, "Like Mary, I am pondering this trip in my heart." I had no idea how to take a life-altering experience and put it into words.

While I earned my master of arts in TESL, I continued preparing to move to China by participating in another summer trip by writing pre- and post-trip newsletters. I, um, dreaded writing the letters because, for the most part, I had only been exposed to boring newsletters. I wish I were the super-spiritual, think-lovely-thoughts-about-all-situations kind of person. I'm not. I'm on the other train with Person A getting as far away from tedious newsletters as possible.

If I were to articulate at that point what I had picked up about newsletter writing after being on the missions committee at church, it was this:

1. Standard formula for a newsletter: greeting about how busy the cross-cultural work is; share random details about the land they are living in; make what they are doing sound super important ensuring supporters will not "cut them off"; and promise they will be better about keeping in contact.

2. Newsletters are a boring part of both serving cross-culturally and supporting those who do. Being a friend, family member, or supporter does not make them more interesting to read.

3. Because it is "holy" work with current and eternal realities at stake, people are given a pass on being decent storytellers. Decent, because perfect is not even a goal! It seemed that organizations in general do not invest in training people how to communicate in interesting ways.

Really?! Really? I didn't know how I was going to change these unspoken truths about newsletter writing. But I knew this: life is interesting, God is at work, and people love stories. I committed to myself to write to my supporters once a month. I admit that at first I wrote out of an "obligation" that since they were paying my bills, I "owed" them reports on how their money was being invested. Over the years my theology of letter writing deepened and broadened to include seeing newsletter writing as a way to minister to those who read them. Quite a switch, eh? Before it was fear based: "Please keep the money and prayer coming." But it evolved into a more gift-based approach—what could I offer my readers?—by allowing them to see God at work in my life, a different part of the world, and in our organization.

The Rest of the Story

In those early years few people on the field owned laptop computers, so my newsletters were handwritten and mailed with photos I wanted included in the newsletter back to the home office. I got to see the finished product twice a year and the main question was if I liked the color of paper they were printed on. Turns out, I did have strong opinions on this, particularly when it came to tying the color into the holidays. I found it distracting to try to read on bright red or green paper and asked for my newsletters to be printed on neutral colored paper.

Not only did I write newsletters, I wrote long handwritten letters that I would mail to my parents, who then graciously photocopied and mailed them to my sisters, grandparents, aunt, and dear friends. Moving to China in the '90s was like stepping back in history at least fifty years in the cities and eighty years in the countryside. Everything was different from the life I had known in America, and the only way to share it was through letters and photos. My faithfulness in writing was helped by the consistent feedback from my supporters: "We love your letters. Keep them coming." I could tell when a newsletter had been mailed out because the next phone call I would have with my parents, they could not wait to tell me who commented on reading and benefiting from my newsletters.

Letter by letter I came to see how my newsletters were not merely a report home; they were another slice of my calling and ministry. I did not set out to write a memoir. But that is ultimately what I did. While newsletters have primarily been seen as a way to communicate updates and prayer requests with supporters, I believe they can cast a wider vision and communicate a story. What you hold in your hands are my newsletters, though they have undergone both my editing and been professionally edited for the sake of compiling and polishing them into this book form. For the sake of clarity I have also omitted photos and text related to photos that are no longer included. That being said, certain aspects of the newsletters I left unaltered to show the progression and changes I made as a writer. For instance, I did not start off with catchy titles to my newsletters and in later years I went through a phase of quite a few subtitles.

This book is primarily the story of my first nine years living and serving in China. At the end of each year, I have included a short page or two called "If you write newsletters." In the spirit of choose your own adventure, skip them if you want and move on to the next year. You still get full credit for reading the book (wink).

However, if you are currently writing newsletters, let's talk directly with each other for a moment. I wrote this book and compiled these letters with you in mind. I do not want to add to your shame and discomfort in this area. Several excellent books exist with useful tips on how to write newsletters, but while those are necessary and helpful, I do not believe that all you need is more information. In your heart, you know why newsletters are valuable. What you might not believe is that they can be fun, that newsletters can actually connect you to people, or that in an unexpected way they can connect you to yourself. I want you to move a couple to the right on the "dread–dislike–tolerate–like–love" continuum of newsletter writing. If you dread them, I know it might be a bit much to expect that you will *love* writing newsletters by the end of this book. But, if hope is sparked and you have a few ideas and over the next year you write a few more newsletters, we can start there. Okay?

I did not set out to prove that second-year teacher wrong, but thank God . . . she was ☺.

Year One in China

*Letters are among the most significant memorial
a person can leave behind them.*
—*Johann von Goethe*

August 1995

Dear friends,

By the time you receive this, my three-week training period in California will be over, but right now I feel as if it will never end. I'm anxious to be on my way to Chengdu, and find out exactly what I'll be teaching, where I'll be living, and how daily life is going to unfold for me. Training has taken place at Cal Poly in Pomona, California, and has covered the areas of Chinese culture (most interesting!), team building, witnessing, and curriculum. The coursework has been helpful, but the highlight has been meeting the people, especially Erin. To meet this person who will be the closest contact with my culture, who will listen when I vent, and laugh when I joke, is a bit like entering an arranged marriage.

She laughs at my jokes, is easygoing, and is also kind of messy (and horrified that I said she's kind of messy, since this observation is based on two weeks of dorm life). In all fairness, I am these things too, which is probably why I appreciate them in Erin. Do you remember Hans and Franz, the German body builders in the *Saturday Night Live* skit from a few years back? They became popular for saying, "Hear me now and believe me later." This is extremely important that you hear me now and believe me later, when I ask you to follow the enclosed (with the original letter) correspondence guidelines.[1]

Assume that I will not be the first one to read your letter in China, and that you won't be the only one reading what I write to you. I will not be at risk, but please don't put someone close to me in a difficult situation because of your carelessness. This is not to say that you need to be overly concerned about what you write. I'm sure the

Chinese don't care that little Sally is walking or that the Broncos beat the Raiders, but I do. Read and follow the guidelines, and everything should be groovy. Short of begging, I do hope you will all write to me. This will be the last time I can explicitly state, "Prayer Request," unless the letter is hand carried out of the country.

Please pray for our transition and settling in. In particular, we need to know how to buy food (smiley face). Sichuan College of Education, where we have been assigned, was one of the six founding schools of Teach in China (TIC) in 1982. Because of the long history, pray that opportunities will arise for us to continue on where others have spiritually left off. In today's session the importance of open communication with teammates was stressed. Please pray for this not to become a problem for us.

In closing, I would like to offer a huge thank-you for the phenomenal support you all have provided. The phones calls, notes, meals, and gifts will buoy my spirit in the months to come. I can't wait to write to you next, because it will be from Chengdu.

God Bless,
Amy

September 1995

Greetings America,

After our flight from Los Angeles being canceled and delayed and then four days of sightseeing in Beijing, we are finally in Chengdu. Beijing was an excellent opportunity to practice the few Chinese phrases I know, and to learn a few new ones to use in purchasing things. However, the entire time, we just wanted to go home to Chengdu, finally unpack and stop looking at our suitcases!

We arrived late Thursday. The next day was filled with meetings, being shown the markets, and learning how to do laundry. Erin and I have decided that laundry is like a twelve-step program in China. Filling the machine with water, washing, draining, refilling to rinse, draining, spinning, hanging, and finally, resting. We found out the hard way that the draining tube needs to be in the bathtub . . . if not, then the bathroom floor is soaked for many hours. However, the joys of clean laundry are worth the effort.

The day after we arrived, we learned what real Sichuan food is like. For months I've been hearing how lucky I am to be in Chengdu, because the food here is great. I would have to agree, but I wasn't quite prepared for my mouth to tingle and go numb as I ate a fancy eel dish. About ten minutes later, feeling returned. I wonder if American dentists know about this?

The weekend was filled with several shopping adventures. Erin and I practically danced around after successfully buying toilet paper. We also passed a restaurant called American Fried Chicken, complete with chicken feet being sold, like at the Colonel's. Eating out has been fun too. The first two times we got jiaozi (dumplings), because I knew what they were and how to order them. We only noticed the second time that others paid first, whereas we paid when we left. We're still learning.

Last night we decided to try something new, and we pointed randomly at the menu on the wall, paid, and sat down wondering what we had ordered. As luck would have it, I think we ordered the hottest noodle dish, and I had to leave in the middle of the meal to go and buy another bottle of water. It was delicious, and I can't wait to point to something else.

My classes started this week, and Erin's will begin next week. On paper my schedule seems light, because I only teach twelve hours a week: six two-hour classes of composition, selected reading, or conversation. However, think about me as I try to build friendships with my 120 students. Another thing to think about is my selected reading course, which is actually British and American literature. The last time I had this stuff was when I was in high school, ugh.

A final area I would like for you to remember is our health. We have heard from many of the Chinese that the Americans are always sick during the winter. Even though Erin and I brought enough medicine to open our own dispensary, I would rather not need to use it. Life has gone unbelievably well for us so far. It reminds me that we are not alone. We remember you daily and look forward to hearing from you.

Miss you, but glad to be here,
Amy

PS: The students have asked for more magazines to read, especially *Newsweek* and *Reader's Digest*, if you happen to have any old ones lying around.

October 1995

Hello, I wanted to let you know that Erin and I have both changed our names. I am either called Ah-may or Army, but rarely Amy. My *waiban* (Foreign Affairs Officer) always introduces me as Army, A-M-Y, which he spells out, sometimes even on the person's shoulder with his finger. It takes all I can not to laugh. The other day I answered the phone, and the person wanted to know if it was Amy or Harry. I said, "Amy," and she wanted to know if she could speak to Harry. I asked, "Erin?" "Yes. Harry." Second languages can be hard, can't they? Thus this is Army and Harry with an update.

The big excitement around here was the purchase of bikes two Saturdays ago. Students went with us to the used bicycle market to help select bikes and then bargain for them. They decided it would go better if we stayed outside and people wouldn't know they were selling to foreigners and jack the prices up. Whenever my student rode a bike out for us to look at, a huge crowd gathered and pushed in to see what the foreigners would do. I felt like Moses parting the Red Sea, as I got the crowd to separate for my test drive. Erin said it was funny watching all of the heads turning in unison following me.

I chose my bike because she exudes character—as she has faded blue paint and seems to have stories to tell. Only later did I learn that her brakes are about 20 percent effective. I named her Lucille so I can sing, "It's a fine time to leave me loose wheel." We're enjoying our added mobility.

My students are wonderful, and I'm thrilled to be beyond basic questions, like what we eat and what we do in our spare time. They have been helpful in buying bicycles, train tickets, and food. Each week my female students take turns taking me to the open market for food. This week, as we were walking past the water pools that contain live fish, one flopped out onto the street and had to be kicked into the gutter before being captured. Something about seeing a fish kicked in the street, and the students asking if this was like shopping in America, made me chuckle.

I was teaching another group how to play UNO yesterday. Since they're my low-level girls who won't even make a peep in class, it was fun to hear them erupt when a Skip or Draw Two card was played. I'm eager to get to know them better. A major blessing for us is one of the TIC teachers from last year, Mark, is still in Chengdu studying Chinese and Sichuan opera. I'm glad he's still here, because sixty of my students were his last year, and he's able to continue relationships with them. Among his talents are speaking Chinese, which is handy in restaurants, playing the guitar, and teaching us Rook. Erin, Mark, and I get on exceptionally well, and he is basically a third member of the team, so please remember him as you remember us.[2]

This month, specifically remember my students.[2] This is their last year of English study, and they have unrealistically high expectations of what their English progress should be, ugh. I feel the pressure, and I know that it won't happen. They are also far away from family and friends and living with five other people in a dorm room. Sometimes when I visit the women in their dorm, they are knitting clothes for their child (remember the one child policy), and one of my students even had a baby this summer and left the baby with her own mother. In this way, being apart from loved ones, we can relate to each other. I miss all of you, especially as we're entering the holiday season.

Thank you for your letters, cards, and thoughts. More than ever before I am aware we are not in this alone, others have come before, and others will come after us. We need you, your faithful remembrances have already found favor. Keep it up. Our health has been good. The food is usually good; I have even learned how to make applesauce and tortillas. (What? You can actually make them and not only buy them at a store? Part of our learning curve is a crash-course in food preparation.) I'm glad to be here with Erin. It's important that I don't take these things for granted, so thank you for your help.

Often when I see the students on campus, they yell their room numbers at me, as a not-so-subtle hint that they'd like me to visit them. As you can see, my address is written below, as a not-so-subtle hint that I would like mail. Thanks for all you've written already.

This is Army signing off

November 1995[3]

The adventure in Asia continues. [I had originally included here a picture of our friend Mark. As a brief reminder, Mark taught at the college where Erin and I teach.] Since Mark is the first foreigner ever to study Sichuan Opera, he is quite a novelty. When he had his first public performance, the TV cameras followed him around for a week. We were allowed backstage to see him before the performance and I was asked to sit next to him while he was interviewed for TV. Why? The obvious answer—I am a foreigner. Erin and I were even filmed watching Mark's performance. Thankfully, he did wonderfully.

However, this whole experience highlights something I have been feeling. The Chinese want foreigners to do well and admire us for trying, but they are quick to ridicule us and point out Chinese superiority. This has been frustrating and has definitely strengthened within me the assurance of whom it is I am serving while here.

Since I last wrote to you, Erin and I have had the opportunity to travel outside of Chengdu by train and bus. We have seen another side of China and are slowly being exposed by our Maker to the Chinese mentality. This is not always an easy lesson. On the bus trip we hit an old man who was crossing the road (his head bled, but he was able to walk) and had to sit out in the rainy, muddy Chinese countryside for three and a half hours, waiting for the authorities to arrive and fill out a report. We found why we were waiting later—because we were traveling alone and don't know enough Chinese to communicate outside of the market. That day was a huge lesson in patience and accepting something that does not seem logical. The Chinese are much better at this than I am.

Thanks for remembering our health. We continue to be remarkably well, sometimes tired but overall fine. My students also seem less panicky about dramatically improving their English. Please continue to remember both our health and our students. The holidays are coming up, and while I am excited to share them with my students, I am sorry that I have to be away from friends, family, and a place that feels right. I am thankful for Erin and Mark and the sense of family that has developed. May we continue to be an example to our students of our Father's love.

Seasonal blessings,
Amy

December 1995

"Here is your duck. Please have a look." With these words Thanksgiving dinner was served. Actually, our attention was directed to the man who hacked our duck into chunks. When we ordered half a duck, I did not realize it was literal and included the head, or half of it. The highlight of Thanksgiving was our culture lecture, where we got to explain why and to whom we are thankful. The students chuckled when we said, "We feel like the pilgrims who have gone to a new land and been wonderfully provided for."

We decorated for Christmas the day after Thanksgiving, and when students visited, they asked, "Didn't you decorate a little early?" I think because Spring Festival does not have the same kind of buildup and is more celebrated after the date, they think it's too early. "No," we adamantly told them. "We did not decorate too early. Do you want us to plug in the tree?" At this they are rather impressed. I am always more impressed that our socket is still working since many are dead.

Recently we experienced social dancing, which is different from discoing, we learned. Instead, ballroom dancing was always referred to as "social dancing." Even though we tried to explain that discoing went out with the '70s, the term lives on in China. Of course I took a picture, but what the picture could not capture is the blue halogen light that made me glow like a beached whale. Erin's shirt glowed, but my whole outfit was unbelievable. It is incredibly hard to be inconspicuous when you are a major source of light for the entire room, but it was fun and good to see the students in another light, even if it was halogen.

The Christmas culture lecture went extremely well, considering it had been a terrible day, which we classified as a "bad China day."[4] Eleven students helped us act out the original Christmas story. During the question-and-answer part, we were asked if we believed the story — now the students know where we stand. Remember [another way of asking for prayer] all the questions and discussions that we have in light of the season.

One of the special moments came when I went to pick up some film we had developed. The little picture girl, as we call the clerk who hands over our photos to us, had a Christmas card for me. We had grown to like each other, even though we can't communicate well. When I pick up my pictures, we look through them and say, "Amy," "Erin," or "Mark," each time one of us is in a picture.

I can't imagine how long she worked on writing this note:

> "Dear nice Ayi (Auntie), Christmas is coming, Merry Christmas to you. Our long-term cooperation build-up our friendly relations and I wish the relation will be forever. It's only now that I get the opportunity to send you a message of deep thanks for the cordial association. Although we can't communicate on language, I think that our hearts are identical. I look forward to your visiting again and do my best to make your joyful. Sincerely yours, LHM."

Isn't that touching? I still cry when I read it and wish that we could talk. Slowly, I am learning Chinese, but I hope that she realized my love for her goes beyond this world.[5]

Our school break is in February for the Spring Festival. We have about six weeks off and are going to Hong Kong for the TIC Conference. When I think about it, I get excited to see my friends and hear what is happening in their cities. Please remember traveling safety and refreshment for TIC teachers. My students are also eager for the break because they have been away from their spouses and children. Thanks for all the letters. I can't stress enough how it helps.

I was reading through important Proverbs and thought of you: *Like cold water to a weary soul is good news from a distant land.*[6] Please remember the Hong Kong conference, our health, opportunities to share with students, and consistency in acting on what we believe.

As a student wrote to me, "Merry Christmas to you and yours from I and mine."

Love,
Amy

January 1996

[In one picture included with this newsletter, I am on my bike at an intersection waiting for a green light. It's like a Where's Waldo? image! Where's Amy?] Where is Amy in this picture? Biking in Chengdu, the city of a million bikes. Specifically, I am at an intersection waiting for a green light. This intersection always has heavy traffic, but Chengdu is great for riding because it is mostly flat and all major streets have separate bicycle lanes on either side. I have decided that riding is a little like rushing in football. You are always looking for the open hole. Sometimes you slip through and sometimes the hole simply closes on you and you bump into someone who is muttering, "Lao wai" ("Foreigner"). I have been known to mutter back, "Zhong guoren" ("Chinese"), when they bike into me.

The bicycle lanes are patrolled by retired people who wear yellow vests and ball caps. They stand at intersections, and when the light turns, they leap out waving a red flag, blowing a whistle, and making sure that no one crosses the magic line they determine. I think they were denied any kind of power earlier in life. They can fine you for things such as not having a bell or two people riding on a bike. As well as fining, they can make you stand and waive the red flag for thirty minutes to stop traffic. This seems to be a terrible, horrible thing that my students dread more than the fine.

The bicycle lane is a fantastic place to people watch. In the 1970s, having a dog was illegal because it was a sign of wealth. I have never seen this many little dogs in my whole life. Instead of seeing a dog sticking his head out of the window, he is standing in the front basket with his paws on the rim. Children are allowed to ride on the back. What a sweet sight to see a child standing on the back with her arms wrapped around her dad's neck. It's safer than it sounds. Car seats are not needed, just a long piece of rope to tie the baby to the parent's back. People in love hold hands while they bike. How many people have you seen pedal past on a bike, talking on the cellular phone?

It never ceases to amaze me what you can have on the back of your bike. We have seen, in a given instance, things such as whole sides of beef or pigs, buckets of food waste, computers, skinned whole calves, twenty live chickens hanging upside down, a standing mirror, bamboo poles that are twenty feet long, bunches of vegetables for cooking lunch, and ten rolls of toilet paper. While riding double is illegal, it is sometimes necessary because of a flat tire. One day after a basketball game with students, Erin and I goofed around on campus with her pedaling me around. Tonight my chain broke off again and I had to hold on to Erin's handlebars while she pedaled—aka towed—me, Chinese style.

By the time you read this, I will be at the TIC Conference in Hong Kong. We are in need of rest and replenishing. This includes the students, many of whom are parents and have been away from their children for five months. One of my students gave birth last summer and only sees her baby on weekends. Thankfully our health has remained good and classes have gone well, but five months without a break, we are all ready for one.

I have had to move out of my room because a family from Michigan is coming for the spring semester. Being someone who enjoys ruts, I don't have a great attitude about it. My stuff is in boxes, and I will move into a room on the second floor when I get back. I won't have any laundry or cooking facilities, and I will have to go down to Erin's room to cook or to wash my clothes. You can be remembering the situation. I know it's a small thing, but it feels big. Thanks for all the Christmas and birthday cards and presents. It was a definite help through the holiday season. I have been impressed with your creativity and thoughtfulness. I will write a more open letter from Hong Kong.

In Him,
Amy

February 1996

Hi, let's dive in.

The worst culture shock of my life was not adjusting to Chengdu, but the first two days I was in Hong Kong. There are many camera and clothing stores, people, restaurants, signs in English, and signs in Chinese, crossing guard signals making machine-gun-like noises for blind people, and many foreigners. You could tell who was a mainland foreigner (me) and who wasn't (most of the other foreigners).

Everything about Hong Kong seemed materialistic and overdone. My friend Cynthia and I referred to this as our meltdown. I have been able to bounce back to not hating the decadent West with the help of Diet Coke, blue skies (only seen five percent of the time in Chengdu), and hearing birds. I hadn't realized that I don't hear or see any birds in Chengdu, but it makes sense since I can buy pigeon in the market.

My spirit is also being refreshed with singing and teaching from the Book of John. It is therapeutic to be with others who have been walking down the same path I have and to hear their experiences. It puts many of my complaints and frustrations into perspective. Two young women in Mongolia went without electricity for two and a half months. To cook and keep warm, they burned dung. Through story after story, I was reminded how good God is and to be thankful for all that I have been given.

Since this will be my only open letter, I want to share what God has been doing and what I have observed about the Chinese view of God. Keep in mind that I have only been here for six months, don't speak the language, and work with a well-educated slice of the population (most Chinese are peasants in the countryside).

The phrase that has haunted me all semester was said by one of my students: "We are not like you Westerners; we Chinese don't have souls." She went on to explain that when Chinese die, they simply cease to exist. "We are not like you" is the lie that is perpetuated over and over by the government through schools and the newspaper.

Another student told me, "Nowadays it is very fashionable to celebrate Christmas in large cities in China." Something about the word "fashionable" doesn't sit right with me. Unfortunately, it accurately captures what we experienced in Chengdu. The two days before Christmas, a few of the larger hotels hung up Christmas lights and had displays in their lobbies, like the ones you see in Western shopping malls. Part of it was funny because it was an attempt at being "Christmas cool." But being close does not cut it when the display has a snowman and a giant stuffed yellow bunny.

Christmas night we went down to look at the lights and were with the upper crust of Chengdu, who used the whole thing as a huge photo opportunity. While it may have been fashionable, it was also empty and devoid of meaning. I left feeling disgusted and mad. After Christmas, all of the articles in the *China Daily*, the national newspaper, referred to Christmas as a Western holiday. Western, Western, Western. As long as it is kept foreign and fashionable, it will be tolerated. Not all was bad; there was a candlelight service at the foot of the Chairman Mao statue, and the mere fact that it was public is encouraging.

I have told you that we are at a school with a long tradition of TIC teachers. This is exciting because we can step in and continue the work of others. Two of our students became Christians during the summer TIC program and shared with one of their roommates the first week of school, and he also became a Christian. From what I understand, one of them has totally transformed and even given up smoking, a huge big deal in China, where you are a true man only if you smoke. Another has gotten involved in a house church. He has wondered whether God can accept him because he is a Communist Party member. The smile on his face after hearing our reassurance is great. Remember him as he is growing and would like to give up smoking as well.

The final piece of news from Chengdu is that at the end of the semester several crises occurred that have shaken our students. The brother of one of Erin's students has a degenerative problem in his feet, and one of my students found out that her brother is dying of cancer and has less than a year to live. The Chinese way of dealing with this is to not tell the sick person and pretend that things are groovy with their health. She asked me to pray for her brother. We learned of these crises in the last two weeks of school, so we will be dealing with a lot next semester.

Your continued generosity far expands beyond my ability to thank you, really. When I showed up at the conference, people I did not know said, "Good, Amy Young is here. We can finally empty the mailroom." I love all of the mail because it helps me feel like I am still involved in your lives. Your generosity in sending your used stamps, magazines, holiday goodies, or newspaper articles is noticed by my students, and they are impressed, too.

Bless you big-time,
Amy

PS: When I get back to Chengdu, I will meet the Varland family, the visiting scholars who will be here for a semester. I will also unpack my stuff in my new room as the Varlands will be living in mine since it is the largest. Please pray for my attitude.

March 1996

Howdy,
The first day of spring semester classes, I was walking up the stairs and a man approached me and asked if I was Amy. When I said yes, he said he had heard I was from Colorado. True. Then surely I

knew of Colorado. Well, yes, not only knew of it but had lived there. Great! (He was excited at this point.) Could I please tell him whether the statue of Kit Carson in front of the capital faces East or West? Ah, to be back in China, the land of unusual questions — where I'm viewed as an expert on anything Western.

The five weeks of traveling was a refreshing break; however, my concept of a long plane flight or car ride has been severely altered after one train trip of forty-eight hours and another of thirty-six. It became almost comical on one train when the train ran out of hot water, standardly supplied in thermoses, and we had to eat our ramen noodles uncooked. They do taste like Doritos when you crunch them up and sprinkle the flavor packet over them. I also learned through my travels that bathing, doing laundry, changing clothes, and even changing underwear are overrated when living out of a backpack for five weeks. I literally kept my long underwear on for ten days straight without changing since I slept in them (I did peel them off to bathe on the few occasions that we found warm water.) I know this sounds disgusting, but it's not bad. Try it on your next family vacation. Remember that I did begin this section by saying it was a refreshing break.

With some fellow TIC teachers, I spent a week in Shanghai, a week and a half in Hong Kong, eight days in Thailand, four more days back in Hong Kong, and then up to Chengdu again. The highlight was Thailand, creating a short break from China. As much as I enjoy where I am and what I'm doing, it is exhausting to function in a culture that is vastly different, or at least where I'm always the outsider to be stared at. And where there is no Diet Coke. For the first time in my life, while on the break, I actually enjoyed sitting for an extended period of time, not feeling the need to do anything.

We arrived back in Hong Kong in the middle of the Spring Festival, which is China's largest festival and celebrates the beginning of the Lunar New Year. I don't know much about it except it is important to be with family and China basically shuts down for two weeks with no shops or restaurants open. This is the year of the rat or mouse, which has been capitalized on by Disney. Erin and I find it ironic after all of our mouse problems!

Hong Kong has displays like our Christmas ones except that they center around mice. In a mall there was a Buddha for the kids to sit on his lap. Very weird combination of East and West. China does not seem to be that commercialized (yet.) I came back a week before Erin to unpack my new room. It is nice to return to Chengdu and have it feel like home. My new room is fine, but I'm glad the weather is warming up a bit since it's unheated. Erin's parents are able to fly in for a few days, and her dad even baked a loaf of bread in our toaster oven! It was fun to hear their reactions to the dirt, bikes, spitting, throngs of people, and for them to get to meet some of her students. Our team has grown to eight. The four Varlands and Steve are new additions. Steve is a friend of Mark who has been in and out of Chengdu this fall and is now here to study the language.

Please remember us all as we try to work together and reflect the One who has sent us. Things are beginning with the semester and team, and I don't have major requests except for one. I was told that one of the Chinese teachers and I will be assigning a graduation paper together. It's to be two thousand words and follow Western guidelines of citing sources. The challenge will be that most students don't write such long papers, have never written a research paper, and have a concept of plagiarism that is different from ours. For the Chinese there can be no higher flattery than to use someone else's words. Some of my students may have written these papers in Chinese and will try to pass a translation off as original work. Are you smiling yet? I know that was my response. Oh well.

> By the way, which way does
> Kit Carson face?
> Amy

April 1996

Knowing that I would miss March Madness, my wonderful father called me Wednesday nights during the tournament to first give me the brackets and then subsequent updates. The students are always crying for culture, culture, culture, and more culture. We decided to have pools in each class with the winner receiving two copies of *Reader's Digest*. Teams seated number one were good common choices and several students chose KU to win it all. Go Jayhawks! The most popular upset team was Drexel. I think because they like the name.

While the students were busy with the NCAA, we had our own little in-house tournament between the mice and spiders. At last report we killed two mice and three hand-sized spiders. Since we got back, Erin had a mouse that came into her room at night. Even after blocking his hole, the silly thing chewed through our attempt to block it each night; we finally set out sticky paper to catch it and had Erin sleep in my room.

The first night, all we caught was some mouse hair. I thought, "This is the stuff sitcoms are made of!" We got him, but it was ugly. Only his hind legs were caught, so he sat up and looked at me. I realize this may be more detail than you need to know, but it was traumatic. Several mornings later, Deb Varland found one floating in the toilet. In case you're wondering, it didn't flush. As is fitting for the year of the mouse, the score is now mice four, spiders three.

Erin and I met a wealthy man who insisted on taking us sightseeing. We agreed to climb a mountain with him and his friend—three of his friend's relatives also came. It rained the whole day, but all was not lost. My student Maggie got to come and act as interpreter. Our lunch conversation proved to be especially memorable. The man started telling us about his believing relatives. He's too busy now, he explained, but will consider these kinds of issues when he retires. We had an interesting discussion and the meal ended with him asking us if we liked it, which we said we did. He responded with a twinkle, "Well, the God arranged it." Erin and I looked at each other and nodded in complete agreement.

Lastly, our Father has been blessing us with numerous opportunities to share.

- On an outing with Erin's students, we took a bus and I chatted with a student as we rode. When the bus pulled into our destination, he asked out of the blue if I was a Christian and if I would talk with him about Jesus. He had written twice to Erin in his writing journal for class about a Bible he was given over Spring Festival.

- Two students saw the movie The Scarlet Letter the same weekend we did; we invited them over to dinner and had an interesting discussion about adultery and true love.

- The Easter culture lecture was a chance to share why we have a reason to celebrate. It's ironic that what we did in our culture lecture would not be allowed in American schools, and we even had a member of the English department in the front row. Most of the students have never heard about Easter and laughed out loud when we said that we believe it. The idea that there is something greater is foreign and contrary to what they've been taught, it's difficult for them to comprehend.

As we only have two months left of school, please pray that Erin and I may be lights that the love of God has to offer. Since we got back from the break, two of my students have had abortions, and another student's husband publicly beat her to shame her into minding him. Other students have received results of acceptance or denial to graduate school. Many do not want to return to teaching after graduating and are desperately looking for any out. May God use us to make himself real in the midst of complex situations and problems. He loves them more than even we have grown to love them in only one year. Thank you for your letters, news clippings, magazines, cartoons, Jayhawk updates, postcards, and any form of mail. You are used to encourage us and keep us going.

Happy spring—we actually had sun for two hours yesterday.

Love ya,
Amy

June 1996

Da Jia Hao or Good morning, class! The literal translation is, "Big family good." This semester I started taking Chinese calligraphy lessons twice a week from one of my students who would like to go to graduate school in art. I'm glad to have some direction in learning Chinese, and for Erin's patience as I point to a sign and say, "East," or "That has something to do with a river."

These lessons have also been instrumental in helping me understand the culture. When my work is corrected, I'm often told that my stroke order is wrong, some strokes are too weak or thick, or the proportions are wrong. Other times, there are several acceptable ways to do something, because, as I'm told, "That's your style, Amy." It's a struggle to understand where the line between rule and personal style is. When I try to say something is just my style, my teacher laughs and quickly tells me I'm wrong. I think this is true in much of Chinese life. The line between following a rule and personal style is thin and not to be crossed.

For example, people must be married by age thirty or there is something wrong with your personality (rule). Whom you marry is more open (style). I've been taking tai chi lessons with Deb and Luke Varland. Tai chi is a slow exercise routine for relaxation. It consists of twenty-four movements that flow together. The goal is to be moving at all times. I move too fast during the parts I know well and not smoothly enough during the parts I don't know well. In tai chi, there is also a set standard of what a beautiful move is. No personal style here. Learn the standard, memorize and perfect it, and then you have done a good job. It's certainly a different way for me to learn something and helps me see my students and where they're coming from more clearly.

I would like to thank you for the various sympathy cards I received about the graduation papers my students are writing. As long as I keep my sense of humor, I'll get through. When we talked about bibliographies, only one-third remembered to alphabetize on their practice bibliography. I've never answered this many questions on publishers or which date is the copyright. Last week we hit plagiarism and source citations hard. Definite cultural differences on this one. I feel that the papers handed in are going to be something that we can all be proud of after a semester of labor. The papers are due on June 3rd and I have to grade sixty of them. Yuck!

Erin and I are meeting with students weekly to discuss spiritual questions they have. I have a student whom I'll call Peter. The conflict in his heart is great, as expressed on his face with anguish like I've never seen. He wants to believe, but it's hard when none of his friends do and he has been taught his whole life that there is no God.

Peter's friend, whom I will call Robert, has also come with Peter to talk with me. Our prayer is that they will both become Christians and can encourage and support each other. Both are reluctant to make a hasty decision that they will quickly fall away from. Peter has asked me tough questions like, if he becomes a Christian, how will he tell people in his hometown after he graduates this year? Wow. Pretty exciting. As one of Erin's students was leaving this week, he turned and casually said to her, "I think next week I'll become a Christian." We're excited because he won't graduate and will be back next year.

All of this thrills me, knowing that Erin and I will both be back next year to continue in the work God has chosen for us. I've enclosed a new picture card for your refrigerator. I'm on Lucille, my bike, in front of the building we live in.

Erin and I will be returning to the US on June 24th. The thought of my students graduating and leaving fills me with great sorrow. Remember them as they have to make the transition back to being a full-time parent and spouse. We both want to thank you for all the support you've given. You have reached through us to touch the lives of our students. The magazines, stickers, audiotapes, and videotapes, and canceled stamps they collect have been incentives for them and a demonstration of love. It shakes their worldview to think of people far away caring for them. Thank you. This is Army and Harry, signing off after an eventful year in Chengdu. We can't wait for another. I'll write again on the plane home.

Love,
Amy

July 1996

The year ended well with only seven students flunking the graduation papers; five of them rewrote and corrected their errors, meaning fifty-three did a good job the first time through. I was proud of the quality of their work, but I'm glad I don't have to deal with research papers again until next March.

Erin and I also got our rooms packed up. I had to totally pack up and move back downstairs, and Erin had to store stuff away. The school is going to do some renovations in our room while we're gone. They plan to take down the dirty, old blue wallpaper and paint the walls white. Yay! Maybe it won't be so cave-ish, but the hardest part of leaving was saying goodbye to Mark because he'll be in the US next year, recruiting for TIC.

We are extremely excited for Peter and Robert have been given permission by their work units to return to Chengdu next year for further education. It is quite unusual that they would be allowed to do this. We feel that God has worked this out, and we have told them that.

Robert wants physical evidence of God that he can see, and Peter wants Robert to decide in order to not be alone. Neither of these young men have churches in their hometowns or Christians in their families. May God continue to work mightily to reveal himself to them.

If life were a movie, the credits would be rolling as we come to the end of this year in Chengdu. To be true to Chinese culture, we would all be standing and shoving to leave the theater, and the movie would be turned off as soon as the credits start. In China, when something's over, it's over, but I'm not writing this from China as I am in the US, so I'll relate a few scenes from this past year.

- "Where do you spit in America, Amy?" "Um . . . we don't really." "Well, where do you spit when you're sick?" I had to ask Erin when I got home if she spits when she's sick. She doesn't either.

- The sound of spoons clinking on bowls as we walk with students to the school dining hall for lunch.

- The mouth numbing taste of huajiao (aka flour pepper — what a deceiving name). Actually, I've grown to like it a little.

- "I don't like the city, Amy. There's nothing to do, not like in the countryside where I spend my free time catching eels."

My student explained to me five different ways to catch eels. Who knew?!

- Riding Lucille, ringing her bell, and yelling, "Watch out, laowai"—(foreigner)—"coming through," which does nothing because everyone rings and everyone else ignores.

- God's continual faithfulness to us—Erin and I enjoy living and working together, relationships with students are good, and we can get around the city like old pros.

- God has been especially faithful with our health. Grace's (age six) foot got torn up in a bicycle wheel, Roger had a long bout with intestinal stuff we thought at first was his appendix, and Mark and Steve were both sick on and off, but Erin and I were untouched. Not that God loves us more! Thank you for all of your prayer. You truly are a blessing to us and through us.

In Him,
Amy

#1 If You Write Newsletters

What Gets in the Way of Writing Newsletters

1. Reworking and reworking a newsletter to the point the information contained becomes out of date.

2. Not prioritizing newsletters as a part of your monthly or quarterly routine, therefore almost guaranteeing a newsletter will not be written.

3. Fear that your life is not worthy enough and that what you are doing is not spectacular or lacks "Wow!"

4. Having a weak theology of newsletter writing.

5. Confusing newsletter writing with academic writing.

6. Being frozen by the thought that others will analyze your letters as much as you do and forgetting that many people read them only once.

7. Bad memories from high school or college English papers being graded.

8. Lack of passion and vision for how to share your life, work, and ministry.

9. Shame over an aspect of newsletter writing, such as infrequency, lack of writing ability, or uncertainly over what material to include.

10. Considering your own experience of reading poorly written newsletters, wanting to spare your supporters of that experience.

Which obstacle gets in your way the most?

Year Two in China
1996-1997

*Letter writing can be seen as a gift because someone
has taken his/her time to write and think and express love.*
— *Soraya Diase Coffelt*

August 1996—How I spent my summer, by Amy

Let me start by confessing that I didn't practice my Chinese
calligraphy. Not even once. Oh, I began the summer with grand plans
that included an hour of practice a day. I now chuckle to think I almost
assigned my new students to read a book over the summer.

The summer started off with my ten-year high school reunion. The line
"I don't remember growing older. When did they?" from the *Fiddler on the
Roof* kept going through my mind as I caught up with classmates who had
three children, a different figure, or a receding hairline. Three classmates
are dentists! I don't know why this struck me particularly, but it did. I
realized we are grown-ups when most of the goals were to have children
and raise them to be responsible adults. Wow.

[The letter goes on to chronicle what I did in the summer and people
I saw. It ends:] Thank you for all of the love you poured out this summer
through cards, calls, and teaching aids, (e.g. canceled stamps, old calendars,
or books on tape). My batteries are recharged and I'm anxious to be back.
Everyone says that in the second year the letters from home drop off. What
does Everyone know? I look forward to hearing from you.

> Fondly in Him,
> Amy

September 1996—We're back!

Before coming down to Chengdu the TIC teachers spent one day
in Beijing hosted by our school officials, and then all TIC teachers and
school officials took a four-hour train ride to Bei Dai He, a beach resort.

Erin went to Florida to visit a friend from Germany instead of coming to Bei Dai He. Given the change in her skin color and the lack of change in mine, I would say her experience was more of what I think of when I hear "beach resort."

My beach time had more of a Chinese flavor—the more, the better. Here, more means more beaches in a day. All of the teachers and school officials would load up on four buses, be escorted to the beach by police cars with flashing lights, and then be allowed fifty minutes until the TIC teachers were herded back to buses to go to the next beach. It was good to have time to hang out with Cynthia, who also teaches in Sichuan Province, and meet the new teachers. I had a stomach virus, or food poisoning, and was glad our trip was low-key, since I was doubled over for twelve hours.

Erin met up with us when we returned to Beijing. Our *waiban* (Foreign Affairs Officer) gave us each a box of Oreo cookies for breakfast, prompting us to sing, "Who's that waiban with the cheery disposition, handing out a box of cookies 'cause she knows it's good nutrition?" I had to stifle a laugh the next morning when she said, "Those crackers were sweet." Yes, they were.

Last year, the waibans asked what kind of renovations we would like done in our rooms. We came up with about six things, mainly suggestions to bring more light to the rooms, but we were told, "So sorry, no money." This can be irritating— why ask if you're not going to do anything? But before we left for the summer, they brought the money department to visit and showed them around. I was glad the money department was mainly women who kept shaking their heads in disgust. Action was imminent.

When we got back, the dingy blue-green wallpaper was gone, and the walls were painted white. Amazing, but wait there's more . . . florescent lighting, sockets that aren't hanging out of the wall, non-termite-eaten door frames, a phone in our hallway, and new toilets (the old toilets were better, but hey, they tried). With all of the renovations, our personal things were coated in dust and shuffled around, but now that we've cleaned, it's bright and cheerful.

With the renovations,·our hall was extended to include two more rooms. The Varlands have returned to Michigan, and two students from their college are now living here and studying traditional Chinese medicine at another school. We get along well and have even gone jogging a couple of times in the evenings, looking like a herd of *laowai* (foreigners) running wild.

Peter had to go home three days before we returned. He has already written of his "desperation of losing the opportunity of further study. What makes me more desperate is I realize I don't have power to control my future." He is having a rough transition back to his hometown, which now seems filthy, noisy, and crowded. I hope to be able to visit him to understand more completely the life that my students live. Peter said we could go fishing. Please think of him, that he may find the One who does have the power to control his future.

My classes are the same as last year: two composition, two selected-reading, and two conversation classes per week. All of my classes are on Monday, Tuesday, and Wednesday. Being a person who feels even a three-day weekend can be too long, remember me, as I will need to adjust to this type of schedule. Maybe I'm supposed to learn to be laid-back and not as Type A.[1]

As a reminder, we teach at the Provincial Education College, and all of our students are adults who have been English teachers. They come here for a two-year program to improve their English. Many are married and have a child. It can be understandably stressful to leave family and share a dorm with five people.

This month, remember us as we transition back to life in China. We have killed a mouse, Erin's bike was stolen, a huge cockroach was in her shoe this morning, and ants are all over our apartment this year. From the right perspective, this is great comedy. May we find that perspective, and as always, may Erin and I accurately reflect the One who is faithful, and may our students be drawn to Him.

Thank you for the letters. I knew you wouldn't disappoint us. If you happen to have extra packets of hot chocolate lying around in your cupboards and don't know what to do with them, I can think of a few people who would be grateful.

> Happy leaf-turning fall,
> Amy

October 1996—What life could use

This past summer one of my adventures was traveling to Scotland. While there I laughed each time I saw road signs warning "humps" for speed bumps. After our first six weeks back in China, I wished life came with similar warnings. Adjusting back to Chengdu was rougher than I expected, and since we didn't foresee the bumps, we felt each one. We have a few classes that have more students than desks. Getting chairs for these students has been a joke. Excuses from the English

---

1 It worked! I now barely recognize the version of Amy who had a problem with three-day weekends.

department range from "The person in charge of chairs can't be found" to "The department that the new students transferred from should provide the chairs." Bump.

Mice, where to begin? They are getting into our food, eating through screens, and I've seen one climb up our kitchen door. One night while at the movies I was sitting next to the carpeted wall and glanced at the wall only to find a mouse six inches from my face. We've caught four mice on sticky paper and had to kill them by smacking them with a frying pan. Bump.

We've had several situations where workers—generic Chinese word for someone who has a job you don't know how to describe—decided our requests are unrealistic. For example, the worker in the photocopying department thought we didn't need one copy of an assignment for each student. The worker who repairs water problems said that the other people live with water leaks and we should too. Okay, but what about the damage it does to the walls? Bump. Bump. Bump.

While I may not see the bumps in the road ahead of me, I know the One who made the road and have been reminded of His love and faithfulness. We had a weeklong break for National Day, and I was able to go on a bus trip with twelve other foreigners (six Americans, three Japanese, two Koreans, a Palestinian, and a Malaysian) to several national-park-type areas. It was a cross between the Rocky Mountains and the color you see in the Midwest in the autumn. Color. Fresh air. Four-wheeling in a minibus.

I understand people who don't bathe because when you don't have hot water and the weather is cold, the desire to bathe disappears. The entire week was gorgeous and I felt refreshed, though maybe a bit grungy. Standing at the top of a hundred-meter waterfall, I remembered that He is "the Creator of the ends of the earth. He will not grow tired or weary and his understanding no one can fathom. He gives strength to the weary and increases the power of the weak."[7] I was weary and weak, and He gave me strength and power.

We even went on a horse trek for two days. Camping Chinese style, our guides cut up bamboo for us to use as chopsticks. When we arrived at camp, the guides unsaddled the horses and made them run around the hills in search of food. It took three hours the next morning to round up the horses. One guide took a fancy to me and even proposed—quite a fetching couple we would make.

I've heard from several of last year's students who have returned home. The following is an excerpt from one who is dear to me. It reminds me of why we, you and I, are here and the difference we can make.

My students like me very much, one of my students wrote these words in his journal book. "Our English teacher has a strange way of making her class lively and interesting and her lessons are not easily forgotten." Why do they like my class because I did what you have done, I taught them how to read, how to write. Sometimes I give them stamps, which I got from you. I told them these stamps are earned by my hard work I think it is precious but if you work hard I give my favorite to you. They all think it is an honor to get a beautiful stamp from me. Like you I love all of my students and they love me too. I often tell them "Amy is my American teacher and she is so kind and I respect her from the bottom of my heart." They want to see you very much. Amy, although you are American and I am Chinese I think we are sisters. You not only taught us how to teach English but taught us how to be a man in this society.

I can't guarantee the road will be smooth from here on out, but I know that we have a purpose and we are making a difference one student at a time. As long as we can laugh a little to balance the bumps, I will be satisfied. Today, while visiting a student at the tourism school, I had to laugh as another class practiced right outside our window how to carry a tray using bricks to simulate food. The little joys of life in China outweigh the bumps.

When you remember us this week, don't think about the bumps but the blessings—our students. May we serve them with happy hearts showing them the compassion and love of the One who sent us.

Love,
Amy

PS: Yes, we still cook in the pan we use to kill mice.

November 1996—One of my favorite parts of the week

It's Tuesday night, almost seven o'clock, which means that Erin and I will get on our bikes and head over to open our library for an hour. Erin works the front desk checking books in and out, and I answer questions, find materials, and re-shelve books. It's fairly zooey as the concepts of orderliness, both standing in line and waiting your turn and then putting something back where you found it, are radically different from those in the States. As with other parts of life, a sense of humor, well, at least means you're laughing in the madness.

"Amy, I want a book on dogs."

"*Okay.*" Me.

"How fast is this tape?"

"*Medium speed. Have you ever read Where the Red Fern Grows?*"

"Amy, this tape doesn't have anything on it when I listen to it. Can I keep my book for another week?"

"*Sorry, sure.*"

"You look especially lovely tonight, Amy." (This was whispered with spittle into my ear.)

"I want a book with a lot of dialogue."

"*Okay.*" (I'm looking.)

"I want a tape with short stories."

"*Just a minute.*"

"What do you recommend for me to read to learn how to write research papers?"

"*Over in that area. Start looking and I will be there in a minute.*"

"Amy, can you proofread this speech for my friend who will give it tomorrow?"

"*Sure, let me find a pen.*"

"Amy, I read about a 'strip mall' in *Reader's Digest*. What is it?"

Oh my, how to explain that while proofreading. "*Just a minute and I'll try to draw a picture.*" (Heavy groans because she knows I can't draw. I guess a sense of humor is needed by our students as well, who have to try to learn from these totally foreign teachers.)

"*Okay, Jane, I finished proofreading the speech.*"

"Thank you from my bottom!"

And I had to laugh. The craziness went on, but so did the warmth of being connected with our students and involved in their lives.

In composition class we have been working on comparing and contrasting; I used one of Shakespeare's sonnets and felt inspired to have them write their own sonnets. I didn't realize that it was the first time that they had ever written poetry in English, and there was a considerable amount of groaning and complaining. However, besides the fact that they thought that words like "rememberable" and "capable" were rhyming, they did a nice job.

The following excerpt is from a student who misses his wife and daughter:

She came by bus already a few times
telling me good news of our daughter,
each time I gave her some leftover dimes
here or home we have no cocks to slaughter.

A few were downright hysterical because they must have used a thesaurus to find other words of body parts (in particular, words we don't commonly use for breasts). We are trying to develop a casual relationship with English allowing them to play with it and not always be formal in their use of English. I was delightfully surprised by a few journals where the students thanked me for the opportunity to write a sonnet.

Now that you know my focus is on the students, let me tell you the truly big news. Brace yourself, this is BIG. A shipment of Diet Coke came to a department store downtown. I know it is probably a onetime thing, but when Erin told me to go to the next aisle because there was Diet Coke, my heart started to beat faster. I mean *really* fast. I hung the receipt on our refrigerator door as a reminder of His goodness and providing and indulging in even things that seem little.

Since the last letter we have no new mice; however, the road is still bumpy. A friend near to us is depressed. Obviously it is a challenge to be depressed far from home, and it is hard to watch her be depressed. We know that she is where she is supposed to be and doing what He wants, but sometimes those can sound like empty words.

Thankfully our students and foreign friends are here to help us. Simie, one of the students who lives in our hall, has become especially close to us, and we will miss her when she leaves in January to return to college in America. In parting, I hope that the busyness of the season doesn't rob you of joy, a sense of humor, and a dose of perspective.

> Thank you from my bottom,
> Amy

December 1996—The Packers versus the Broncos

Putting our petty differences aside, or not so petty, depending on your point of view, we decided to collaborate on a newsletter. As a side note, in case you have forgotten, Erin is from Wisconsin and Amy is from Colorado, meaning this football season has been especially interesting.

With fall and winter being a festive season, and this being an election year, we have been busy attempting to share our culture with our students. Usually, we're successful, but there are those moments when we realize . . . we have not been. Here are a few of the funnier misses:

- After spending a class period talking about Halloween, the origins and present-day traditions, a student wrote in her journal about what she had learned. She wrote about the famous "Hallowmas" that could be compared to the Chinese New Year. It was a time when Americana dressed up or went door to door with their jack-o'-lanterns saying, "Trick-or-treating." The trick-or-treaters would be invited in to eat pumpkin bread and chat. After that they would go to the next house and the whole process would start over again.

- At Thanksgiving I read a book to my students called Pilgrim Voices. It contains excerpts from the pilgrims' journals. After each entry I had my students write a summary and had to laugh at one student who wrote about the migrates. You know, those famous migrates or migrants or pilgrims. I wonder what she'll teach her students.

- Unusual questions at Thanksgiving included:

  "Why don't your turkeys have heads?" (It's an honor to eat the head of an animal. An honor Erin and I are both willing to avoid.)

  "If you put stuffing in the turkey, what do you do with the organs?" (To the Chinese, the obvious answer would be, "Eat them.")

  "How do you harvest cranberries?" (Good question . . .)

In trying to lecture about the US elections, we realized that it's hard to explain the electoral college system when you do not fully understand it yourself. While all of this may cause you to laugh or seriously consider our effectiveness, it can remind us not to get too hung up on details.

On the positive side, we have had students tell us, "Now I know who you are thankful to," or, "I wish you had said more about Christmas. We Chinese are walking in darkness." Several students from last year are having their students act out Matthew and Luke. A student from last year, who called to let us know how she is doing, told us that "Silent Night" is going to be played over the school PA system to teach it to all of the students. Wow. Thus we continue to sow seeds knowing that some will grow in humorous soil and others in more fruitful soil.

The week after Thanksgiving we bought a "Christmas" tree from the flower market. Since we could not tie it to the top of our bikes, we hired a bicycle cart to follow us home. Walmart decorations never looked this good! We took a photo of our tiny, seemingly frail, sixty-year-old housekeeper, Shen Yang, and the tree. This is the same woman who, as part of her job requirement, is to protect us from burglars. We're not kidding. The waibans told us this. She can be found up in the window ledges cleaning and even gestured that the best way to get a flat stomach is to do push-ups, and demonstrated them by getting down on the floor. She is amazing and fun. We love her and are blessed to have her.

As one student put it from last year,

> "Merry Christmas to you and
> yours from I and mine,"
> Amy and Erin

PS: See you at the Super Bowl. Go Broncos, Go Packers, but in the end, may the Broncos be victorious. (Apparently Amy has the computer at the moment.)

PPS: See you at the Super Bowl. Go Broncos, Go Packers, but in the end, may we have a repeat of the last game! (Apparently Erin took over.)

PPPS: Excuse me, Elway was out with a hamstring and we have already clinched the division titles.

PPPPS: Broncos, Packers, Broncos, Packers, Broncos, Packers. Apparently the collaboration is over . . .

January 1997

[For the sake of this book, I will summarize a letter here and there as they do not make much sense now, looking back; but for those of you who write newsletters, I want you to get a sense of how often I wrote and the general content. In the January 1997 letter, I wrote about the new holiday, "Santamas" because pictures of Santa are splashed around Chengdu this year with the word "Xmas" in lights. I also talked about how we had heard from former students and the ways that they were teaching their students about Christmas.] I ended:

Even if our students themselves have not made any kind of spiritual decision, they're still telling their students. This is encouraging since it helps Christianity not to be perceived as foreign. Their students are also hearing at younger ages. Please pray that they will get accurate facts and that opportunities will come up to teach about Easter.

Love,
Amy

PS: The students go ape for the old calendars, stamps, and magazines that you send. Thanks. With all of the stamps they say, "Boy, you get a lot of letters," and I have to explain that the stamps are from friends who care about them, not actual letters.

February 1997

I originally wrote this newsletter from Thailand over a month ago, but it was lost somewhere in transit. The news is kind of old, but I still want you to have it. It's an eye-opener.

Amy.

~ ~ ~

Sawadee Ka, or "Hello," from Thailand. An encouraging aspect of going to a country where I don't speak the language is to realize I've picked up more Chinese than I had been aware of. Not to give you false hope, I probably can communicate on the level of a two-and-a-half-year-old, which, isn't much, as anyone who has actually tried to have a real conversation with a two-year-old knows. But some communicating does go on.

If we were playing Jeopardy and the answer was "flowers," the question would be, "What is your impression of Chiang Mai, Thailand?" This impression is influenced by several factors:

1. There are flowers and flowering trees all around.

2. We are here during the Flower Festival, complete with garden scenes set up and a parade with floats, kind of like the Rose Bowl Parade.

3. I live in Chengdu—not exactly a floral mecca. The Chinese attitude towards flowers is to stick them in a potted plant and

enjoy them as long as they can live without water. We do have lovely pots of dead flowers sprinkled around the city.

By the time you read this, we will be back in the classroom. An emotionally taxing part of last spring was the amount of abortions our students or their wives had. Because we work at an adult college where a majority of our students are married, conceiving during the semester break is not unusual. I was able to have a candid discussion with six female students who were dorm mates last year and found out that many do not use birth control pills because the hormone levels are extremely high and the side effects severe. Their husbands don't like condoms, and you can only get "the ring" (I think an IUD) after you have a child. Pregnancy during school is very inconvenient, so abortion is used. I even had a student tell me that she had sacrificed her baby to her education.

In a country where only forty out of every ten thousand people have an education beyond high school, education is understandably valuable. Due to China's large population, each family is allowed to have one child. The Chinese accept this as a painful but viable solution to a population problem we can only imagine.

While they accept it, I would like to share a student's journal entry from last year to help personalize this situation:

> School has been open for a whole week but I still have to stay home. This morning, my wife and I went to a hospital to check whether she was conceived or not, for her period didn't appear at the usual time. The fact is that she was. When my wife heard the doctors diagnose, she began to sob. I knew she felt both sad and frightened because of the Chinese population policy. The would-be child had not the license to come into the world, it must be got rid of it soon as possible. The doctor asked us to choose a time to have the operation, which seems somewhat cruel to Chinese women. After a short time of discussion between my wife and I, we decided to follow the operation at once. One reason is that the doctor had warned us over and over again that the sooner the easier. The second reason is that I could not stay at home for a long time.
>
> Ten minutes after our decision, my wife was send to an operation table and the operation began. I stand beside her somewhat paralyzed. The woman who was

lying here was my wife? Is she crying? Where did the blood dropping into the big bottle come from? Her hands gripped on mine. She asked for what? Break! Break. What was that sound? 'Dad ... Mum ... Dad ... Mum ...' It echoed in the air. I dare not pay my attention to it. I was a robot at that time. It seemed a decade when the doctor declared that the operation was over. I made sense of the word 'over' immediately. Yes, it was over. The misery was over. Let's go home. I caressed my wife, kissed her cheeks and wiped her tears, then I carried her out of that damn room quickly, as if it were hell. Now I can still recall the red blood, the scream, and the groan. It was cruel. Here I don't mean our population policy is not proper, I appeal for a better solution to make women suffer less.

Abortion is not an option but a fact of life in China. What is an option is our response to it. Pray that Erin and I may demonstrate in real ways compassion, understanding, love, patience, and kindness. May the hope in us be evident and intriguing.

Thank you for your prayers. As we go through the various phases, both in our relationships and serving in China, you are used by God to keep us afloat. Your generosity and consistency truly leave me at a loss for how to adequately thank you. Thailand has been a refreshing time. One of the highlights was watching the Super Bowl; seeing this year as a football game, halftime is almost over, and the game clock for the second half is set.

Love,
Amy

PS: Congrats to Erin and the Packers. We always have the Avalance.[2]
PPS: In the original letter this is where I encourage the Jayhawks in the NCAA tournament but alas, we already know how that turned out. [They didn't advance far.] As my dad says, "We always have the Avalanche."

April 1997

[Because of the lost February newsletter, this letter was also included with the delayed February 1997 newsletter.]

2   The hockey team in Colorado.

"Erin, I don't think we're in Thailand anymore." Confirmation of this came the other night as we were eating in a restaurant. Fish are kept alive in tanks to guarantee freshness and are paid for by the *jin* (about a pound). When you order a fish, the waitress will catch one with her hand and bring it to you for you to agree on the size, and therefore the cost. This happened, no big deal. However, the waitress tried to kill the fish by repeatedly throwing it on the ground. I kid you not. At first I thought, "It slipped out of her hand," but she kept picking it up and throwing it down. Later, when they brought out a live rabbit to be agreed upon by another customer (same process: freshness, size, and cost), I thought, "If they start throwing this poor thing on the ground, I would've seen it all." (Luckily they didn't.)

After the TIC conference, I traveled to Hong Kong and spent six days with my parents. The highlights, in no particular order, were the blue sky, talking, a stand-up shower with hot water twenty-four hours a day, the Star Ferry (every city should have a boat ferry!), the skyline, real bakeries, the Peak (what a view of Hong Kong), tuna, talking, Diet Coke, the Hong Kong Museum, parks with flowers, boats, school children in cute British-looking school uniforms, dim sum, Dad videotaping nonstop, riding double-decker buses, and talking. The best part was being with Mom and Dad.

My parents were able to come to Chengdu for a few days, and they got a fairly accurate slice of life, starting with the English department dropping off our schedules at four p.m. the day before we started teaching. The pipes in our building are being replaced, and unfortunately, when they were there we had slight problems with the water, gas, and electricity—and there was pounding pretty much all the time. I've also discovered that bricks are only moved at 10:30 at night. However, the bright, shining spot, and the reason we are here, is not for the accommodations but for the students.

Mom and Dad got to meet each of my classes and had fun answering questions. The most commonly asked questions were about Deng Xiaoping (since he had recently died and was a famous Chinese leader) and what I was like as a child. Three days passed quickly, but now at least they can picture Erin, our home, the classrooms, the open market, the traffic, the buses, and my students. Their overall impressions were that the food is good and the students a delight, but "We didn't realize it was this dirty."

Since all of my new students will be graduating at the end of the semester, they're anxious about their futures. Their feelings vary from excitement to go home and try new teaching methods to dread over returning to a small, undeveloped, remote hometown and a job they hate. Some have taken and passed a test to get into graduate school, while others have failed that test. Their sense of control over their own lives is rather different from my sense growing up in America. On the flip side, the need for control, or to feel control in control, is not as strong as mine. We know where their true hope should lie but the call of money for them is loud right now. Ask that Erin and I may be consistent in living with the hope that we have.

As we look to next year, Erin knows that she will be returning to the States. I don't know what I'm doing—I do know that if I stay in China, I will stay at this school. At this point, I'm mostly ignoring the decision because what I do next year doesn't affect what I'm doing right now. You could ask for guidance in this area.

I don't know if you remember, but last year was the year of the rat, according to the Chinese lunar calendar, and we had a massive mouse problem. This year, it's the year of the ox, and we certainly don't want to have an ox problem! I don't know where to find sticky paper big enough to hold an ox, and I don't fancy beating one to death with our frying pan.

> As always, living and laughing
> in Chengdu,
> Amy

April 3, 1997—A note from TIC

Many of you have probably heard by now that Amy has been through some fairly serious health problems in the past week. In the last week leading up to Tuesday, April 2nd, she had been suffering from "flu-like symptoms" bad enough to cause her to say that she had never felt more sick in her life. On that Tuesday she was taken to the hospital after her "flu" became more serious and she started suffering seizures. As Amy underwent several tests and a subsequent CAT scan, doctors in Chengdu determined that she was suffering from epidemic meningitis. That afternoon she went into a coma that lasted until the next morning. As she regained a groggy consciousness, doctors became much more optimistic about her prognosis, but also suggested that she be taken to Hong Kong where the medical facilities are more familiar to Western patients.

As of this writing, it is expected that she will be flown to Hong Kong over the weekend where her parents will be joining her. Her parents, of course, have run the whole gamut of anxiety, heightened by the fact that Amy is about as far away from Colorado as she could get.

Also involved in this situation is Amy's teammate Erin who has been integral in the information doling and the decision-making process. After the first highly stressful day, much of the stress was greatly reduced as Amy woke up from her coma and showed a remarkable amount of lucidity for someone in her state.

We urge you to pray for Amy that she'll make a full recovery and that she'll be kept safe in all of her travels between Chengdu and Hong Kong. Also, lift up Amy's parents as they travel and for Erin as she recovers from her 24-hour-a-day job as a go-between.

May 1997—Cultural experience #712: A week in a Chinese hospital

[I remember handwriting this newsletter in Hong Kong while my brain was still recovering. You will see that my brain was still not fully healed in my simple, staccato-like sentences.]

April 2nd was day two of what I thought was stomach flu. The waiban visited at 9:00 a.m. to see if there was anything they could do. I told them it was the flu, no big deal, no need to worry. When I went to change my clothes, I discovered that I had red spots all over my body. I called the waiban office and visited the clinic on campus to get some medicine. At 11:00 a.m. I got the most severe headache I have ever had, and by the time Erin got home from classes at noon, I could hardly walk. She called the waibans and I was taken to the hospital. The pain was so bad I prayed to die. Erin kept saying, "Amy, don't say that." The doctor said, "Next month, I'm going to Alabama." How nice.[8]

The doctors gave me a shot to put me to sleep, and the last thing I remember is being wheeled on a stretcher outside onto the streets of Chengdu as we went from one building to the next. At this point I went into a coma—which I now refer to as a comma in my life since it was a long pause—and had seizures. Erin said it was nothing like comas on TV. My eyes were open. I was moaning and kicking and had to be tied down to the bed or I would have flipped myself out. Thirty of my students were in ICU with me, and it was upsetting to Erin to have them see me like this. They knew it was quite serious and kept telling Erin, "You need to trust the doctors." She told them she did trust the doctors, but we have someone who is even more trustworthy. And now for some miracles.

- We live five minutes away from what we have been told is the number-four medical facility in all of China.

- A British neurologist, Dr. Smith and his wife, are studying Chinese in Chengdu, and he said I was getting the same treatment I would receive in the West, third-generation antibiotics. The chances of me being near the exact medicine I needed were unbelievably slim.

- Dr. Smith said I would be in a coma for forty-eight hours, but it was fewer than twenty-four, showing the power of God undeniably.

- The prayers of literally thousands of people in North America, Europe, and Asia.

When I woke up from my coma, the first thing I wanted was a chocolate milk shake. I don't remember this, but I guess I repeatedly asked for a chocolate milk shake. Not only are chocolate milk shakes impossible to get, Dr. Smith told me that he wasn't sure that was a good idea for my stomach. I honestly don't remember my response, but Erin tells me I said, "It's a risk I'm willing to take." Can you believe I was this cheeky in my weakened condition? ☺

I do remember Erin telling me I was lucky to get the catheter I had been saying would be so convenient to have on cold winter mornings. Thanks, Erin, but I've changed my mind.

Chinese hospitals are not like Western hospitals in their basic philosophy. They provide medical care, and the family of the sick person provides all other needs. Erin and another TIC person who flew in from Beijing to help had to provide all of my meals, clothing, toilet paper, water, cups, straws, everything. My room, however, came complete with cigarette butts on the floor, dirty walls, and my urine bag dripping on the floor. I was in a teaching hospital and was considered a novelty as the only foreigner. Several times a day a herd of interns would come in and discuss my case. The intern assigned to me was an obstetrician. Isn't that funny?

Here may I publicly thank my beloved teammate who went above and beyond the call of duty. She was an absolute pillar, spending hours with me in the hospital, organizing students to spend the night with me, and reading aloud to me. I even threw up on her and she merely took her sweater off and cleaned me up. She gave my parents much-appreciated updates. She was righteously indignant when she felt I wasn't treated right, and she even tried to remember the song I wanted played at my funeral. Erin, I love you and can never thank you enough for taking care of me when I couldn't take care of myself.

I am now spending time resting in Hong Kong, which is far more difficult for me as a Type A person than being in a coma. I'm restless and eager to get back to my students and tell students that God has healed me and that they have seen His power in action. I am aware that I am not what I was. My spelling is off, my handwriting is different, and the way my brain processes things is a bit odd. All will be normal again, but it takes time to heal, time I am frustrated to spend.

I would appreciate your prayers that this will open students' hearts to the purpose of life and the power of God. They have seen me healed and Erin calm in the face of death. Before all of this happened, I had decided to return for year three in Chengdu, and now I know why . . . my work is not done.

Thank you for your prayers, letters, and gifts. I think this was a good reminder for all of us what a truly precious gift life is.

Grateful to be catheter-free,
Amy

June 1997—Back in the saddle again

After my first day back teaching, Erin and I commented that it hardly seemed I had been gone. Routine will do that to you. You slip right back to where you were, even though much was not as it had been. The students were excited to see me but didn't comment much on the whole situation except to say how I looked. The Chinese are big on comparing. "You looked better last Tuesday," or "We decided your red shirt looks the best on you." (Who is "we"?) "You're not as energetic as you used to be," or "Today's lesson was quite informative." (What about yesterday?) The endless commentary can be wearing, except that this is how the Chinese show concern and care. I have to remember to read it that way.

Because I don't remember from Wednesday when I got into the hospital to Sunday afternoon, I had my students write about what I was like. Through this, I was reminded that they were affected, but culturally it wasn't cool to show it. Nike says, "Just do it." The Chinese say, "Just bear it." Without any further ado, my students [unedited]:

> I hurried to the hospital far ahead of my other classmates because I rode a bike while the others walked on foot. When I got there, Amy was carried to a CT room to be examined. I hurried to CT room and I saw Miss Amy was lying a moving bed, and she

didn't know anything at that time. I saw her moving from side to side, and she looked worried, but she couldn't utter at all. I joined the nurses to carry Amy to the fourth floor where infection patients stayed. I ask for looking after her, so I was permitted to stay with Amy. Amy opened her eyes, but she was unaware of anything about her. A doctor put a long needle to fetch her blood to be test, which astonished me. Although the doctors give her medicine for calmness, she moved in bed. I wondered she was too sick, while why she so strong that two men cold hardly calm her?

When we saw Amy lying in the hospital bed with our own eyes, we all couldn't recognize her, who was dizzy, moved continuously, groaned loudly. Although Amy was in so deep dizz. she had powerful strength. Her face was also red, but when I felt her body, it was cold. I must take hold of her hand to try to control her and make her quiet. I failed many times because my strength was not enough and didn't give up. I couldn't bear the situation and my tears came into my eyes. This was not my teacher Amy.

I didn't realize how serious it was until I went to see her in the hospital. The scene was horrible. Amy stayed in the bed surrounded by all kind of machines. Her face was pale, and her eyes were half closed, and her teeth sharped tightly. When I stood beside the bed, observing her carefully, I found there was no a little usual bright sight slipping out of her eyes. The only phenomenon to prove her living is her eyeballs were still moving slightly. She moved violently, not like a patient.

Several of Amy's friends came and they prayed for Amy. Most of the students were deeply moved by the devout praying of her foreign friends. Though the Chinese student haven't that kind of habit, I'm sure they were praying in their hearts at that time.

I couldn't keep my tears when I saw that your hands and feet were tied by the thin rope. You lay in the bed, but you wanted to get up because you felt very uncomfortable. Your eyes were open, but you couldn't see anything. Erin stood outside the room with your other friends, each time, when she saw you, she would cry. She told us not to be sad, but she is. Almost anyone who saw the situation would cry. That night, Jill and Julia had a dream, one is bad, one is good. Christina and I couldn't fall asleep for a long time.

At last Amy was out of danger. Several days later when I again saw Amy, though she was weak, she looked much better. When she went to the WC (bathroom) I saw her walks trembly as a child learn to walk again. I couldn't help warning her to take care.

Many students volunteered to take care of Amy, but department leaders only allowed female students to look after her. So many male classmates felt sorry to miss the chances, but they helped those students who were appointed to take care of Amy. And if only someone came back from the hospital, multitude people around to inquire the latest news about Amy.

When I saw Amy in the hospital she looked fine. When I ask her if she got used to the condition in the hospital she joked that she never got used to any hospital. Amy is Amy, I think a happy and strong minded person.

I could hardly believe that she would come back and give us lessons again. As a common person in this situation, he can't come back. It's always regarded as a chance to have a rest for him. It's difficult to have done with it like Amy for a teacher.

Although there was something wrong with Amy's head, she keeps on teaching.

Aren't they precious? However, I had been disappointed that many attribute my healing to being a "good person." To deal with my frustration, I wrote them a letter thanking them for all they did, telling them how I loved teaching them, and then explaining this misconception. I gave each student a copy, and they earnestly read it.

This spring has absolutely passed in a blur! I'm not referring to the coma. ☺ The school year is almost over. The Amy-and-Erin era is almost over and change is on the horizon. As you remember me this summer, ask that my body completely recovers. Remember Erin as she adjusts back to the land flowing with Diet Coke; it's not as easy as it sounds. I will meet my new teammate this August. Her name is Shelley, and you can be asking that we'll function well as a team. For the students, that they will know the truth.

I will be home this summer. See you all on the flip side . . . of the world.

Love,
Amy

June 1997—A letter to my students

Dear students,

I want to write you a letter to thank you for all that you did while I was ill. Helping the doctors when I was quite "active," spending the night with me, the cards and flowers, and the overall concern were appreciated by Erin and me.

While I was in Hong Kong, I kept telling anyone who would listen how much I wanted to get home to Sichuan College of Education and my students. I hope you understand how much I enjoy teaching you and spending time together with you. Next year, I will miss seeing you in the classroom, in the library, over lunch, and around campus. I think some of you have misconceptions about my healing. I have heard some of you say, "I knew that God would heal you because you're a good person." Yes, it is God who healed me. He used the skill of good Chinese doctors and the right kind of medicine, but He did not heal me because I'm good.

Three years ago, two TIC teachers died in a plane crash on their way home. They were good men who intended to keep living in China, but God decided to take them home to heaven. Last September a TIC teacher died of a heart attack, another good man. Why was I healed instead of dying? I'm not sure, but I believe part of the reason is for you to see the incredible power of God. Do you realize I was almost dead eight short weeks ago? You have seen a miracle.

I am not afraid of death, and in a way, I wish I had died to meet Jesus face to face, but it was not my time. We were created to enjoy life, and I hope that the next phase of your life awakens your heart, interests, and energies. Thank you for the privilege of being your teacher.

With much love,
Amy

July 1997

Greetings from blue skies, sunshine in Denver, with one final meningitis newsletter.

I'm at home and visiting friends this summer; in some ways it's hard to believe the whole medical situation ever happened. Was it only four short months ago that I was, as *The Princess Bride* says, "Mostly dead?" It is wonderful to be back to health again, and yet it makes it easier to forget where I've been and what I've been through.

When I returned to Chengdu, one of my students asked me what I had learned from this experience. I don't recall what I said to her, but that question has prompted me to think. Of course Erin and I were reminded of God and His character. But for me, the overriding impression was, what was I investing in? Investing my time, energy, worry, effort, and joy in?

I had the rare privilege of being removed from my life in an instant, and I found out I'm not as important as I like to fool myself into believing. Yes, my students missed me, but did they stop being students? No. Did our college end classes because I was in the hospital? There was a disruption, true, but then life "got back to normal." The quiz I was writing the day before I went into the hospital was still there six weeks later when I returned.

I'm an English teacher, naturally I'm interested in and pleased with the progress my students make. However, after they graduate, many return to small rural towns where the opportunity to speak English is minimal and their ability radically decreases. This can be discouraging. Why am I investing all of this time and effort when it is going to disappear anyway?

Then it hit me. What am I investing in, the English ability or the students? When I was sick, all of the work was still there and not that important. What was important was the difference that had been made in my students' lives. I'm not saying that we shouldn't do our jobs well. I love teaching, lesson planning, and sharing my culture, but God has blessed us with our jobs. We need to use them to be a blessing. I invite you to ask yourself the same question. What are you investing in?

Grr, grr, grind—that horrible sound was me shifting gears in conversation without thinking of a nice transition. When Erin and I became teammates, I talked about us being similar to an arranged marriage. As the school year came to an end, I kept thinking that we were having an "arranged divorce." Not necessarily by specific choice was our team dissolving, but due to logistics. I will be in Chengdu and Erin will be in Wisconsin. I'm looking forward to meeting Shelley, but I will miss the shared history that Erin and I have and playing the "Do you remember" game because no, Shelley doesn't remember; she wasn't there.

Oddly, as part of our divorce, our parents got to meet. This summer Erin and her folks drove out to Colorado to visit relatives, and we all had dessert one night. Due to my NDE, near death experience, our parents had talked quite a bit on the phone and finally got to put faces with voices.

I am excited about this coming year because as well as teaching, I have accepted the position as the curriculum director for TIC. Normally, this is a full-time position in and of itself, but I agreed to do it if I could stay in Chengdu and continue teaching. I will have an assistant who lives in Beijing and will handle all of the office-type work. Basically, I will get to be in charge of training the teachers for both the summer and the year program in how to teach English in Asia. I will also provide additional training at the midyear conference in Thailand. If teachers have questions or problems, or need ideas, they can call me and I'll help them. This is ideal! I still get to teach my students and prepare others to do a quality job.

Summer is blazing by, and I'm savoring the joy of being alive. Thank you for your prayers. I'm 100 percent back to health, maybe even more than that because I am more aware of what a joy it is to be alive. I will get to meet Shelley when I'm in California, and you can be praying for team bonding to begin without it feeling like team bondage. Thanks for being part of this. I hope you realize this journey is as much yours as it is mine and remember to take a minute to consider what you are investing in.

> Written with love and bathed
> in sunshine,
> Amy

#2 If You Write Newsletters

Ideas for Your Newsletters

1. Include a recurring "character" or thread. Do not overthink the character, and realize that it can change over time. I have found that having a recurring character has been more important than I would have thought. Including my ongoing battle with mice provided enough of a connecting point, enough of an anchor for people to track with my life and work in China.

2. Use variety in your newsletters.

   - Quizzes—about a cultural experience, what is needed for a visa, how often you are asked a set of questions.

   - Give a tour—of your website, home, or city. Even something as mundane as a tour of your kitchen, written well, will be memorable and engaging.

   - Interview—of a teammate (what is it like to team with you?), a local, a family member who visits, or a local pastor. Interviews can get long, so be willing to edit to keep the newsletter moving along.

3. Once or twice a year include a "Top Ten" list, such as

   - Top 10 differences in a normal day in your "host" country compared to your "home" country

   - Top 10 moments from your month

   - Top 10 ways you have changed by living and serving in your host country

   - Top 10 silly things you miss about your home country

- Top 10 misconceptions about your life.

- Top 10 language mistakes you have made

- Top 10 random or unexpected comments made to you

- Top 10 random or unexpected comments you've heard

- Top 10 things you love about your host country

Which idea will you try in your next newsletter?

Year Three in China

1997-1998

The tender word forgotten,
The letter you did not write,
The flower you might have sent, dear,
Are your haunting ghosts tonight.
—Mary Elizabeth Sangster

August 1997

When I came home last summer with five photo albums and around a thousand pictures, one of my sisters cheekily pointed out, "You don't have to take a picture of every meal. We get it. You eat food." This summer I toned down the picture taking and only had two and a half albums, but I adore taking pictures. I got to be home for almost two months this summer and had a wonderful time traveling around visiting friends and family. True to my interest in photographs, I took plenty-a-picture and justified my habit by saying, "This is for my newsletter." To keep me honest, I now need (and want) to show you a small fraction of my collection.

[Originally I included six pictures and told some short stories in this newsletter, mostly involving people I had met with over the summer.]

One picture in particular touches me. I wrote, "I visited my amazing grandparents in Michigan who still live in the house my grandpa was born in. Not bad for people in their nineties. We baked eleven loaves of bread and two batches of cookies. I had forgotten that baking doesn't have to take all day when you're not baking in a toaster oven."

[At the end of the letter, I said] If last year's hit phrase from a movie was 'Show me the money,' the phrase for this summer was 'Show me the love.' Thank you for all the Diet Coke, phone calls, movies, chats, cups of tea, and patience in looking at my photos. It was fun, but I'm glad to be headed back."

Love,
Amy

51

September 1997

The flight to Beijing was one of the nicest I've had. We arrived a week later than we normally do, and we only had one day of sightseeing and then off to Chengdu. Luckily, there was time to visit Dunkin' Donuts twice.

Transitions are odd because one minute you're floating high, filled with the thrill of life in China, the rush of traffic, the sound of horns as a taxi nearly takes you out, and then unexpectedly—WHAT? My beloved, framed pictures of friends and families, packed up for the summer, are ruined due to humidity and mildew. I hate this place! Then a student from last year stops by to tell me about his classes, and as he's leaving he says, "I tell all my students that I love my Amy, my beloved teacher." Whoosh! And I'm right back up there on cloud nine. We had a mouse/rat bothering us until he met Mr. Frying Pan. Whack! Whack! Caught on sticky paper. His friend, an annoying mouse, refuses to step on the sticky paper, instead preferring my nightstand.

I had been awakened three different nights by the beast near my head. He even had the nerve to come into the bathroom while I was in there. Grr.

Up down, up down. What the transition?! . . . as the highs were high and the lows low. Life is smoother now as we ride out the transition back into the routine of daily life.

What struck me about returning to Chengdu this time was the unbelievable change in the city during the two months I was out of the country. In one area, huge buildings are gone—GONE—and a finished park is in their place. Near the movie theater that we go to, the road is torn up and the buildings gutted. Torn up is too mild; decimated and unrecognizable is more accurate. As I bike through, it honestly looks like the remains of a war. The cry for modernization is loud and almost unbearable at times. I wonder what the cost is for a whole society to change this rapidly? What is being sacrificed? Who is being trampled? I don't know, as I, too, get caught up in the stream of change.

Balance is going to be the theme word for this year. Between teaching the heaviest load yet, being the TIC curriculum director, and knowing a lot of people after two years, I see how easy it would be to be doing something all of the time. Remember me and my weakness in setting limits and saying, "No." In response to my attempt to negotiate a lighter schedule with the English department, their solution was to give Shelley another class making both of us quite busy. Not acceptable. We have come to an agreement with the department, but it still involves more grading than I like, with eighty composition students a week. Ironically, they keep telling me not to work too hard because that is what caused my illness last semester.

"And how's Shelley?" many of you are wondering. We have some crucial differences, like she's a Pepsi woman when I'm Diet Coke (and missing it) all the way. The other day I was talking about John Elway, and she had no clue who he was. Can you imagine functioning in a world without John Elway? Neither can I. In slightly less important things, like getting a rush from teaching, loving hot-n-spicy food, being readers, and enjoying traveling, we're remarkably compatible. Thank you for your thoughts in this area.

Mail would be a nice thing. So far, I've only heard from my family and Erin. Other than that, the transition is over—let the living begin again.

In Him,
Amy

PS: A quick addition. Last night, at 1:57 a.m., the mouse stepped on the sticky paper in my bedroom. He is now intimately acquainted with Mr. Frying Pan, and I was back in bed by 2:02 a.m. Yay!

October 1997

"Amy, here is my homework."

"Okay, Xiao Wang, but it's late." I said.

"No, it's not."

"Yes, it is. Everyone else gave it to me yesterday because it was due on Tuesday."

"Yes, you said do it Tuesday."

Oh, the unexpected road bumps communicating in a second language: *due Tuesday* versus *do it Tuesday*. How often I hear something close, but oh so far from what was actually said.

My new job as curriculum director is keeping me on my toes. I enjoy the challenge but realize more each day that I'm pretty clueless. I found out the other week that I head the Curriculum Committee. Okay, two questions: what is it? and who is on it? I'm going to Beijing next week for a series of meetings. My main goal is to coordinate efforts with leaders in Mongolia and Vietnam as to what we will be doing at the midyear conference in February. It is my desire that the curriculum sessions are what the teachers need and want to equip them for the second semester. This can be a formidable task because the group is diverse, with some teachers absolutely loving teaching and others absolutely loving the Chinese and living in China and teaching is more a means to be with them. As you can guess, the motivations and interests of these two groups are different. Please be asking for wisdom in this area.

A cool aspect of being the TIC curriculum director is that I got to go to the contract renewal ceremony between TIC and the State Bureau of Foreign Experts, which was held in the Great Hall of the People in Beijing. To put this in perspective, imagine that you were invited to the White House for dinner. Now do you see why I'm excited? The building is actually a series of halls, named after the provinces. The signing ceremony was in Shaanxi Hall, and then all involved had a group picture taken standing on risers, which reminded me of high school choir. I couldn't help making the joke that if we weren't careful we were going to have the Great Fall of the People. Get it? Okay, you can stop groaning now as we move into the Guangdong Hall for our Cantonese banquet.

I wish that our life would be a sitcom on TV. There are only a few problems with this idea, the main one being that the audience would say life couldn't be like what we are showing. Yet I'm here to testify that we don't make these crazy things up; we live them.

The mouse problem has thankfully settled down only to be replaced by . . . bats! Fortunately, they're not in our house, but they fly around outside from 6:00 p.m. to 8:00 a.m. They dive-bomb around, making it hard to bike and duck at the same time. The other evening, as Shelley and I were biking, a bat swooped right between us, causing us to scream. Of course people stared and laughed. We have comforted ourselves, reassuring each other that the bats aren't going for us but using echo-location to find bugs. This little lie worked until one flew directly into Shelley's hand as she held some books to her chest.

Would you believe that on a sitcom? How about the other morning, Shelley woke up and her bottom lip was swollen and looked like something that could take hours to put on by a Hollywood makeup artist. We have no idea what caused it, but I tell you, I don't think I earned the Supportive Teammate Award for as loud as I laughed. The swelling did go down by lunch.

Shelley and I have already seen answers to major requests. One of her students found out that the money her sister was giving her for school actually came from the sister's married lover, causing a moral dilemma for the student. Her sister has decided to get a job so our student can stay in school. Yay. We have had opportunities to talk about why we have a peace and where the saying "Don't presume to be teachers" came from.[9] Many students have been asking for a culture lecture on the role of the Good Book in Western literature. We're going to put the lecture off until next semester when their English is better, please be lifting that one up now.

We are, however, being pushed out of our comfort zone in one part of life. We live in a hotel hallway that has traditionally been occupied by the foreigners and our beloved housekeeper/Chinese mother. To earn money, the waiban office has rented the two empty rooms to four Chinese schoolteachers who are here for a two-month seminar. Dealing with cultural adjustments had been a fun adventure . . . until it came into our home. When you live in a foreign country, home is usually the one place you can escape and be yourself, especially in a country where you stick out like we do. When I go out on a walk to "get away from it all," I can't. I walk too fast, I'm too tall, I've even been told that I'm clever because my hips are so big. Normally this is funny, but the point is, now we have no special place to retreat to.

We (all seven of us) share a phone that is right outside my door and have rather different definitions of what is a culturally appropriate volume while on the phone. For the Chinese at this school, bedtime isn't until 11:30 p.m. and spitting is okay. Shelley has taken to playing music to block out the spitting noise. Please don't take this wrong and be concerned. As I said, we're being pushed out of our comfort zone and need to continue to seek help from the One who knows no cultural boundaries. I'm thankful He does, because we seem to be bouncing into our boundaries more than usual.

For National Day we went on a two-day trip with fellow TIC teachers from Nanchong (also here in Sichuan Province) to the Wo Long Panda Reserve. Boy, are the pandas cute! It was great to be out of the city and do some hiking. We have started biking around Chengdu, exploring. One Saturday we ended up at a KFC with about a thousand other people, so while Shelley ordered I circled around until I found an empty stool and perched. In one picture I took, I'm thanking Mr. Sanders for his chicken and ice cream and asking him when he thinks Diet Coke will come to Chengdu.

Thanks for all of your thoughts and letters. The holiday season is coming up, please be asking that the hearts of the students would be softened and that we wouldn't be too busy to listen. Thanks for laboring with us. If only some of the bats would fly in your direction.

Chow for now,
Amy

November 1997

Having ended my last letter bemoaning our new neighbors, it is only fair to tell you right off the bat (no pun intended) that they aren't annoying anymore . . . and no doubt they are writing (or screaming into the phone) the same sentiment about us. What's changed with them? Nothing. We've adjusted to each other with some help from above. Adjustment is wonderful. When I hear their mahjong tiles clinking down the hall, instead of being perturbed I know that they're home enjoying an evening in. On the funny side, and there is always a funny side here, they had a party the other night and had so much *baijiu* (hard, hard liquor) that my bathroom reeked of it since we share the same air vent. TIC has a no-drinking policy, and I thought, "Well, at least I can breathe it." (I wouldn't want to drink that stuff; I teared up simply standing in my bathroom because it is strong.)

The meetings in Beijing to plan the conference went well. Yippee! I have a plan for what I'm going to do during the curriculum sessions and have been working on it. I won't bore you with the details; I did, however, come home from my time wiped out. Being in meetings and trying to tackle problems the teachers face, is exhausting. I'm grateful for the support that TIC offers to teachers to help alleviate burnout in a land that can leave you dry. Please be lifting up the conference and the time before it as I train new teachers who will be living and teaching in China and Vietnam next semester.

It seems like it wouldn't be a letter from Chengdu if there wasn't something about mice. Well, they're back! The week started off with one obediently lying dead on the sticky paper—my kind of mouse. On Wednesday Shelley was making tortillas, and upon opening our utensil drawer to get the rolling pin, there sat a mouse. She screamed and ran into the living room. I went down to the kitchen and banged around hoping to scare the mouse, and got the rolling pin. A few minutes later I went back to get something and the mouse leapt out of the drawer at me. Okay, he was leaping for freedom and I was in the way, but it was a creepy feeling. He headed into my bedroom and we sat down to have lunch.

During lunch I got a phone call from a student confused on an assignment, and as I was talking, the mouse came out from under my door and I yelled into the phone. My poor student. Last night Shelley and I were standing in the hall talking and heard a mouse right by us. We looked around. We didn't see any but then heard it again. We were hearing the mice run around inside the walls. Gross!

Something I hadn't foreseen myself doing when I came to China was writing letters to Chinese senior high school students. As my students graduate and return to teaching, some ask if their students can write to me. I have about six high school students whom I correspond with regularly, about once a month. They're quite sweet and obsessed with grammar. I've given advice on sibling relationships, accusations of stealing, love, family, and both studying in general as well as studying English in particular. I feel like the "Dear Abby" of Sichuan. The challenge is that their vocabulary is limited, and I have to express what I'm trying to say in simple English. My hope is that in years to come these kids will meet another foreigner (or Chinese) person who can tell them about something much more significant, and the road to communicating deeper truths will already have been partially paved. Remember these kids and ask that they be prepared for something grand.

One of the highlights of October was our Halloween costume party. Can you guess who the two people in costumes at our party were? Amy and Shelley. Quite a few of the students wore masks; but they were giggly and embarrassed, so they mostly carried their masks around. One cultural area I'm still working on is how to throw a good Chinese party. In America we're usually happy with food and talking with our friends at a party. But since the main source of social contact for the Chinese is the work unit where they live, shop, and work in close contact with each other, they do plenty of talking and at a party want instead to be entertained.

Last year I had made pumpkin bread for the students, so during the week leading up to the party I kept being asked, "Amy, are you going to make pumpkin pie again? You're an excellent cooker!" They would giggle because they used the Chinglish "cooker" on purpose, and I would laugh on the inside because it was bread and not pie that I made. In preparation for the party, we made eight batches of pumpkin bread with the help of students and brought three pounds of peanuts and three bags of sunflower seeds. At least we all agree on the importance of food at a party.

We "bobbed" for apples using apples tied on string and played musical chairs. Since the Chinese are proficient at shoving to get in lines, they are vicious musical chair players! The highlight of the evening was when I thought it was over but the camera came out and it was picture time—*take a picture with Amy, take a picture with Shelley, take a picture with Amy and Shelley, take a picture with Amy and your best friend, take a picture with Amy and all of your roommates.* Get the picture? Ha-ha. All in all it was fun.

This week a friend of ours will be giving a culture lecture to our students on the history of Israel and the simultaneous history of China, which tends to help our students draw parallels between the nations of the Bible and their own country. In turn, this makes the Bible more real for them. Our students are tied to it [Christianity] being Western. We are hoping for an eye-opening lecture that will spur them on to want to learn more and lead into Christmas nicely. You can be lifting up the reverberations.

Thanks for your immediate response to my call for mail. I could tell exactly when you got my newsletters because within a three-day period I heard from many of you. It was good to hold your letter in my hand and see your handwriting. This is not the easiest season to be away from home, but it can often be one of the most exciting ones. Your words to us were encouraging. We're remembering you too as you're surrounded by much that can be distracting. When you hear the song "Silver Bells," think of us and all of the silver bicycle bells that ring in Chengdu. With the ever-increasing traffic and the philosophy that only lots of loud noise can get traffic jams going, "Silver Bells" is my theme song for this year and it might as well be yours too.

Ring-a-ling,
Amy

PS: For those of you who haven't heard yet, our dog, Tanner[3] had to be put to sleep.

December 1997

Recently Shelley and I visited another TIC team which lives about a nine-hour bus ride away. Their school is little bit outside of Nanchong, and it was nice to go on a picnic down by the river after living in the heart of a big city. To save time, we took an overnight sleeper-bus home. If you're able to sleep on a lawn lounge chair snuggling your luggage while inhaling smoke, this is a great way to travel. Contrary to what Shelley says, I did not get a full night's rest. I merely rode with my eyes convincingly closed except when I looked at Shelley to see if she was asleep.

When we got home, I was excited to take a sponge bath and do a load of laundry. Upon entering the laundry room there was . . . you guessed it . . . mouse number five. I did a little victory dance waving my instruments of death in the air. I wore rubber gloves because I had to move the paper to get a better whacking angle for the frying pan. Later in the week I changed the words to "Three Blind Mice," figuring

---

3 Our family dog in America—Shelley and I didn't have a dog!

if we're going to live this, we're going to laugh about it.

Five dead mice, five dead mice
How did they die? How did they die?
On to the sticky paper they ran
Where they met up with Mr. Frying Pan
I hope there's no more in His plan
Than five flat mice, five flat mice.

The truth is that number four was found rotting in one of our desks. And the great lesson there was, if you think you smell something rotting, there probably *is* something rotting. No amount of Lysol can remove that smell.

We had a wonderful time inviting students over for dinner. This is a bit challenging because they want to eat Western food but often don't like it. Sloppy Joes (now known as "Floppy Joes") were a complete miss. In general, the Chinese don't like to touch their food and don't like tomato-based things much. The broccoli I served was finally described as "raw," but they did like the "chocolate" (pudding). Tacos have had the most success, and here I let one of my students give her rendition of eating Western food:

> This afternoon, Amy gave Lisa, Grace, and me a special prize because of our good composition. I felt a warm and kind atmosphere in the salon (drawing room) when we reached the room. Amy was busy preparing for the dinner with Shelley. Delicious smell had been filled with the whole room. We wondered how we had a typical western food with knife, fork and spoon. I didn't feel worried at all because two kindhearted American teachers would act as our models.
>
> At first we put a piece of bread in the plate and then I ladled out some tomatoes, cucumbers, beef and seasoning on the bread. At last we rolled up the bread and cut them to eat with forks and knives. Amy gave us the name "taco" which is a kind of very, very typical American food. We had a free talk happily while eating which made us know each other well and helped us stimulate our appetites. After this we tasted the other dessert—Jello, which tasted sour and sweet. I liked it very much. Shelley taught us how to make

it. I plan to make it for my friends and let them share my happiness. I admired Amy's and Shelley's natural and unrestrained temperament, and this causes them to look young forever and have no worry to disturb them.

While I doubt we have no worries, we are grateful to have many opportunities to interact with our students and get to know them. They are highly motivated to know English, which is a blessing and fun in the classroom. Their recent obsession is to speak exactly like a native speaker without any accent. I, on the other hand, am more concerned with their Chinglish mistakes, which will make them stand out more than their accent. No matter how clearly "Wish you happy forever" is said, it still sounds funny to me.

Mark your calendars on February 7th—actually it'll be February 7th on this side of the world so you should mark yours for February 6th. This is the Curriculum Day of the TIC conference in Thailand and the day that I'm responsible for planning. The morning will be a big session for all of the teachers, and the afternoon is split into workshops. The preparation has gone well—thanks for all of your thoughts. I hope you realize what an influence and effect you have.

As this year closes and we begin again, I want to thank you for being a part of this investment in lives. It is a joy to live and serve in China with you. Thank you for your letters of encouragement, your daily thoughts, and the small things you send for the students and us. Students keep commenting on how many friends I have; it impacts them that this is not something I'm doing on my own. For all of this I can say, as clearly as I possibly can, "Wish you happy forever" and may the next year be as fruitful as this one.

Love,
Amy

PS: We were told today that all of the bathrooms are going to be redone and we won't have hot water until the end of February. Think of us, as there is continual pounding in our home. May we be beacons of peace amongst the noise and a sweet odor from our sponge baths.

January 1998—Bummer!

Bummer. Pain in the butt. Bottom out. Kick butt. You're a boil on the butt of humanity. All I need is a good kick in the pants.

Starting December 8th, these sayings came to life for me in a new way as I had a boil in the area of my body that made it impossible to sit (I'll let you figure out where). By the end of the week I could feel a pushing on bone and nerves and was walking funny.

When one of the waibans found out, she told me it was because I slept on the floor (I laid on the floor to watch TV) and told me I was going to the doctor the next day. By that point I was in so much pain I would have agreed to anything, and thus began another medical experience in my life that I can't believe I had. The doctor agreed that it was a boil and that it needed to be lanced. Doesn't that sound harmless?! "It is a boil. We need to lance it." He should have said that they were going to use a Weedwacker on my behind!

Entering the surgery room, we (Shelley, the waiban, and I) put little booties over our shoes and waddled in. The window was open because fresh air is good, and a bucket of previous patient's bloody bandages sat next to the operating table. The doctor wore flip-flops, and when I jokingly asked if he liked foreigners, he assured me he did. What he failed to mention was that anesthesia is too expensive, and the Chinese way is to bear the pain. The surface was numbed, and I didn't feel the initial cutting, but then they had to go about an inch and a half into my flesh. Picture me, lying on a narrow surgery bed with my pants around my ankles, booties on my shoes, squeezing Shelley and Xiao Feng's hands. I told myself not to cry, but at one point I couldn't help screaming, "Stop!" I think the philosophy is the faster the better. Unfortunately, in being fast they sacrifice gentleness. At the end, I couldn't stop crying and lay there in disbelief that this had happened; it was the most traumatic experience I have ever had.

Shelley was such a support to me the whole month of December. She held my hand and described the surgery. When we got home and people left, she cried with me. She went back to the hospital every day to hold my hand and tell me what was happening as the doctors had to check no infection remained—by jamming a long Q-tip-like instrument of pain into the wound. When I kicked the hole in the wall one day due to the pain, she didn't tell me for the millionth time, "Just bear it," like the waiban did. She did, however, dub herself Nurse Nazi and say I was a stubborn patient. I told her she was bossy, and I think we were both right. She is now far more familiar with my behind after bandaging it for two weeks than I would have guessed, when I met her in August, that she would ever be.

Bang, bang, bang. Welcome to our home. By the time I leave for the semester break and travel to our mid-year conference, we will have had pounding in our home for four and a half weeks solid. Our home looks like a construction site with a hole in the hallway, piles of bricks, and construction workers galore. In some ways they are precious as they get brave enough to yell "Hello" or discover the doorbell. When they keep ringing it for days on end . . . Sigh. The other day I yelled at no one in particular, "I surrender, you have beaten me." But there was no one to surrender to, and the banging continued.

With all of the construction, the mice seem to migrate to our place and another three have been whacked into the next world. Mouse number eight, I had little sympathy for him after he visited my bedroom five nights in a row. It got to the point that neither hitting the wall nor shouting fazed him, so I finally turned on the light and told him to leave. He ran across my room and up the hat stand with all of my dresses hanging on it. At the top, he began to spin around, and then he ran down and left. I was happy when he finally discovered the sticky paper.

The circumstances of December brought life to the simplest of terms. We did not get caught up in the materialism that saturates the US; instead, I was thankful to be able to sit, albeit gingerly, on Christmas. The thirty minutes the workers rest at lunch are a precious time of day now. The reason we are here was highlighted by the Christmas note from one of my students, Carrie. She comes over almost every afternoon to listen to tapes of simple English at volumes that would teach the dead English.

> How I excited to be the part of your life! And so did you. Thanks for you warm, love, a very kind heart for me. Maybe sometimes we have different attitude towards one thing, but we can understand each other. We have different culture. You are my respected teacher in the class. In another hand, you are my dear friend, even sometimes like my sister for you loving to me. I really appreciate for its fate or God let us know well. I like best the feeling, especially when I in your home. Happy for your everyday.

We end this semester worn down, but not broken. I'm ready for a change of scenery, but happy to know I will return here after a short breather. This month, as you turn on your faucets and enjoy your hot water, remember our health, our energy level, and our desire to count it all joy—no matter what.

Bang,
Amy

February 1998—We won!

Knowing me, you shouldn't even need to ask what that refers to, but in case you're wondering, the Denver Broncos won the Super Bowl! Shelley and I left Chengdu to start traveling to the TIC conference and were on the train when the Broncos were playing the Pittsburgh Steelers to see who would get to go to the Super Bowl. If the Broncos play Sunday afternoon, it's Monday morning here so I usually wake up on Mondays and wonder what's happening with the game. Even Shelley, the woman who had no idea who John Elway was a few short months ago, thought of them Monday on the train. We had arrived in Kunming and walking around saw a restaurant that had Internet access for two dollars an hour; what a bargain for peace of mind. Waiting for the news to come up, Shelley said, "I'm a little nervous." How's that for team support? When it came up on the screen that the Broncos were in the Super Bowl and were playing the Packers, I squealed in honor of Erin, who is from Wisconsin.

The Super Bowl started at 6:18 a.m. on the day I was supposed to begin training the new teachers! Can you believe that?! Fortunately, the guy doing devotions felt the same way I did, and we moved the session back to 10:00 a.m. The game was announced in Thai and we had to watch the refs and their signals. The announcer said things like, "Blah-blah Hail Mary! Blah-blah, touchdown!" While you had the battle between beers, I saw a mango drink matchup. I was excited to get to see the game, but it did make me want to be home with my family and all of the festivities. Daily denying myself is hard.

Training the new teachers was fun because of their excitement for Asia, which is infectious. For three days I led sessions about teaching English as a second language and what it means to be a teacher in Asia. I also interviewed about half of the current TIC teachers to see how their semesters went and if they need any help. I certainly got more than I gave as I heard their creative ideas for lessons.

At the TIC conference, curriculum day was successful, in part due to your petitions. Thanks. I felt calm the day before and everything went smoothly. I talked about how we've chosen to be teachers and what it means to be chosen by God for a task by looking at Moses, Jeremiah, Mary, and Joseph. Being chosen isn't enough; they each needed to accept the call and act on it. We, as teachers, have been chosen for this season to be teachers and need to act on that reality by taking teaching seriously. I know being chosen doesn't mean a rosy trip through life and was able to share about the realities of being chosen to teach in Chengdu in December—the boil, the lack of hot water, and the construction noise. Not fun, but God has promised that He will not leave us and He will be with us . . . and He was!

I quoted from my student Carrie's Christmas card in the last newsletter. This semester I would like to ask you to pray for her because she is in our home most afternoons during the week listening to English tapes. She sees us; she sees how we love and respect our Chinese mother, how we react to people coming by. She helps me cook for other students, and she was there for the boil. During the construction phase she stopped coming over because the noise was simply too much. Pray that she will continue to come over and that I will display a life that is consistent with the hope we have.

Shelley and I are restless to go home and get back to teaching. Visiting Fantasy Island (aka Thailand) is refreshing, but I want to go home. Thank you for your continued love and affirmation of me. For the first time, our school has agreed to let a teacher (me) stay for a fourth year. We are thankful to know where we will be next year. This semester pray for our health, Carrie, balance between teaching and being curriculum director, and faithfulness in living out the hope we have.

From a victorious,
in every sense of the word,
Amy

March 1998—I'm clean!

Normally this would not be headline material, but after three months of no hot water, what a treat to hear the hot water running in the pipes at 9:00 p.m. on March 7th. We are back to our typical schedule of hot water for an hour a day from 9:00 to 10:00 at night. On the surface the bathrooms look nice; unfortunately, China suffers from a lack of quality workmanship. I do not want to sound cruel or superior, but the fact is that doing a construction job well is not a cultural value—as long as it looks good on the surface, it is considered a good job. This has been a frustrating cultural adjustment to make.

A hot topic in China right now is the economy. If you talk to two different people, you would probably get conflicting reports. The best that I can tell from a variety of people is that the private sector is booming and the economy couldn't be in better shape for them, but in the public sector many businesses have gone bankrupt and have closed in recent months. Our students, in general, are more tied to the public sector with family members who are suddenly not unemployed, but "retired without pay." It's a great burden to these families as a source of income is gone and with it the medical and retirement benefits.

C. S. Lewis says in *The Screwtape Letters*, "Prosperity knits a man to the world. He feels that he is 'finding his place in it' while really it is finding its place in him. His increasing reputation, his widening circles of acquaintances, his sense of importance, the growing presence of absorbing and agreeable work, build up in him a sense of being really at home in the earth, which is just what we want."[10] As the economy and the security of the future is changeable right now, our hope is that our students can find something that truly is secure without being lured away by false hope of prosperity.

Shelley and I were joined this semester by visiting professor Paul Jones from a small college in Michigan. It's been good for me to see Chengdu through fresh eyes—much now seems normal to me, and I forget how it might look to an outsider. Paul started laughing the other night and said, "If you had told me a week ago that I'd be eating dinner with a roll of toilet paper in the middle of the table as napkins, I wouldn't have believed you." Oh yeah, we don't do that in the US. It's normal now, but with Paul's arrival I realized how much more strongly I'm associating with the Chinese. He'll say things and I feel something well up within me and I want to say, "Hey buddy, you don't understand China." Yet he's not saying anything I didn't say two years ago. It's good to know that my love for and understanding of the Chinese are deepening.

I was ready to send this off when something unusual happened last night and I needed to add this paragraph. The doorbell rang about eight o'clock; it was Carrie. She had a blue plastic bag and said something about a rabbit. I thought that she had brought us some cooked rabbit. Silly me. Out of the plastic bag came a cute, live, baby rabbit. I asked Carrie if she was a pet or for food. "You decide." Clue number one. I then asked, "What's her name?" "You decide." Hoping I was wrong, I asked several other questions that made it clear I was now the proud owner of a little white rabbit. Carrie had bought it for me the day before and all of her roommates knew she was giving it to me, so I had to keep it or cause her major loss of face. Fortunately we have a backyard our new rabbit can hop around in. Last night we put her in a cardboard box. When I went to check on her later, she wasn't in it and I found her sitting in the trash can nibbling away. This morning I'm off to buy a cage and some vegetables. As I wrote this, she hopped on my foot.

Carrie hasn't been able to be around as much because she spends her afternoons in classes preparing for the entrance exam for our college. Even though she is already a student . . . don't ask. Part of the system is that you can take the entrance exam repeatedly until you pass. I don't get it.

Yesterday I was in the boy's dorm playing cards. When we finished, the boys started imitating what I'm like in class. "Talk to your partner!" Carl said, waving his hands like a fish. "Does my behind stick out like that?" I asked in mock horror. No, it was an exaggeration. Well, it had better be. ☺

Then Robert said: Amy, are you in charge of TIC?

Amy (laughing): No!

Robert: You're in charge of a part of it, aren't you?

Amy: Yes.

Robert: You write articles for *Readers Digest*, right?

Amy (smiling): No, I write articles for the TIC journal.

Robert (he was already standing but sort of puffed out his chest on this line): On behalf of the Chinese people, I would like to thank you for living in China for many years and making such a great contribution.

Amy (sticking out my chest a little and chuckling): Robert, on behalf of the American people, you're welcome!

I pass on that thank-you to you. Together we are slowly changing people. You are making a *great* contribution and I am now making a *cleaner* one.

> Squeaky clean,
> Amy

April 1998

Well, let's get the tragedies out of the way from the get-go. Both my bunny and Carrie are gone from my life. FB (Fluffy Butt, the bunny) had horrible diarrhea ten days after we got her. She loved to sit in the trashcan, eating trash and no doubt ate something that disagreed with her system. Don't ask me what kind of mother lets her little one do this—obviously a bad one. The poor thing became dehydrated, went into a comatose state, and lay there kicking and twitching for an hour before she died. I sat on the floor crying and petting her through this. Shelley dug a hole out back, and FB was buried in a Broncos hand towel.

With Carrie, I had no warning—she simply wasn't in class one week. The next week when she was still gone, I asked the other students if she was okay. One student said she had dropped out of school and moved to Shanghai to work. Another told me that she said something about an operation and looked sad. Who knows, all I know is that I miss her. I mentioned several letters ago how Carrie would come and spend her afternoons studying in our home. Who would have guessed that I would grow to love simple English played at extremely loud volumes all afternoon.

I feel like I have done more living in the last month than most people do in six. I had the privilege to visit two of my former students and got to see both of their homes and the schools they teach in. The two experiences were rather different which, as you will read, is a bit of an understatement. Taking a bus, I set off to visit Alice first. It was a great honor for her school to have me visit, so I was greeted—as I stepped off the bus—not only by Alice, but also, by the head of the English department.

In her class, Alice gave a teaching demonstration, which meant that all sixteen of the teachers from the English department observed her class. Afterwards we went to a meeting room to tell Alice what she had done wrong. I learned that the Chinese way is to point out what is wrong allowing you to correct it, thus bettering yourself. There is no need to say what you did well because you did it well, you know you did it well, and you don't need to improve so why mention it. The affirming person within me was having trouble functioning in this meeting, but that was okay because the focus wasn't actually on Alice. Since I was there, we rapidly spiraled into technical grammar questions they all had been dying to ask some native speaker. What fun! (Sarcasm, grammar is not my forte or of much interest to me.)

That evening I was to give a lecture to the high school students about learning English and then open it up to questions. No problem. There were two things I didn't grasp before entering the hall for the lecture: A) these kids are starved for any form of entertainment even if it is a lecture on learning English, and B) there were 1,500 students with a few hundred more curious people thrown in.

A + B = a frantic mob of humanity who went wild when I entered.

I was to give the lecture sitting at a table on the stage and speaking into a microphone. Some of the questions included the following:

"Do you know Miker Jodon?" (Michael Jordan)

"I think you are very beautiful. I want to know why you are so tall."

"Can you say this sentence in Chinese: I like China?"

After three questions there was a power outage in the city and the crowd went wild. Some of the students stormed the stage to ask for my autograph. When it became apparent that the lights weren't going to come back on and the crowd had to be controlled lest it truly turn into a mob, I was escorted off the stage.

During this visit I was treated like royalty with each meal being a banquet and my accommodations being in a hotel. Alice stayed with me because the Chinese think that if you are alone, you are lonely. The only chance I got to be "lonely" was in the bathroom. The weekend ended with me being driven back to Chengdu in a police car because they don't have to pay at the tollbooths or obey speed limits. I have already received a number of letters from the students because of that visit and hope to return there next fall.

Another enlightening experience for me was when Shelley, and our student Robbie, and I went to visit Peter, who lives out in the countryside. This experience was more like visiting a friend because we stayed with his aunt and uncle and were treated like part of the family. The first night we stumbled into a bit of a cultural faux pas as we prepared for bed. When Shelley and I emerged from the bathroom, it was obvious to the six sitting in the living room that we hadn't washed our feet. Looks of shock, horror, and disgust flashed across their faces. As Peter's aunt hurried to boil more water for us, they sat the bucket in the middle of the living room—to be sure that we used it—and told us to wash our feet. We convinced them that we would wash them, but we were more comfortable in the bathroom. Live and learn!

The next day we went on an all-day picnic with Peter and his forty-three students. Since we had a two-and-a-half-hour walk to where we were having lunch, I had plenty of time to chat with my pen pals. These students spared no effort in having a "picnic." I later referred to it as a Martha Stewart moment as they hauled wood, woks, cutting boards, knives, spices, bowls, pots, chopsticks, and all kinds of meats and vegetables and proceeding in teams of six to cook a gourmet spread. Since Shelley and I weren't on a team, we were invited from team to team to eat. Martha herself never had it so good. After a short program of performances we walked home.

That weekend was eye-opening on the reality of life in the countryside. We came home and rejoiced in the life of luxury we live. Our clothes are not washed by hand in the river. We don't work seven days a week up to our knees in mud doing backbreaking work. Life does not consist of surviving. One of my pen pals walks four hours once a month to go home and visit her family. The bus (at thirty-seven cents one way) is usually too expensive.

From one extreme (a ride home in a police car) to another (walking through rice fields), it was a busy month but a good one. As we were reminded of the importance of loving people and being faithful and serving them where they are, I wonder what next month has in store.

Love,
Amy

PS: As always, I humbly say thanks for your time, effort, and love for us.

May 1998—She's back!

A month after my friend Carrie "disappeared," I got a phone call from her.

"Hi," she calmly said.

I think I yelled in slow, simple English, "Carrie, where have you been?"

She was sick and had gone to a hospital in a city far away. Since phone conversations are not the easiest in a second language, I left it at that, but I'm eager to see her and find out what happened. The Carrie Saga is a little slice of the ambiguity we often find ourselves functioning in.

The aftershock of visiting Peter and Alice at their schools, and getting to meet their students, has been good. Both have written that their students are more excited about studying English after meeting a real *laowai* (foreigner). I don't care too much about that. I'm glad to help make what appears to be foreign (*wai* means "outside") not as outside. I have about six new pen pals and received the following advice from two girls who write together: "The spring is coming. Amy, are you wearing skirt now? Please do show your graceful bearings in your skirt. That's every girl's privilege." I don't know how well I show my graceful bearings, but I now smile more at women in dresses.

The highlight of last month was the visit of my college friend Kim and her two friends. I met up with them in Beijing, and we had a few odd moments as Kansas and China, which are normally far apart from each other, shared space. It's a weird feeling to have two completely separate aspects of life coexist, but then the taxi pulls up, and you're lifting and shoving luggage into it, and life continues. We played in Beijing for a few days and then came down to Chengdu for another five days.

I appreciate how Kim and company made themselves accessible to the students. Of course, the students wanted to know what I was like in college, and if you want to know, you'll have to ask Kim! They had a hard time grasping that Kim works for a church—she's in charge of the singles' ministry—but is not a nun, can marry, and doesn't appear to be overly poverty-stricken. "You mean, it's your job?!" JoDee is a fifth grade teacher, and was asked several questions about the Jonesboro shooting; and Natalie is a speech pathologist, and in general, she focused on trying to explain what she does.

I had forgotten how much fun it is to hang out with a gaggle of women and talk. They treated us wonderfully, bringing little touches of home, with bagels and recent newspapers topping the list. I know it will help to have others to talk to who have seen where I live and what I do. I'm thankful that whenever I do return to the US, a support system is being laid to help me with the transition. As we're heading into the home stretch of the school year, remember our energy level, our ability to focus on the task and not kick it into vacation mode, and above all, to love, love, love our students. I'm rather pumped because my next visitors will be my two sisters.

> Bearing gracefully,
> Amy

PS: The day Kim arrived was the one-year anniversary of when I went into the hospital with meningitis. A far more fun day was had by all.

June 1998—Three giant golden flowers

What do you call a family that has three daughters in China? You say they have three golden flowers. In the case of my sisters visiting, we were more like three *giant* golden flowers let loose on Chengdu for about ten days in May. After sharing much of our lives together, it was incredible to have them here, gaining insight into who I am becoming and where I live.

More of my separate little world collided together while the three of us were in Beijing. John and Barb White were like pinch-hitting parents for us when we were growing up. If Mom and Dad were out of town, we often stayed with them. Who should be in Beijing on business the exact same weekend my sisters arrived? The Whites! John has fallen in love with China and reads every book about China that he can get his hands on, and he has even taken Chinese lessons. Are we on a Disney ride with "It's a Small World" playing in the background? Actually, we know that this is a blessing and not a coincidence. Bearing gifts of contact paper and Dove soap, their visit was appreciated on many levels.

Back to my sisters. We got to go on a weekend trip out into the countryside, which let them see field after field with people doing backbreaking farming and lots of water buffaloes, as well as spend time with my students. Here are random thoughts and comments I overheard them say:

- You can speak Chinese.

- Your students are so sweet.

- You're right: the best analogy for being a foreigner in China is like being famous in America. People watch you walk down the street, look to see what food you've ordered, and want to know what you've bought.

- It was great to eat with your students and see them spit on the floor. We knew they did that, but to see it was another thing.

- After visiting the hospital where I recovered from meningitis: "It's a good thing Mom and Dad didn't see this. We were told it was like a hospital in the 1950s. We weren't told that it was more like the original '50s, and filthy."

- The food is great.

- Now we understand why you love China and continue to prolong your life here. (The ultimate comment for me!)

Their visit also made an impact on my students. I think my favorite question was whether we "warred" as children. They loved Laura's voice and Elizabeth's gentle nature (ha!). I think it made it more real that I am not this random person, that I am part of a family. Obviously the students knew this, but to have my sisters stand there, and for them to see the love between us, makes it real, that I have left my family and have chosen to live here. The following student's journal shows some of their ponderings on this issue:

> Amy must be very happy these days, because her sisters, Elizabeth and Laura, came to China to stay with her. Two sisters of hers went around the campus.

Love, Amy

I wonder if they want to know what is Amy's life like here in China. This Monday they came to our classroom to talk to us. After their introduction, we asked a lot of questions, but there is another question in my mind. Amy has stayed in China for about three years. She is familiar with China, its culture, its everyday life, and even its food. When she goes back to the States, how can she go well in the "new" society? Is it possible for her to live in China forever? If she just wants to look after her parents, will she live happily as she is in China? I want to know more about Amy.

Our hope is that the students will continue to ask questions that will get to the heart as to why we are here and continuing to stay. Through consistent living out of our lives, may our living be worthy of such questioning. Living in a fishbowl can be draining. Ask that we have the strength and the desire to keep on shining His light, and not our small frustrations.

After my sisters got home, both wrote to me about how much they were affected by China; it is that kind of place. Elizabeth said that what she didn't like about life here is oddly what she'll miss. Being stared at is not fun, but having the freedom to stare at others is the trade-off. I understand these contradictory feelings. I feel them daily.

It was hard to have them leave. In Luke, a person said that he wanted to say goodbye to his family and was told, "No one who puts his hand to the plow and looks back is fit for service in the kingdom of God."[11] This is not easy stuff. It is hard to know that I won't see Laura for more than a year. I'm thankful that China is such a good fit for me, because it makes the staying easier. It makes it easier on my family too, but they have to plow on as much as I do. Part of being a family means that we're all in this together. Thankfully I hear the words of my sisters, "We know why you continue to prolong your life in China," and I'm grateful to have their blessing in returning next year.

Love,
Amy

PS: Much more has happened, and I'm eager to share how this semester has gone in general. His hand is evident, and I'm continuing to grow. I'm on my way home for the summer and I can be more candid in the next newsletter. XOXOXO

June 1998—Home sweet home

Am I talking about Denver or Chengdu? Yes. This may seem like a Chinglish answer, since an "or" question isn't supposed to be answered with a yes, but anymore those lines are blurred. The reality of this blurring hit smack between the eyes the last month we were in Chengdu.

The waibans want to buy new furniture for our apartment. This sounds nice enough, and yet I felt the territorial American rising within me. Technically the apartment is the school's, not ours. However, it's been my home for the last three years, so to me it feels like mine. It was hard to have the furniture committee traipsing through my home, criticizing, and even saying the cute bamboo bookcase I had bought must go.

This is also a trust issue. Do I trust them to provide not only what I need but what I actually want and would enjoy? I'm embarrassed to say no, I don't trust my school officials. Culturally our tastes are different. What I think is comfortable to sit on is not what they would choose. After having nothing overly comfortable to sit on other than my bed for the last three years, dangling a sofa in front of me is almost more than I can take. I'm not kidding. I've had more furniture fantasies this year. Big fluffy cushions. My feet curled up, a footstool that has no bamboo. Do I trust my school officials? Do I trust the furniture committee? Ultimately, do I trust God with things that are out of my control yet such an integral part of my life?

For me this is the reality of living in China. Furniture, the little things, can get blown out of proportion in my mind. I was feeling crazed, more so than Shelley, and was doing all I could to control the situation.

"Can we come to the store with you?" I think we indirectly asked this more than five times. "Do you have to replace the furniture? If money is a problem, I really like my bed, and I don't need a new one." Isn't this the same bed I complained about the first semester? See what I mean about crazed, desperate attempts to control the unimportant and yet the oh-so-distracting?

Trust. And so we left Chengdu without going to the furniture store. The furniture committee has still not been given the funds to purchase anything. If I return to a green, floral, soft sofa, I think I'll cry. The reality is that it will probably be wooden, brown, ugly, and uncomfortable, but I can already hear myself saying down the road, "Are you sure we need a new sofa? The wood finally bends to our bodies, and brown is a great color for hiding the Chengdu dirt."

A sad trend that we've begun to notice in China is a casualness towards divorce. I think it is a bit like the attitude in the '70s when the stigma of divorce decreased and the idea of a no-fault divorce grew. We, as a society, have come to realize that there rarely is an "easy divorce," and while it may be necessary, there are both positive and negative consequences. I fear that as the pendulum swings in China towards an easier time of getting out of a bad marriage, they are racing past the agony and looking at it as a quick and easy solution. More than in past semesters, this spring my students would say casually, "I'll just divorce him," or write in their journals about leaving their spouses. I'm not saying that divorce can't or shouldn't be an option, but they sound so flippant, so loose.

One morning in May, my dear Chinese mother, Shen Yang, was emptying our trashcan and told me that her daughter-in-law left her son. This is a woman I've known on a surface level for three years, as she visited Shen Yang. Her young daughter, Lan-Lan, Shen Yang's granddaughter, is around on the weekends. The sadness in Shen Yang's eyes broke my heart. I hugged this precious woman, and we wept over the brokenness in her family. She told me that her daughter-in-law had left to be with a man who is taller, better looking, and richer than her son. He has lived in Holland.

Given the limited extent of my Chinese, we can't go much deeper in conversation, and I don't clearly know why she left. I do know that Shen Yang needed many hugs the next few weeks. Her sparkle has come back, but I see little Lan-Lan on the weekends. I wonder how this six-year-old will be affected by her mother living in another province with a tall, good-looking rich man who has been to Holland.

There are many more things to share, but that is enough for this letter. Mouse number nine was caught and drowned a few days before I left. I guess the saga of living and loving in Chengdu continues.

Love,
Amy

August 1998

Home, wedding, Shelley, and parents, summer program training, Fourth of July, class, Erin, aunt, grandparents, playing, year program in training, gone, happy. There you have it. My summer in a nutshell. A small nutshell, leaving out all of the phone conversations, book reading, movie seeing, lawn mowing, sister/parent hassling, couch lounging, Diet Coke drinking, family hanging out with, or cat petting.

Basically that was the Cliff Notes version of what I've been up to. For some of you that would be enough . . . But for the rest of you who cry out, "Details, I want details," I've written the rest of this letter.

[The body of the letter contained pictures and updates of what I was up to in the summer, but I will share a couple of direct quotes from the letter that work well in book format.]

Side note as I readjust to the US, I have these thoughts: Two liter bottles are huge. Are fifty thousand different kinds of toothpaste necessary? Sixty-five miles feels like flying after walking, biking, or taxiing in slow city traffic for a year. I was ever so happy not to hear the Titanic song played in every place of business I entered, and I hope China is obsessed with a new song by now.

As we return for another year of loving and living, our prayer is that our students will see and know Jesus, not so much that they will see and know America. Two journal entries highlight this situation:

> Amy is also an example for her good qualities, characters and moralities. The Communist party often ask us, serve people heart and soul, but there is less and less people can do that nowadays China. On the other hand, from Amy, I can see foreigners have the better qualities and moralities than us. I do not mean to look low on our Chinese nation. I would say Amy is a mirror of foreigners. I find the reason why our country is behind America. Amy has a good nature. She always smile when we meet. The two years will be past. I would say to Amy: You're a great one for giving up better situation in US, and can enjoy teaching in China. We'll never forget you.

> It is said that it is hard to understand people with the development of the economy, but I don't agree to that. Yesterday evening, Amy and I visited Jennifer in her home. By means of our talk, I found out that we three shared similar ideas, that we have different culture and religion background, especially Amy, who is a Christian from America. The reason of our understanding is mainly because we are teachers, and we all have good qualities of human beings. Amy is an excellent teacher with pleasant characteristics. She is also humorous, warm-hearted, and just. Since we will all graduate from our college, we don't have enough

time to get along with Amy any longer, but we won't forget her. Her happy smile stay in our heart forever. I love you Amy, my beautiful American teacher. I love Amy, a real Christian.

We all know I am not that great. America is not that great. If there is any goodness in me, it is the Holy Spirit living through me. May this be what is seen and received by my precious students. Thank you for your faithfulness to me. Many of you have asked what you could pray for this year, and I jokingly said that I had learned my lesson the last two years and was putting health at the top of the list. Cultural insight, language skills, patience, good team relationships, and new furniture that I like (being real) would also be on that list.

Go Broncos!
Amy

#3 If You Write Newsletters

How to Write Readable Newsletters with One Easy Tip

The most common mistake newsletter writers make is that instead of *showing* their supporters about their life and ministry, they *tell* them. One of the cardinal rules of writing is "show, don't tell." Too many newsletters read either like a list or like a report. You list the cities you visited in a month. You report on how many people you are meeting with.

For instance, readers and supporters know you travel, but their eyes begin to glaze over when they read a list of cities they have never heard of. Worse than that, their emotions aren't engaged, and though embarrassed to admit it, they are bored. Instead of a list, write about an interaction you had with someone in the airport. Yes, you need to be accountable for the prayers and money people are investing in you, but if they are hearing from you regularly enough, they trust that you are doing your "job." They don't need a report; they want to sense what your life in ministry is like. They need to *feel* what your life is like, which they are a part of.

Here are a few ideas to practice showing versus telling:

- Share a conversation you had.

- Walk them through the process of paying a bill, finding a new apartment, or making tacos.

- Take them to school with your children, and let them in on a typical day for them.

- Explain a part of the gospel that makes serving in your context challenging or fun.

- Coach them through a cultural interaction.

- Share a ministry victory that may be so small you almost overlooked it.

- Take a part of your day that is different from a day in your passport country, and paint a picture for your supporters.

In general, show them what has gone on in your life since the last letter. You don't have to hustle for your worth in your newsletters. Trust your supporters. They are for you, they care about you, and they want to share in your life and work.

Where could you start to show more (versus tell) in your next newsletter?

Year Four in China

1998-1999

Please write again soon.
Though my own life is filled with activity,
letters encourage momentary escape into others lives and
I come back to my own with greater contentment.
—Elizabeth Forsythe Hailey

September 1998

Your questions and interest this summer regarding the furniture situation were warmly welcomed, as they showed you read the newsletters and you care. Thank you! When we first arrived back, I had a difficult time not crying right there in front of the waibans. I guess my hoped-for fluffy, green floral couch is somewhere in my future, because it's not in my present. The actual furniture isn't bad. What set me off was that my wardrobe was shoved to the gills with some of our stuff—shoved in total disarray and lack of concern. Somehow, for me it symbolized that I am pseudo nomadic, with this not truly being my home. I had not planned to be thirty and moving in and out of a dorm room every year. (The school officials do not want us here during the summer because they want to be able to use our space to house summer teachers.) So, the tears ran as I unpacked the wardrobe.

However, now that my possessions are settled and I have rearranged the furniture—to avoid comparing it to previous years—I am fine. It feels homey to have a matching set of bedroom furniture. Air conditioning was even added this summer, which will supposedly also work as a heater in the winter. Life has become rather lush by Chinese standards. I wrote Erin that the apartment now is nothing like the dark cave we moved into three years ago, and for that I'm grateful.

The changes in our home merely reflect the changes in Chengdu. Society is improving and changing at such a pace that this is simply not the same city it was even a few short years ago. The modern conveniences that are now available (usually at a price) grow by the day. I wanted you, dear reader, to be aware that I am in a fairly modern city, and at first I struggled with some guilt over how many things are now available. I'm still definitely in China, but it's a China that is learning how to cook Mexican food and has great ice cream. A Kentucky Fried Chicken is even going to open up right outside our front gate!

With the changes in diet, exercising is becoming more of a focus. For the first time, I'm hearing of workout places springing up and have even checked out a few. The first place was too far away, and way too macho for me, with the guys strutting around and trying to look buff and women in aerobic leotards that reminded me of the '80s. Last night I went to an aerobics class with my waiban and think I might start regularly going to the class. It is women only and has a Chinese feel, but it's nice to be doing something different than running. The first thirty minutes were kind of low impact, with lots of arm flinging and leg bending to popular music from the '80s. Even though I couldn't understand the instructor, I could sing along with the songs!

When the thirty minutes were over, we suddenly stopped. The tape was changed to waltzing music, and we did a kind of ballet routine. It was rather gracefully performed by all but the large white woman in the middle of the back row. Shelley came to observe, and at one point I looked back at her and yelled, "Well, I guess these are the ballet lessons I didn't have as a child." So there I was, trying to be graceful, and in my head hearing the waltzing beat of one-two-three, one-two-three. We did a bit of stretching/toning to the modern music, and the class was over.

The best part of having been here for several years is getting to continue relationships with former students and see them as their lives progress. One guy has fallen in love, and I've never seen him this gooey. It is hysterical. Another former student I have supported through an abusive boyfriend and an abortion with another boyfriend is now happily married to a wonderful man. Her husband can speak some English, and she feels like a friend. We lie on her bed and talk, not sit in formal Mao chairs, and have formal conversations. She held my hand while I was in the hospital with meningitis. We have a past, and that feels good.

It is comfortable finally to be at the point where my students and I have a track record. This seems to be meaning more and more with the students. Weekly now I'm asked if I'm planning to immigrate to China, or if I want a Chinese boyfriend, or when I will become a Chinese citizen. Slowly we are moving from bizarre outsiders to beloved outsiders, and we're seeing "interest" beginning to happen.

Conversations are taking place around significant topics. Such as, do I really believe? Why do I believe?

In a journal, a student, who lost both of her parents to cancer last year, told me that she was given a Bible to read by her sister who lives in Singapore, and she wonders what I think of this. We are asked difficult questions about family members who don't believe, people who are good but don't believe, and about evolution. One student who has been studying but hasn't made a decision yet found out her husband has inoperable cancer. As you remember us, ask that we have clear, culturally relevant answers that reflect truth accurately, and that we will say enough without saying too much or too little.

You are an encouragement to me as we go through the ups and downs of life. Thanks for faithfully remembering us . . . and for all that you do to remind us we are loved. It's working. I only cried for an hour instead of days!

Your beloved outsider,
Amy

PS: I'm learning to write my address in Chinese, so if you write to me, I promise to write back and will try to impress you with my Chinese characters.

October 1998—It's begun . . . mouse one!

I've seen two mice this year, both while I was on the phone in the hallway. Each mouse ran down the hall towards me, scaring the bejeebers out of me. With the second one I screamed, "Mouse! Mouse!" and stamped my feet trying to get it to turn around. It became confused and kept running at us, as Shelley was also in the shared public hallway. He ran right into our laundry room. Slam! We shut that door fast.

My poor Chinese friend on the other end of the phone became confused and asked me why I was yelling about a cat. What? I'm not. "Mouse" sounds like *mao*, the Chinese word for cat. She called me several days later asking if I wanted a cat or was I talking about cats. How do you explain . . . neither. But it was sweet of her to offer.

Back to the mouse. The scared creature was trapped in our laundry room, and what did we, as two well-educated, brave women of the '90s, do? Call for our Chinese mother, Shen Yang. She went into the laundry room with a hose and emerged fifteen minutes later with the mouse still hidden, scared, and by now probably soaked. I went in to set out poison, saw the mouse again, shrieked, and left thinking we would never have clean laundry again at this rate. I looked in the laundry room the next morning and still saw him. Due to a miscommunication, one of our friends opened the door later that day, and he escaped.

Sunday morning I started a load of laundry and let the water run a bit to let the obvious rust run out. I turned the water on and glanced into the washing machine to check the color of the water. There sat one soaked little mouse with rusty water cascading all over him. Oh yes. This is true. There was a mouse, a little, adorable, scared mouse, sitting in my washing machine being soaked by me. I must confess that I entertained thoughts of filling the machine and turning it on to either drown him or agitate him to death, but he looked helpless, like one of the hamsters we had when I was a child.

Instead of great bravery, I cried again for my Chinese mother. She quickly evaluated the scene and then went for Chinese instruments of death and destruction. She came back with a small blue plastic bag and a chopstick, captured the mouse, and I have no idea how she killed it.

National Day, October 1st, was on a Thursday this year, giving us a four-day holiday. The school invited us to travel in Sichuan Province with our waiban, Xiao Luo, and her friend. The four of us went to Yibin to see the famous bamboo sea and then to Zigong, one of the self-proclaimed "Top 40 Tourist Sites in China." Dinosaurs have been discovered in Zigong, and I had been itching to see how the Chinese would set up a dinosaur dig and museum. The Chinese word for dinosaur means "terrible dragon." The door seems to be opening up for more and more contact with Xiao Luo as she also tutors us in Chinese, she attends my class, and sometimes we go to the same aerobics class. You could be remembering her and asking for her to have some spiritual interest.

Following up on those who have walked the Romans Road is both a blessing and a frustration. Of the three in our school who made decisions this summer, two seem taken with this road. In addition, a former student who is a tour guide was talking with me on the phone, and it came out that while leading a group of foreign tourists, she now believes the truth too. Unfortunately, all three have believed the "busyness lie," hook, line, and sinker, claiming to be too busy to study or grow. We have tried to talk with each of them about the importance of growing spiritually. It is exciting to see the changes that have taken place, and we ask for this time to be a time of protection letting them develop a firm foundation.

Issues continue to be raised in journals and tough questions asked. A former student visited me and told me that she had started having an affair with an older married man. She knows it's wrong but longs to fill the hole in her heart. We're going to spend more time together as she gives me cooking lessons.

Busy, I like busy. Those who know me joke that if I'm not going 110 miles an hour, I'm not happy, and this is true. But unlike other years, this year we have a lot of company on the weekends. Our last weekend without having any company or having to be out of town was on our first weekend here. Being hostess to a bunch of foreigners isn't where my heart is. I would rather focus my attention on students, both present and former, and on being the curriculum director with the work that commitment involves. The visitors are a reminder that I need to be willing to change and not become so narrow in whom I want to serve.

We eat lunch in the dining hall with our students, and on Monday I was a little startled when someone behind me touched my head. The following note was in her journal today regarding the incident: "Dear Amy, I apologize to you for offending your tidy hair, because when I touch it I see your annoyance. And I really feel sorry. I don't realize the difference between in the USA and in China. If I like something, I show my love with touching, but obviously it's no use for everyone or everything. I want you to know that I have no malice to you or to your hair. Best regards."

While I was obviously not offended—surprised, yes—I was deeply touched again by their love and concern for me. I thank and encourage you for helping this to be my life. Together we are reaching out to show our love by touching lives, and when misunderstandings occur, our hope is that they know we bear no malice to them or their hair or culture or whatever it is that I'm touching.

> From malice-free hair and heart,
> Amy

November 1998—It's all about the food, baby!

As I sat reflecting on my month and trying to decide what to share, nothing leapt to my mind. I asked myself, "What did I do for a whole month that for the life of me I can't think of now?" I pulled out my calendar, wondering where all the time had gone, and there it was—food.

This past month has been spent feeding and being fed in both body and mind. We've been celebrating the birth of children and the birthdays of my students, learning to cook, having another taco party, going to students' homes, eating more gross meat than I have ever cared to, and making pumpkin bread. In general, living . . . and having a blast.

The month began with a cooking lesson by a former student. I'm learning about learning in China. Whenever I'm taught something, it means that I'm shown how to do it without being given a chance to try it myself. No wonder my students think I'm a freak when I'm teaching, because I haul them into whatever they are learning. I had a cooking lesson, but I'm not sure how much I learned. I was reminded again that Chinese cooking is not low-fat cooking, as Anna generously poured oil into each dish.

Shelley was gone two weekends on business trips. One weekend I had a gaggle of girls over for tacos. Our dinner conversation was about "the Annie Books" (aka Anne of Green Gables), and I told the story behind my own ear-piercing experiences. The ear-piercing story was later reported as the highlight of the evening. They reciprocated two weekends later, when it was Halloween, because the students were afraid I would be lonely on a holiday with Shelley gone. Each girl was in charge of a dish. Since we had a fairly small kitchen, they took turns cooking, and it seemed like a never-ending feast, as dish after dish emerged with its proud cook. We ended the evening with them carving a jack-o'-lantern and me laughing at their attempt—definitely a Western learning experience.

Another weekend I went to one of my students' homes, where she proudly served me steak. I want to find the book that told the Chinese that Americans love steak. No matter how many times we say, "Really, we love to eat *vegetables*," it falls on deaf ears, because they retort, "But the book says you like steak." If it came from a book, heaven forbid we question it, even if a real live American is telling you it might not always be the case. Boy howdy, that was a tangent. You've probably picked up on the fact that I wasn't all that keen on the steak, but I appreciated the spirit in which it was served, and ultimately that is far more important.

In case you're wondering, the steak was more like short spare ribs with lots of fat. At one key moment when I was left alone for a minute at the table, I put most of the meat that had been put in my bowl back into the serving bowl, making it look like I had eaten it. Tacky? Yes. But also face-saving for all. That evening ended with two hours of talking with a junior high boy whom my student tutors on Friday nights.

The next night, Shelley and I were invited by one of her students to visit the student's former English teacher and eat dinner. We were delighted to learn that the teacher had been a student at our college in the '80s, when the first TIC teachers taught here. While she has not believed all that she was taught, it was an awesome reminder that I see the here and now of 1998. Life is long, and others can cross the paths of our students with good food. Here it was, sixteen years later, and we were eating dinner at her table, talking. Wow.

The flip side to all the food is my aerobics class, which I'm growing to love more and more. I go to a class that keeps the ballet-type dancing to a minimum, but even "ballet aerobics" is growing on me. I'm hoping I can learn more about what defines a graceful woman in China, even though it will never be me. For several weeks I danced around in my socks, while everyone else wore ballet-style shoes. I thought it might help my dancing if I looked the part more and wasn't leaping around in gym socks, so I bought a pair of ballet-style shoes. Well, that hasn't happened. I'm still klutzy. But now I'm klutzy in ballet shoes.

Thanks for remembering us. We still have visitors most weekends. It seems like having visitors is going to be our life for this year. On the other issue I mentioned last time, two of our students have found follow-up in a local fellowship. Exciting! And we have another soul to tend. I'm eager to tell you more, but it'll have to wait until Thailand. Please remember them. That seems to be about all from the kitchen of Amy and Shelley, where the eating is good and the cooks are clean. So I heartily say . . .

Pass me some more,
Amy

December 1998

I've enjoyed studying Chinese characters, and as a visual person, it seems to be the way for me to crack the language. Not that I have learned all that much considering how long I've been here, but it encouraged me the other day at lunch when students told me they're afraid to speak Chinese in class because they think I'll understand them. I even had a long chat with Shen Yang last week, using as much of the family vocabulary as I could.

(Side note: family vocabulary in Chinese is a huge insight into the cultural importance of your rank in the family. There are eight words for "cousin"—based on whether your cousin is on your mother's or father's side of the family, the gender of the cousin, and whether they're older or younger than you. And that's only for "cousin." I could tell you more, because I find all of this fascinating, but I realize that nuances of the Chinese language don't speed up everyone's heart rate the way they do mine, so I'll get off this side note now.)

Last month I spent a long weekend on an official TIC visit visiting one of our teams in Hangzhong, Shaanxi Province. The team is probably one of our most remote teams, and yet after visiting them, I'm convinced more than ever that China is rapidly changing. I had visited the school three years before in my first month in China and couldn't believe all the changes and all the stuff that is now available for purchase. It was also my first trip by myself. While I would far rather travel with somebody—especially Shelley because we're compatible and she's loads of fun—I was encouraged to know that I could do it alone.

I'm not sure many Chinese want me to, though. In trying to upgrade from a hard seat to a hard sleeper, I got all flustered by the paperwork and turned to the man nearest me, handed him the form, my green card, and a pen, and made him fill it out for me. He was gracious and did it. Yay, strangers. Be kind to those around you, because you never know when you will need to shove a form and a pen into a stranger's face.

This month Shelley and I also visited one of Shelley's students and her family in their hometown of Mianyang. Before we went, all we heard was, "Mian Yang is so clean!" It got to the point that we would roll our eyes—yeah, yeah, clean city, whatever—as we stepped over orange peels, spit globs, and trash mounds. But can you guess the first words out of our mouths when we got off the bus? "It's so clean." Amazing what littering and spitting fines can do to clean up a place. Desiree's family was inviting and thoughtful. Desiree had called ahead to tell her father that foreigners bathe daily, so he needed to clean the bathroom extra well. We didn't end up bathing. (Shelley did have to wash her feet. I was already tucked in bed with socks and gloves on, and there was no way I was coming out only to stick my feet in water.) However, that kind of thoughtfulness engulfs us.

It has been encouraging to see the growth in our new sisters. Ms. Mao, who became a Christian last summer, regularly attends a Chinese church and is instrumental in getting Chinese Bibles and taking new friends to church. It's cool to see how she is being used and to see her eagerness and desire to be used. I'm also meeting regularly with Ms. Li, who became a Christian this semester. It is amazing to see how dedicated and solid her faith is, though she's young. Her aunt is depressed and looking into religions. Ms. Li wants to give her a Bible and talk with her. As these women will be going home for Spring Festival, you could be remembering them and asking that their families will see a difference and that they will not feel isolated or be vulnerable to attack.

We're in the middle of celebrating Christmas now. I am a bit sickened by how the holiday is presented as Western and foreign. Department stores have Christmas carols blaring away . . . in English. Christmas cards are all around, and many students are sending them to friends and family. Why? Because it's cool. This letter is getting long and I didn't mean to go off on a tangent, I'll save more about our celebrating for next month's letter.

Thanks for being here with us, be it in your thoughts, prayers, cards, and presents. We are warmly loved and encouraged by you. I hope it comes back through this letter to you.

Merry Christmas,
Amy

January 1999—"In my eyes you are foolish"

How would you like to be told that by your student? I've known Ida for three years, and this is the second time I've been her teacher. In her journal she wrote, "All the people who fall in love will become crazy and foolish, so do I. I'm a happy fool . . . In the world, there are many foolish people the same as me. They would pay anything for their lover or their loving thing. For example, Amy, you would leave your homeland and relationships for your teaching. In my eyes you are foolish but great. Maybe teaching is your lover."

She's right: in the world's eyes we are foolish—year after year to return to a place that can no longer be defined as a "cool cultural experience." The older I get, the more this concerns my students. They want me to return home so I can get married and have babies. (Little do they realize this sounds to me far more foolish than living in China. Can you tell we had a slumber party with three kids? ☺) I literally jumped up and down last week when the school told me that Shelley and I had been invited back for another year. Fools that we are.

December passed in a whirlwind of Christmas and birthday activity. We had several Christmas parties in our home, and the hit activities were making cookies and acting out the Twelve Days of Christmas. Bakeries are quite common, but having an oven in your home is still rare, and the students loved using cookie cutters and decorating the cookies with colored sugar. And boy did they chow down on the cookies after the cookies came out of the oven. The actions they made up to the songs were hysterical, and knowing Chinese culture, it was a given that there were tons of pictures taken in front of our Christmas tree.

In class we read Matthew and Luke and pretended that we were investigators. Using the two eyewitnesses, we reconstructed the chronology of what happened and looked at how the original story has influenced current celebrating.

Again, and I'm sorry that I say this often, but it's true, I can't believe how rapidly things are changing. Christmas is alive and well in China. It's mentioned extensively in the Chinese newspapers, but the focus is completely secular. The good thing is that Christmas is now a common topic to discuss and not something we have to bring up.

Interestingly enough, several students wrote after Christmas about how Chengdu celebrated Christmas. One of my male students wrote about a girl he tutors and how she talked and talked about how *fashionable* Christmas was. It annoyed him that she went on and on and never mentioned the name of the One who was being celebrated. Now, mind you, this student doesn't buy into the reason behind the holiday, but it bothered him that she had no idea of why Christmas was significant and felt that the Chinese were being misled. He ended by telling me that he knew the Real Reason for celebrating and would tell others.

Fashionable. That is a good word to describe Christmas festivities here. Christmas cards are all the rage, and not only to give to us. Our students mailed them to friends and family members. "Jingle Bells," "We Wish You a Merry Christmas," and "Silent Night"—all fashionable. Father Christmas, having your picture taken with Christmas decorations, a Christmas disco party—with all of this the Chinese are finding ways to celebrate. It is an internal tension that awareness is increasing (good!), albeit devoid of deeper meaning (disheartening).

In one short week we'll be leaving for TIC's midyear conference in Thailand. Thanks for your faithfulness this term. This was one of the best semesters, and that is due in large part to all of you who lift us up. The small tangibles that immediately come to mind include having no real illnesses and only one mouse. Funny how victories are now defined! I think being in aerobics and learning more Chinese have influenced me positively.

As we leave, remember students who are going home to spend a month with their families, especially those who are not returning as the same people who first left home. May this time reinforce the changes and not challenge them as they go home and have time to think. May they wonder more and more what motivates us to be "foolish."

From one grateful fool,
Amy

February 1999—Wait, don't I know you from someplace?

Well, you might recognize us from the made-for-TV movie, *Class Is Over*, which is about unemployment in Sichuan. Shelley and I ended our semester with a Saturday acting gig. Our friend, Jason's girlfriend's father, is a movie director and needed two foreigners. We were supposed to have been filmed riding in a pedicab driven by an unemployed person. Unfortunately, that day it was raining, and they decided he would be a taxi driver. The best part was that the actor didn't know how to drive, so after we climbed into the backseat of the cab, about four people pushed the car to make it look like he was driving.

Some of the great leaps in logic in the filming were killing me, but I had to release logic and keep acting. Shelley and I both got in the backseat of the cab, but when we were pushed up to the hotel, I was in the front seat and Shelley was in the back. Why? So they could zoom in on the suitcase we forgot on the backseat. In the next scene we had to explain to the hotel manager that we had lost the bag, and the directors wanted us to act angry. Not wanting to fuel the idea that foreigners are animals, we merely acted frustrated, which became easier with each annoying take.

The so-called driver ran in with our bag, and the director wanted Shelley to kiss him. It threw them for a directing loop when we refused—their attitude was that all Westerners are loose. What's a little smooch? We compromised with Shelley trying to hug the driver and him shaking her hand. At first Shelley and I were excited to tell our students we were going to be on TV in May, but after realizing there is a reason we are teachers and not actors, I'm going to make sure they have plenty of homework that night.

Here's a more open update on what's going on with students.

Miss Mao, who became a Christian last summer, continues to be rooted in her faith. She's involved in the Chinese church, and her family knows of her conversion. Before she left for the holiday break, the reality of her family's eternal destiny was sinking in. Please be praying for her husband and that when she returns home, after her final semester, she will find a church to be involved in. It's wonderful to see her being used and deepening in her faith.

Ms. Li heard about the truth last summer, and we met several times this semester to discuss questions she had. Going out for tea one Friday night, she told me that the evening before she had decided to believe. We met several times a month for follow-up study. She tells me that she prays every night in bed and talks with God about the good and the bad in her day. I like her, because she's a bit fiery like me. One day a man was annoying her and she wanted to punch him (she's not your typical Chinese female and has hit several people before), but she reminded herself that Christians don't hit people, and so she didn't. What a fun example of the Holy Spirit.

Curriculum Day of the conference went well. Thank you for praying. I spoke on Luke 2:52: "Jesus grew in wisdom and stature, and in favor with God and man." It made me think of TIC, because Jesus had balance among a variety of areas in his life. As teachers serving in Asia, we too have a variety of areas (teaching, team, Chinese culture, and sharing our faith) that we need to do well in. If we compromise one area, we may have compromised all.

I looked at three biblical people who did well in their jobs and were culturally sensitive in waiting for God to open doors. Because Esther, Joseph, and Ruth had done well in their respective situations, when the doors opened they were able to walk through them. The final person they considered was themselves—asking how are they doing in teaching, their situation? I'm passionate about teaching, because if we do not take it seriously, we potentially compromise all else that we do.

Thank you for standing alongside and praying for us and our students. I haven't been in a Chinese hospital yet this year, and I haven't had worms in over a year, yay! This truly was a fun fall and winter, and I'm eager to get home to Spring pineapple in Chengdu.

> Here's my autograph in case my
> Chinese acting career takes off,
> Amy Young ☺

March 1999—The panic has begun!

Remember "The Graduation Paper" I teach in the spring? Actually, it's a research paper, but for my students it's the first time they have ever written this kind of paper. The process of choosing a topic, taking notes, organizing the information in a linear fashion, citing sources, and not plagiarizing—all in a second language—can be daunting. Learning about writing in a foreign language is, in fact, learning about the thought patterns of that culture. I tell the students this process is a small glimpse into how bizarre we Westerners are.

Discussing the cultural differences of academic writing in China versus America, the students go through varying degrees of shock. When I'm feeling cheeky, sometimes I want to say, "Welcome to my world. Now you have a wee taste of how I feel at times." Last Tuesday night in the library was the first chance that the students had to borrow material since we began talking about the graduation paper in class. The following is a real conversation between me and a delightful young man who normally has a great sense of humor.

Robin: Amy, I need help finding material.

Amy: Okay, what's your topic?

Robin: Methodology.

Amy: Well, that's a bit general. Do you remember when we brainstormed topics in class to help narrow it down? Were you interested in any of the topics we brainstormed?

Panicked look.

Amy: Think about it for a few minutes, and I'll check with you after I help Owen (or any number of other crazed-looking students mobbing me).

A few minutes later . . .

Amy: Robin, have you come up with something that interests you?

Robin, proudly holding up the book titled *Language Teaching Techniques and Principles*: Yes!

Amy: Robin, dear, that is basically the same as 'methodology.' Which technique or principle interests you?

The crazed look returns . . .

The graduation paper is an opportunity for me to demonstrate love to my students. Being patient and kind jumps to the front of my mind. I had the above conversation over and over. "What's your topic so I can help?" "I don't know." Ugh. They know they need at least five sources and often they want to check out any five books or journals they can get their hands on. Because writing a research paper is such a new experience, it is hard to tell them it doesn't help to grab random material; maybe the source will be useful and maybe it won't be. It makes me wonder what I grab and cling to like a security blanket, in the face of the realities of China I'm having a tough time grasping.

I also find that I'm a bit bored with teaching how to write a research paper, because it's the fourth year I've taught this. There isn't much I can change in teaching bibliographies. But I know it's the first time for these students, so I want to love them through this process.

With the beginning of the second semester, many journal entries contained lofty goals for the semester: I will memorize 250 new vocabulary words, read a novel a week, go to the English Corner, study Japanese, improve my handwriting, find a job in Chengdu, knit sweaters for all of my roommates, do morning exercises, and lose weight.

The freshness of a new semester comes with the hope that all of this can be accomplished, but we know the reality of life. Our desire is for students to truly see what is important and needs to get done. As you think of this semester, may it be that we would also see what is important and do it—not what looks like the most fun or what cries the loudest for our attention, but what is pleasing in light of eternity.

Love ya,
Amy

PS: A student's husband died around the end of February. She's back in class and obviously going through the grieving process.

April 1999—Can you pass the test?

After being in China for a while, I'm having fewer culture tests where I'm put in a situation I don't know what will happen or what my response should be. However, earlier this month I went home for the weekend with my student Xiao Hui. Right before we left, she found out that a high school classmate was getting married. She called him and invited me to his countryside wedding—not to be confused with modern weddings that take place in large cities.[12]

The following is a test I have devised for you to see how you would do at a countryside wedding in China. No cheating and looking ahead to the answers because real life tests do not allow that option. You may feel free to discuss options with your teammate (in my case, Shelley) as long as you keep smiling at those precious Chinese around you, often they don't realize you are also trying to figure out what you should do.

~ ~ ~

1.   The night before the wedding, how many people, including Xiao Hui, did Xiao Hui bring to the groom's house for a party and to spend the night?
a.   two
b.   three
c.   four

2.   What did I do at the party while Xiao Hui played *majiang* (mahjong) with her classmates?
a.   I played too.
b.   I slept on the couch.
c.   I practiced Chinese.

3.   How many people slept in the bride and groom's double bed

with me?
    a. two
    b. three
    c. four

4. What time did the groom's party wake up on the day of the wedding to go in a caravan to the bride's home with the purpose of getting the bride and bring her back to the groom's home?
    a. 4:00 a.m.
    b. 5:00 a.m.
    c. 6:00 a.m.

5. After arriving at the bride's house and setting off firecrackers, we were fed an egg as a symbol of fertility. Who went with the groom to the bride's house?
    a. only single people
    b. the groom's family
    c. anyone who spent the night at his house

6. Upon leaving her home, it is tradition for the bride to do which of the following?
    a. bow to her parents
    b. sprinkle rice in front of her new husband
    c. not look back

7. When the couple arrived at his house, they first burnt an offering and bowed to the ancestors. After burning the offering, what was the bride's first household duty?
    a. cook an egg for her husband
    b. make a cup of tea for her new mother-in-law
    c. make the marriage bed with brand new bedding

8. It is now 9:00 a.m. and about 150 friends of the groom are seated outside for a banquet. (It seemed a bit early to be eating a dinner banquet, but when in Rome, pass me the chopsticks!) The bride and groom went to each table to toast their guests. What small gift was given to each guest?
    a. two cigarettes and a red envelope of candy
    b. a can of Pepsi or Sprite
    c. a picture of the bride and groom

~ ~ ~

The answers are below. I hope you passed the test! We are taking little tests like this all the time; you could be asking that if we don't do well, at least we will learn quickly!

> Gan Bei! (Chinese toast meaning
> "bottoms up"),
> Amy

PS: In *The China Daily* newspaper, the lead story was about Premier Zhu's visit to America, and it had a picture of him visiting the Broncos headquarters—there is a man with taste!

Answer Key:

1. C—Xiao Hui, me, her mom, and a high school girl who lives in a boarding school. She spent the whole weekend with us without telling the school officials. Ugh!
2. B—Hee-hee!
3. C—Oh yes, there were four adults in a double bed.
4. B
5. A
6. C—Very good visual picture of not looking back; she wasn't supposed to turn her head at all.
7. C
8. A

May 1999—Have boil . . . will travel

I woke up on a Tuesday morning with the instant awareness that dreaded boil was back and in the same place. Since it was beginning, I went directly to the waiban and said I needed to go to the hospital. Xiao Feng, who went with me last year, hung her head and said, "Oh no." I think we both had flashbacks to me screaming and kicking a hole in the wall. Instead, Xiao Liu took me and we opted for trying Chinese medicine because it is "pain free"—those words were like music to my fearful behind. A nice woman doctor gave me penicillin pills, a N-A-S-T-Y liquid to drink after I eat, and this gooey stuff to spread over the boil and be taped into place with gauze. In three to five days, I was supposed to be boil-free. Yay.

Now comes the traveling part. My dear friend Wendy invited me to her father's junior middle school to guest teach in the English department. I was thrilled to go, mainly to get to spend time with Wendy, and now she was going to get to see more of me than she had planned on!

The time in Zitong was a whole lot of life crammed into a little space. The first night, I met and spent time with the six English teachers. One had attended the TIC summer teaching program, so we knew several of the same people. Another had never spoken to a foreigner before and was petrified of me. A third proceeded to tell me how fat his wife was. "As fat as Ms. Zhao," he said, pointing to a fellow English teacher. Oh brother. Speaking of culture tests, how do you answer that one? "My, that is fat." "I don't think Ms. Zhao is fat." "Beauty is in the eye of the beholder." I think I said, "These peanuts are delicious."

The next day began my marathon teaching of fifteen different English classes to be taught over the course of two days. Word spread that a foreign teacher was in town, and both newspaper and TV reporters showed up. Teachers from the high school came and sat in on my class and begged me to come to their school. Every teacher in the middle school was required to watch me teach at least once, and many watched several classes. A few even brought their young children in to see the foreigner teach. The back and sides of the classrooms were often lined with adults.

The students were delightful. I autographed many English textbooks, smiled for seemingly endless pictures, and answered questions like this:

"No, I don't like to play basketball."

"Yes, I do like oranges."

"I think your school is wonderful."

"Yes, I like you."

I felt the weight of Zitong on my shoulders. Much was wanted of me, and I was acutely aware of how limited what I had to offer was. The great Yang Laoshi (Teacher Young) was in town, and people wanted a piece. Riding to the school the first morning, Wendy asked me what my WWJD bracelet meant (it was only the second time I had been asked), and I told her. Later her father wondered how I was able to be patient and serve graciously. Wendy told him it was because of my bracelet. I'm thankful that even though I have a finite level of patience, kindness, and goodness, I can use Somebody else's because I needed it!

And so my boil and I went home. Three days came and went. Five days. Ugh. It began to grow. Because I was going to Beijing for organizational meetings, I decided to have the boil treated at an international clinic in Beijing. You should have seen the look of relief on Xiao Feng's face when I told her. I simply wanted to make sure she and her coworkers weren't offended and they weren't.

Arriving in Beijing, I hobbled off the plane, painfully close to the point where walking was exceedingly painful. I told my friend Becky to take me directly to the clinic, even though we had an hour before the appointment. A wonderful doctor from Jordan, with a big syringe of anesthesia, performed the minor surgery. The Chinese nurse and the doctor kept saying in Chinese, "*Hen da*" and "*Ji dan*," meaning the boil was very big, the size of a chicken egg. He wondered what was wrong with my immune system, and I am beginning to wonder, too.

My bandaged bum and I took it easy for a few days in Beijing before attending the meetings. Not that there is ever a well-timed boil, but this boil was poorly timed because after the meetings, I was on my way to Mongolia for a brief visit with the curriculum people there. Imagine the wife's joy when I showed up as her houseguest and explained to her she would be bandaging my bottom.

The meeting was held at a TIC teacher's house in a small town in the middle of the Gobi Desert. Our road trip was Mongolian-style, not AAA-style, that's for sure. We headed out of town in my host's Land Cruiser and soon came to the end of the road. Driving in the direction of the town, we stopped often to ask people if we were still going in the right direction. After the meetings, I had the opportunity to visit a Mongolian student in her home (yurt/ger) and eat Mongolian food. The next day we returned to Ulaanbaatar, Mongolia's capital, and I flew back to Beijing.

A follow-up doctor visit verified that all was healing well, and he said words that made me want to kiss all of those around me: "You don't need to bandage it anymore." After almost three weeks of gauze in a precarious place, and a conservative estimate of eleven people seeing or bandaging my bum with varying level of skills, (Wendy, wear your glasses and don't bandage everything down there!), I was happy.

And so, virtually pain-free I boarded a plane for home. After two weeks of my students returning to their schools to practice teach, I was happy to be coming home to greet them (even though they will soon be handing in their long research papers). I arrived as some international excitement broke out. [The US bombing of the Chinese embassy in Yugoslavia.] From crowded bus to seated baths soaking the boil, from doctor's appointments to meetings, this has been a month ripe with opportunities to ask, WWJD.

Sitting happily now,
Amy

July 1999

"Clinton is the devil!"

What is Rush Limbaugh doing in a newsletter? He's not. I saw a student doodling this statement in his notes as I walked around checking that they were on task. He wrote it two weeks after the bombing of the Chinese Embassy in Yugoslavia.

It amazed me how quickly life can change, how feelings can change, how what I see in someone else's eyes can change. I happened to be out of town when the bomb was dropped and the students started protesting and attacking the consulate in Chengdu. Riding on the crowded shuttle bus from the airplane to the terminal, a nice young Chinese man asked me where I was from. I told him and he said, "You know Chinese people hate Americans now." Being on a crowded bus, surrounded by passionately nationalistic people, I simply said, "I know. I know. I'm so sorry." When we got off the bus, he smiled at me and said, "Goodbye, teacher!" and bounced off.

This captures in a nutshell how the last month has been: extremes and compartmentalization. Anger towards the US government and love for foreign teachers—a complex array of emotions on both sides. A couple of weeks after the bombing happened, I received the following letter from a former student and wanted to share it, giving you a glimpse of what I considered to be a common Chinese person's reaction:

Dear Amy,

I don't know whether any student talked with you or not but I'd like to. I have a frank character and don't like to hide my opinion. As you know, I'm not a Party member and I'm not interested in politics, but I am a Chinese. I'm concerned deeply with my motherland as all the other Chinese. It's easy for you to understand this kind of feeling, for you love your country, too.

All the Chinese and I know that your President, Bill Klinton, said, "Sorry," and apologized to China. His words may be true and out of heart, but we can't accept that. This attitude is not only our government's but our, which I can know from the talk of people among me. I'd like to explain the cause in my letter.

First, it is maybe the cultural difference between China and America. For you, it's true (Clinton's apology). It is okay. For our Chinese, it's greeting in the daily life. It's only use in trifle. For example, if someone stamped your feet carelessly, "Sorry" is okay. This accident concerned with our people's lives, our country's dignity, can "Sorry" be enough? Also, a person with some scientific knowledge can know that the attack happened not by mistake but on purpose. Can the bullets miss, hit our embassy once, twice, and three times? NATO almost has the most advanced system in the world. Even if in daily life you'll feel bad if someone stamps your feet on purpose, how can you demand our Chinese keep quiet as such things happened?

For another, most of us don't believe in your President though he acts as speaker of your country. As an educated person, I do not like to pay attention to one's private life, but it's a fact that he has become the talk around the world in previous period. Of course, President is also an ordinary person and can have his own feeling, but everyone should have a sense of responsibility to his wife and child let alone a President. He gives us a feeling of a cheater. How can we believe in him? His action isn't fit for his words either. When he visited China last July, he said that he liked China and Chinese people. When our President visited America lately, he welcomed him warmly. Now, why attack our embassy? That day in your home, I didn't continue our words about the matter. One reason is that I don't want to hurt our feeling. Another is I believe in your words. I think your "sorry" is true for I know my teacher is an honest one.

[I deleted several paragraphs about the victims.]

Lately, Amy, if you can read Chinese history of recent time, you'll know why Chinese is so angry before this accident. In recent time, our country was poor and invaded by the Western countries, including America, again and again. It can be said that our Chinese recent history is a history of humiliation. We tasted enough, the taste of humiliation. Most Chinese don't think our embassy was just hit but think our motherland was invaded by NATO, which no Chinese can stand that whether he is old or young, poor or wealthy, educated or not educated.

Why I write the letter to you? I'd like you to know what the Chinese really think about the accident. I also like the American people behind you, your parents, your siblings, and your friends know what we think. Let's be open-minded. Maybe our idea is different, but it is because we are different that we need more communication.

Yours,
Miss J

We have heard this over and over from students and friends. Turning the other cheek is hard, especially for me as a former debater where the situation seems to cry out for a response. On the Chinese side, there has been misinformation about the war and the bombing, so we can't discuss it at all, nor do we want to. However, this has provided a good opportunity to talk with a Christian student about forgiveness and our ability as Christians to forgive. We are different.

I can see why God has Shelley and me in Chengdu another year. This is a key time to build on relationships. When the bombing happened, students in other departments wanted to "attack and damn" us. (Not sure what that means.) Our students said, "No. Amy and Shelley are our friends. This has to do with the government."

It's nice to be home for the summer. I'm writing this from a bagel shop, plan to see a movie later, and will mow the lawn—does it get any better?! Still, we're looking forward to the possibilities of next year. Shelley and I recently found out that a good Chinese friend who is spiritually seeking is gay. Another has major gambling debts that nobody knows about. Thanks for sticking with us as we live with real people with real needs.

Satisfied with life,
Amy

August 1999

Right before the end of the school term in June, one of my students was giving a cultural report. In it, she explained the differences between the Chinese and Americans when it comes to time orientation. Most of the students were nodding, "Yes. Yes. We know this." After her report, I told them that even though they had heard about time orientation several times, I don't think they grasped the difference and asked them what they would be doing on July 17th. I might as well have asked them what day they thought they would next have the flu.

To hit home the difference, I took a big breath and laid out my summer plans: fly to Minneapolis where I have a two-day layover with my sister Laura, go to Denver four days . . . and I continued on for a long paragraph with rough details on what I would be doing each day of the summer. When I got to the end, I said, "And then fly back to China." Phew. They looked at me with huge, wide-open eyes. *The foreigners truly are as bizarre as we have been told.* (Now for your culture shock: even though they were graduating in two weeks, most had made no attempts to find jobs! We American are quite time-oriented.)

Of course, not all went according to plan, but the mere fact that I had a plan was key in my American mind. The trip to DC was canceled because the Chinese teachers couldn't get visas. This ended up being a good thing because instead of going to DC that week, I had surgery on my behind. The dreaded boil had turned into a fistula, meaning a permanent tube had opened allowing continual oozing out of my bottom. Lovely. The options were to leave it open or to operate—not a hard call to make. Unfortunately, it did not heal as quickly as hoped, and the surgeon had to do another brief surgery to finally resolve the problem.

Unexpected highlights I had not foreseen on the schedule:

- Getting to see my sister Laura three times.

- Seeing friends more times than I anticipated.

- Spending five fun days with my grandparents and my sisters. Great family time.

- Speaking at quite a few churches and small groups about China and pleased with how interested people were. Thanks!

- The weekend after Dad's birthday party was the first time we five in my immediate family had been together in several years. I love my family!

Life is real, however, and there were a few lowlights. Two friends are getting divorced, and another ended a relationship with someone she thought she might marry. The visit to my grandparents was the last time I'll see their house because they are moving to assisted living. My surgery was surgery—knocked me out, woke up groggy and nauseous both times.

The bottom line (no pun intended) is that with the ups and downs, I'm glad it was my summer. As Shelley and I head back home to Chengdu, please pray for

- Health. No joke. Get on your knees, people! ☺

- Continued relationship with school officials, students, and friends in the aftermath of the bombing.

- Follow-up for several students who I have heard became Christians this summer.

As we return to China, I have no idea what is scheduled for the fall. That's the nature of China. I'll keep you posted as we get to it.

Love,
Amy

#4 If You Write Newsletters

Five Common Newsletter Mistakes

By Davita Freeman

After three years on the field, Davita Freeman returned to the US to work in the home office of her organization. She worked in the communications department and primarily with paper newsletters and mailing list support. Over the years, she read more than five thousands newsletters. I contacted her asking for *Five Common Newsletter Mistakes* and *Five Things Newsletter Writers Do Well* (after Chapter 5). The following is Davita's answer to "What common mistakes have you seen newsletter writers make?"

~ ~ ~

Here are the top five common newsletter mistakes I have noticed over the years.

1. **Stream of Consciousness writing.** I have read far too many of these types of letters in my years working with newsletters. The writer sits down at her computer and starts to write the first thought in her head. This is followed by another unrelated thought. And another. By the end I am just confused and ready to move on.

2. **Apologizing**. There may be a few times where an apology is needed during your years of newsletter writing but never at the beginning of your letter. Avoid such statements as:

    a. I'm sorry it's been so long since I last wrote. I've been really busy. (Your readers know it's been awhile and they've probably been busy, too.)

    b. I'm sorry for taking so long to write. I don't have much to write about. (Again, your readers know and now you've just told them you have nothing much to say . . . why should they read on?)

Also, never apologize for a financial update or a financial appeal.

3. **Infrequent and long updates.** Try to be consistent and frequent, but life happens. The best-laid plans fail. Don't beat yourself up. Also, don't try to tell your readers everything that's happened since your last update. Instead consider these:

   a. Consider if a Top Ten list might be a way to capture the highlights of the recent months, such as "Ten Times God Moved in the Last Year" or "Five Surprises in Six Months." Still keep each point short and, if possible, upbeat.

   b. If writing letters fell off because of a difficult time you could share a prayer or lesson God has been teaching you during times of grief, transition, uncertainty, etc.

4. **Getting too personal.** Typically your newsletters go to a broad audience and you won't have a close connection with everyone. That's normal. But, that means you need to consider carefully what you share that will encourage and enlighten them.

   a. Your newsletter is not the place to share about your addiction to computer games.

   b. Nor is it the place to share about all the things about the culture you live in, or your work, that anger and frustrate you. Cultures and work are broken and ignoring it all isn't ideal, but your newsletter is not where you should be venting.

   c. Nor is this the place to share about how hopeless you feel in your work and how you wonder why you're even doing this.

   d. Such struggles need to be addressed but with people who can help you work through them in a more private setting.

5. **Never Communicating.** Surprisingly this is common with

cross-cultural workers. Writing a good letter does take some time, and for those less inclined to writing, it does feel difficult, but it is vital to sustainable work.

a. If you stop communicating, your supporters often end up confused. I've had a number of phone calls from supporters wondering if their worker is even still overseas and what she is doing, wondering if their donation is still of any value.

b. Value your supporters (financial and prayer). Communicate with them. You don't have to be the next Shakespeare or Maya Angelou, you just need to connect. They will appreciate the effort.

c. Practice and it will get easier, and with a little effort, you'll probably see your writing improve. Your supporters are worth the effort just as you are worth their support.

Which mistake will you work on in your next newsletter?

Year Five in China

1999-2000

*A letter is the most basic—yet the most
flexible—mode of correspondence
regardless of its subject matter.*
—Scribendi

September 1999—Expectations

At first glance, "expectations" doesn't seem such a powerful word; however, what are you expecting from this newsletter? I imagine you would say, "To hear about Amy's life in China." If you said that, you're in for a surprise because Amy was too busy to write this and asked me if I would. Since I'm new to Chengdu and don't know many people, I said sure. My name is Isabel and I don't know much about China, instead I've decided to write about the passions of my heart: aboriginal languages of Costa Rica.

Wait, don't scan ahead to see if this is true or not! My question to you is what are your new expectations of this newsletter? Maybe you're excited to learn about the aboriginal languages of Costa Rica. Maybe you're thinking, "What is going on?" Perhaps you'll only look at the pictures or throw it away, but don't. Keep reading.

Okay, okay, okay. It was me, Amy, writing all the time, and I don't know anything about aboriginal languages of Costa Rica. (I like the sound of saying it. That's why I picked it.) I wanted to give you a little taste of our transition back to Chengdu. Small expectations we didn't even know that we had weren't met, like you expected this letter to be from me. You didn't even know that you had that expectation until you thought it might not be me. Then you started thinking, "Hey. Wait a minute. This isn't how it's supposed to be." Expectations can be far more powerful than I realized.

Three things happened that got me thinking about this topic. First of all, we live near the back gate of our college. For the last four years, with ease we have come and gone as we pleased. The market where we buy most of our food is out the back gate. It is also much easier to get a taxi out that way, instead of having to walk to the front gate and try to get one on the busy road. Our favorite *jiaozi* restaurant and a restaurant that we call The Pink (because it used to have pink walls) are an easy walk using the back gate.

But the school is building a new apartment building between the back gate and us and have deemed where we live a construction site. Seeing as having steady traffic going through a construction site may not be the safest thing, they have locked the back gate. "How inconvenient," Shelley and I cry. "Don't they know what a hassle this is for us?" Why is it a hassle? Because we expect the gate to be open. If we didn't have this subconscious expectation, we wouldn't mind. In fact, if it was our first year here, we would even think that this was the way it was supposed to be.

The second obstacle in the smooth living of Amy Young is the arrangement of my schedule. For the last couple of years, the classes I have taught have all been nicely lumped together during one part of the week. I had gotten used to that arrangement. This year, my classes are spread out throughout the week. By Friday, I'm singing to myself, "It's the week that never ends. It just goes on and on my friends." Now again, it's not that I am teaching any more hours. The pain point comes because my schedule does not fit my nice little expectations.

For the grand finale of examples, I present Shelley's teaching load. In the past (Are you noticing the pattern of our dashed expectations? We keep comparing them to the past) . . . Anyway, in the past, she worked with the new students, who have typically comprised three classes of thirty students. This summer, the government in Beijing decided that all colleges and universities in China needed to double their enrollment. Our enrollment went from two thousand students to five thousand students overnight. The decision was made by the government in July and was implemented in early September. There aren't enough dorms, so the school has had to convert office space to dorms. Watching that process has been unreal, but I digress. This year, Shelley will be teaching seven classes of new students. Because there aren't enough teachers, all seven classes (about two hundred students) will be combined for her to teach them US History and Culture. Boy howdy, we did not see that one coming at all.

The good thing about expectations is that they don't have to stay fixed, and we already have positive things to report in each area. The back gate is open daily from 11:30 a.m. to 12:30 p.m., so we've changed the time when we do our shopping. I'm adjusting to my new schedule and am more used to it with every passing week. Originally, Shelley was told that each class would have forty-five students, but they all turned out to have about thirty. We continue to be faithfully provided for. If there's anything we should have learned in China, it's don't expect things to be like they were. Don't expect to know what's going to happen. Yet we are human and sometimes forget this tip for life in China. Hopefully, we will remember to turn to the One with a bird's-eye view, instead of basing expectations solely on what we see.

Expectantly yours,
Amy

PS: Seven things I didn't expect and was delightfully surprised by:

1. Hot water in both the evening and morning. Morning showers are nice.

2. I brought back bed sheets with me after using towel sheets for four years. The "real ones" sure feel nice.

3. Letters from my students last year—they are precious.

4. Peter, a dear student from my first year, is here as a student again.

5. More and more students have email, there are new chances to communicate with them.

6. In my aerobics class, many people warmly greeted me back after the summer.

7. Also in my aerobics class, more people are getting brave and talking to me, giving me a chance to practice in Chinese.

October 1999

This letter will start off with a little word association. I'll give you a word so you can give a brief definition to whoever happens to be around you:
Picnic.
Sports fan.

Good marriage.

Holiday.

Parade.

In linguistics these might be examples of notions. A notion basically refers to your concept of something. Usually people don't realize how deep their notions are until they live cross-culturally and encounter a way of doing something that's different from the normal way of doing things. Normal, of course, refers to their way. ☺

What got me thinking about this topic was the celebration of National Day this year. Seeing as it was the fiftieth anniversary of the founding of the People's Republic of China, it was a big one. As I retell what happened, see if you pick up on three notions I bumped into as I continued to learn about China.

Rumor had it (code for our students told us, but no official notice from the English Department) that we would have a seven-day holiday. I went to ask the English Department when the holiday would be, but ten days before the holiday they still hadn't decided when and how long our break would be. How can this be? The government in Beijing eventually declared that most schools would have a seven-day holiday, and so it was decided. The English Department let us know that we would make up Wednesday's classes by teaching them Saturday after the holiday and Thursday's classes would be made up on Sunday. Wait a minute? Doesn't a holiday mean you get the days off, not that you shuffle them around to the weekend?[13]

Erin, my first teammate, visited for three days during the National Day holiday. It was great to see her and have her see all of the changes Chengdu has gone through the last two years since she left. On National Day, there was a two-hour parade on TV broadcast from Beijing, and I would bet that 90 percent of the population watched. Erin and I were among the 90 percent (Shelley was travelling with a student for five days). As we watched the parade, the first hour got a little long because it was troop after troop of soldiers followed by tanks—for an entire hour.

Before the endless viewing of marching troops with serious faces, I hadn't realized I thought of parades as happy, kind of goofy events, with people smiling, waving, and having a good time. Later I asked Chinese friends what they thought of the parade. They said that due to the last 150 years of China being invaded and poor, they felt proud and safe to see all of the soldiers and tanks.

Before Erin returned to Hong Kong, I asked her what she noticed that was different in Chengdu since we first came here. She said,

- I hear less spitting and more cell phones.

- Some parts of the city are completely different because small roads have been torn down and replaced by larger ones.

- Man, do you have a lot more stuff in your room. What are you going to do with it when you leave?

- The food is still awesome.

Of Mice and Money

This summer, several of you said to me, "We loved your mice stories last year." Well, it was two years ago that we were plagued with mice, not last year, but for your entertainment delight, they're back. Ugh. The current batch is the most aggressive I've seen. They eat anything left out—anything—tea bags, potatoes, bread, oranges, chocolate. Part of the kitchen is near my room, so the mice have been disturbing my sleep.

Shen Yang and Shelley got one while I was gone, and this morning I woke up to two caught on sticky paper. Now that I realize that Shen Yang will kill them, I have given up whacking them with my frying pan and call for her. Today, she came into the kitchen to kill them with a knife and a pair of pliers to pry them off the sticky paper. I told her to wait a minute until I could go into the bathroom and turn on the water to avoid hearing them die. Pathetic, I know, but it's what I did.

The money part of mice and money means that for the first time in over four years with TIC I am in the hole. I know I will be provided for because I always have been, but I thought I should share this part of life with you.

Again, as I look back over the past month, I'm thankful to be here and share with you a little bit of life in China. As you pray for us this next month, you could be asking that our notions of what is right will be more and more in line with those of the people we love and live among. Also ask for God to reveal Himself to our students. There seems to be less and less interest in spiritual topics and more and more interest in money, education, and good jobs. Thanks for the encouraging letters you send after you get my newsletters. I appreciate them.

Living La Vida China,
Amy

November 1999—Welcome to the China Vortex

Sometimes Shelley and I are sucked into what we call the China Vortex, where the situation is totally China, totally out of our control, and totally not how we are culturally programmed. It used to be that I would try to fight the vortex and bring order to what I perceived as chaos. Now I'm usually more comfortable with going with the flow, knowing it is the China Vortex and to just hang on for the ride.

Case in point: a friend of my parents, Mr. White, was recently on a tour group in China that came to a city near Chengdu. I was going to take a public bus, pick him up, and bring him back to Chengdu so he could see where we live and attend my classes. During lunch the day I was going to pick him up, I was talking with some of the students and explaining my plan. Horrified, one girl said, "No. You will be lonely on the bus and it's not safe for you to travel alone." She insisted on calling her father and arranging a car to take me in order to save me time. This all sounds lovely, but looks can be deceiving and this situation was crying out, "China Vortex, China Vortex."

I tried to explain that I was actually looking forward to having time alone on the bus to read but that I appreciated the offer. The captain of the Titanic had a better chance of saving all of the passengers than I did of resisting the Vortex. Dreamy, her English name, is one determined young lady, and later that afternoon her father's cousin, her friend May, Dreamy, and I boarded a minivan to go pick up Mr. White. Though I didn't get to read, I was entertained with a long story about a ride and a broom in a countryside wedding (aka bride and groom ☺).

We arrived, picked up Mr. White, and then the Vortex swept us off to a restaurant where, of course, the cousin paid even though he was doing us a favor by driving us. We finally left the restaurant at eight and headed back to Chengdu with the Vortex holding us firmly in its grip. The cousin is, no kidding, the slowest driver I have ever ridden with in China. We passed nobody. This is simply unheard of in China. It was the Vortex in action. Arriving safely at home at 10:30 p.m., the Vortex spit us out saying, "Ha, and you thought you were going to go alone on a public bus and miss all of the fun. Not a chance. I'll see you again when you least expect it." That's one of the things I love about life in China. It's never quite what I think it will be.

Speaking of life never quite being what I expect it to be, my plans for next year aren't quite what I thought they would be either. Some of you knew that I thought the plan was to finish this school year and then probably head back to the US for some more schooling and at some point in the future return to China. In October, "the plan" was modified a bit.

I will still be leaving Chengdu, but for Beijing instead of Denver. Most of you know that I am also the curriculum director for TIC. This is a job that's usually done from Beijing, but I have been less than thrilled to leave Chengdu, and have only agreed to do the job if I could stay here. To help the arrangement, I have an assistant who lives in Beijing but is going on home leave next year. Because she will be gone, I have been asked, not by TIC but Someone with a bit more authority, to move to Beijing for a year and pull the pieces of the job back into one position.

As painful as it is, I know that it's time to leave Chengdu. I had thought leaving Chengdu meant to be in the States for a while, but I was wrong. The irony about this change is that as I mentioned in my last newsletter, for the first time I'm in the hole with TIC . . . and moving to Beijing will require more support. The human side of me says, "Excuse me, there is a problem with this plan."

The past month or so, I've been pondering what it means to be a person of faith. It's rather easy to talk about, especially when things look neat and tidy and don't require much faith. What went through Abraham's mind when he was asked to sacrifice Isaac? No wonder Moses came up with all of those great excuses as to why he surely couldn't be the one to talk to Pharaoh. Yet being a person of faith isn't limited to thinking and beliefs. So, as illogical as it looks to me now, I'm moving to Beijing next year. I look forward to reporting in a year on the things that I can't see from this side of faith—parts of the journey that I will only understand after I take my own leap of faith.

So much more to say, but space is running out. I hear the Vortex calling, as Shelley and I have been invited to the home of a fellow teacher in the English Department for dinner . . . and I can't wait.

Faithfully yours,
Amy

PS: Random update on the mice. The mice are driving me crazy. One was in the pillows of my bed last night. Gross. They poop around the house at night. It's a good night if they only wake me up once. Three times is a bad night, but the other morning, I ran into our tormentor in the kitchen and he is only about the size of five cotton balls. How can something this little and cute be this annoying?

December 1999—Macao comes home

What do you think could be one of the most horrifyingly embarrassing things that could happen to you? Forget to wear a slip?

Walk around with lettuce on your tooth and no one says anything? Last week I had one of those moments where you think you'll die, but unfortunately you don't.

In preparation for the return of Macao to the Motherland on December 20, our school had an English speech contest. Shelley and I were asked to be judges. The contest was held on an evening when Shelley teaches, so only I was available. A few days later, I was asked to be the hostess of the contest instead of a judge. A little background in hosting something in China will help you understand why I was a bit reluctant to accept.

Any party, contest, or ceremony in China has a host and a hostess, and the physical appearances of the hosts are vital. It's often a handsome man and a beautiful woman who are dressed spectacularly. Keeping this in mind, I mentally ran through my closet, creating problem number one. The host and hostess will use their voices in dramatic ways and give each other these host and hostess looks. I can now recognize both the voice and the look, but there is no way I can reproduce them without cracking myself up and offending the audience. Hence, problem number two. This is a speech contest celebrating the return of Macao from the evil foreigners who ripped her from the bosom of the Motherland. Do you truly want a foreigner hosting the party? Problem number three.

I tried to explain to the English Department that I didn't know how to host a Chinese speech contest and that I was a bit nervous, could someone else do it? Please? "But, Amy, we were having such a hard time getting judges until you agreed to be the hostess. The students and faculty were quite excited and want to see you. Some of the teachers are even canceling classes to see you." Oh, great. Come and see the foreign buffoon make a fool of herself. I thought that these words were going a bit far in trying to stroke my ego, and then an English teacher walked in and said, "Amy, I heard the great news that you're hosting the party and am trying hard to rearrange my schedule to be there!"

Okay, I give in. I'll host the event. Trying to nail down exactly what was expected of me so that I could behave as culturally appropriately as possible, I was told to wear a dress and be myself. This was not helpful. The night of the speech contest came and I still wasn't sure what to wear because all of my dresses are for much warmer weather or at least indoor heating. I finally selected a sleeveless, knee-length dress and wore long underwear on the top and bottom, two pairs of tights over that, two pairs of socks, boots, and a cardigan sweater that was Shelley's. All day I kept thinking, "If only I had my prom dress!" The ensemble I pulled together came pretty close. ☺

My student and co-host Liu Wei and I started off by greeting the audience in unison. He introduced the judges, I encouraged the contestants, and then we took turns introducing the contestants when it was their turn to give the speech. I made some jokes, people laughed, and I thought, "Hey, hostessing isn't so bad." The speeches ended and the woman in charge of organizing the contest hissed at me, "Get up there and make a speech while the judges tally the scores." Make a speech? About what?

Instead, I took my cordless mic and decided to pull an Oprah and walk around interviewing the judges. I had the first judge stand up and asked her how she was going to spend the twentieth of December celebrating Macao coming back. "Watching TV and eating." Next judge, same question—"Shopping" was the answer. And what will you buy? "It depends on how much money I take." The audience was eating up this whole interview thing. The third judge, as he stood, asked if he could ask a question. "No," I joked. "I ask the questions." And the audience roared.

Well, he asked anyway. "Are you cold in a dress?" I'm not sure how I answered. I probably said "not really" or something like that because into the microphone, in front of everyone, he said, "Oh, that's because you are fat." I wanted to die. My worst nightmare had come true. I wanted to scream, "Of course I'm cold. It's December and there's no central heat. I was told to wear a dress." Instead, I asked him to sit down and moved on to the next judge. Not thinking, I asked her if she thought I was fat, and she wondered if I wanted the truth. "No," I said. Diplomatically, she said, "You are more lovely this year than ever." The organizer motioned that they had the results ready and I could sit down.

I did, and tears came to my eyes. I thought of leaving, but then the audience would see and it would ruin the festivities of the whole evening. I knew that he had not intentionally tried to hurt me, and I forced myself to stay. Loads of pictures were taken afterwards, and then I finally escaped home. I slept fitfully, and at 2:30 a.m., I had to say out loud, "Mr. W, I forgive you." Then I was able to sleep.

Here too we find the gospel: even our worst nightmare can be redeemed. Later in the week, Shelley and I invited three of our students over for a Christmas tea. At some point, the incident came up and they said they couldn't clearly hear what Mr. W had said, but they knew it was something terrible and that I handled it well by being funny instead of saying mean things. Somehow we got on the topic of good stories and they asked us to tell them some, so we told the stories of the prodigal son and the good Samaritan and talked about the deeper meaning of both. I said that it's easy for me to love those I love, but I need to love even those who are hard to love. Tearing up, I said it was not easy for me to forgive Mr. W, but I knew it was what I should do and that once I did it, I meant it and I felt released from the hurt. They said I was a better person than they were, and I said it was because I had help and my natural inclination wasn't to be this way.

Two of the three were taken with the stories and want to get together to learn more next semester. I'm glad that I didn't react on my first impulse out of hurt and that I was able to step back and see the bigger picture. I'm sure that it wasn't on my own strength, but with your help via the Helper. Continue to ask that Shelley and I can act in ways that are culturally appropriate and glorifying. You never know when you may be in a dress with long underwear. Your daily faithfulness helps us keep a sense of humor and a sense of purpose. Thanks.

Love,
Amy

January 2000—It's beginning to look a lot like Christmas . . .

This isn't just a song, it's the reality of life in modern China. I used to stress that celebrating Christmas was especially true in the big cities, but this year the effect can even be felt out in the countryside. As usual, we gave two cultural lectures about Christmas. In the first one, we talked about the history of Christmas and why Jesus was born. Most of the students know that Christmas celebrates His birth, but they don't know any of the specifics of His mother being a virgin, His birthplace, the shepherds (pronounced by our students as "shef-erds"), or the wise men. Want to see the story with fresh eyes? Explain it to people who have never heard.

We are repeatedly asked if we believe it and are laughed at, out loud, when we say that we do. An understandable reaction because the gospel does sound too good to be true and even a bit weird. On the other hand, there are usually a few who come up afterwards and say, "Oh, it is wonderful, I wish it were true." We end up hearing the whole spectrum of responses after that first lecture.

The students are especially taken with the Christmas decorations, so it's a good time to invite them over to our home. When we ask them which of the decorations they like best, the Christmas tree wins hands down. As I mentioned last letter, one of the highlights for this year was the Christmas tea we had with three of our students in which two expressed interest in studying the Bible next term.

This was such a highlight because there hasn't been much spiritual interest this fall. Part of it is due to the Fa Lun Gang (cult) crackdown that started this summer and has continued through the fall. Early this semester, the government made it illegal to be a part of the Fa Lun Gang, resulting in people being more leery about religion in general. Also, many of our students put all their eggs in one basket, focusing all their attention on passing the test to enter graduate school. They feel that they have their future pretty well under control and don't need help. A third reason there isn't much spiritual interest is due to the spiritual oppression in Sichuan. A friend of mine who lived in Sichuan for two years and now lives in a province much closer to Beijing said that she can't believe the spiritual difference and that Sichuan is under spiritual oppression. Being close to Tibet and Tibetan Buddhism, I can believe it. Pray for Sichuan.

Back to Christmas in Chengdu. It is interesting to see how Christmas has developed over the last five years that I have celebrated it here. Five years ago, there was no sign of Christmas until Christmas Eve when a few of the hotels decorated. The next two years, there was more decorating, but it was still rather "primitive" with snow being made of preformed Styrofoam (used in protecting appliances in shipping) and kicked into pieces with obvious boot prints. Last year, the displays and decorations were lovely, and there was even Christmas music played in some department stores. This year, it was "Christmas with Chinese characteristics" as places started decorating after Christmas. In most of the department stores the checkout people wore Santa hats as Christmas music blared over the PA system. The Chinese now send Christmas cards. To show you how deep the change is, below is an excerpt from a student's reaction after reading from Matthew and Luke as well as *'Twas the Night Before Christmas*:

> I also like the Christmas reading. I did some Christmas reading. Oh, after I did some Christmas reading, I feel Christmas is a unique festival. It is full of romantic things such as Christmas tree, light, gift, star and so on. Each time is related to the birth and death of Jesus, and Santa Claus is gracious to every child. All these things are full of myth and mystery, but for our Chinese, most important is the Spring Festival. I think it loses its charming gradually. During the festival, the most important thing is to give money to children and invite people over to eat. From my point of view,

giving too much money to children isn't good, this will spoil them, and sometimes people's inviting each other to eat is wasting food and money.

To compare Christmas with Spring Festival, maybe I prefer Christmas. This is due to the Christmas reading and the glamour of Christmas draws more and more Chinese people's attention. I'm a little bit worried about our Spring Festival. I'm afraid that Christmas may surpass the Spring Festival on some aspect. Christmas influenced Chinese people a lot. For example, I found my husband on Christmas. He told me that our daughter is only eight years old, but she knows something about Christmas. Because of our deep love to our daughter, we agreed to prepare a Christmas tree for her. I think this doing can also decorate the house, so we can see how great the Christmas's influence are.

In talking with a number of our students, these ideas are not unusual. Many say that their children are aware of Christmas and want to celebrate it. The consensus is that the next generation will grow up celebrating Christmas. Part of the reason they are drawn to Christmas, I think, is because it is a holiday with meaning and significance that transcend us. If it were merely about gifts, music, and eating, it's no better than Spring Festival, but deep within, many recognize that there is more to life and are therefore drawn to Christmas. Our prayer is that their eyes will be opened to the truth.

The semester break is about to begin, and I'm ready for a short break. In Thailand, I'll be able to find out how my account is currently and what my expenses for next year will be. The big difference next year is that I will have to rent an apartment, and rent is not cheap in Beijing. I will be teaching part-time and will not be earning a salary, meaning that I'll have to raise enough money to cover rent and living expenses for next year. Not sure how much more that will be a month, but I'm estimating about $1,200 more a month. As I said, I don't know yet, and I will let you know the specifics later. Thanks for sticking with me through all of the changes.

Looking forward to fresh fruit, being warm, and sleeping through the night without the pitter-patter of little mouse feet.

Love,
Amy

February 2000—"I like it more than I like eating dog"

. . . Said one of our students one day when we were eating lunch in the student cafeteria. "What, pray tell, could be more enjoyable than eating dog?" you may wonder. Mice. "Amy, do you call it mouse . . . meat?" In my mind I said, "No. We don't call it anything," but out loud, I said, "Yes." It was one of those times when you kind of linguistically wing it.

At first I thought the student was making fun of our recent mouse infestation—one drowned in my toilet, another ran over my head while I was asleep, and one of them destroyed a carnation on my desk. The student was quite serious. A different student piped in that it was her favorite meat too. This was definitely one of those "I'm not actually having this conversation" experiences, but I took it as an opportunity to learn as much as possible. First, I asked if it tasted like chicken. "No, better," came the response. That's what I deserve for asking a snarky question. Okay, how can you prepare mouse? After catching the mouse, you remove the skin before you cook it, but you need enough for one mouse per person, so sadly, they haven't eaten mouse in about four years due to the rat poison that is around now.

Another day I was eating with two of the same students and Shelley was at another table. We were discussing their families. One of the men is single, another recently married. "Oh, what does your wife do?" "She is a doctor. She kills babies." "Do you mean that she performs abortions?" I asked, trying to both insert vocabulary and soften the sound of the job. "Yes. She kills babies because she works in the family planning department." He did say that she would rather have another job because many of the peasants in the community don't like her and it's difficult to live where you are not wanted. Sometimes women are able to hide, but if a woman is found out by the government before the end of her pregnancy, and it's her job to kill the baby by an injection and then deliver the baby.

Putting the whole abortion issue aside, the conversation highlighted again for us how much value life has here, and that's not much. Part of it is due to the size of the population. As you sit in your spacious home, get in your car, drive to a huge parking lot, push around a large shopping cart, you cannot imagine what it's like to live in a country with 1.2 billion people. There are people in your space all the time here. Rush hour traffic may be bad in the States, but you're in your own car, listening to whatever you want on the radio. There are things that keep your space neatly defined. Here, we don't have that luxury. Life is crowded. With crowding comes the cheapening of life.

It's good to be continually learning, to be given the privilege to understand the thought processes a little bit more. As I sit here thinking about the semester that has ended, one of the highlights for me was the benefit of having long-term relationships as I understand the culture more. A former student called me and asked if I could proofread his resume. As I was reading it, I commented that he certainly had a wide range of interests. He had majored in English, taught geography, passed the self-taught lawyer exam—self-taught courses are common here)—and is now finishing up a master's program in international economics. He said, "You know I am neither a Christian nor a Marxist, so I keep searching for some purpose to my life."

I let that go for the moment and kept reading his resume. At the end of it, we had a great conversation that we never would have had when he was my student and on the verge of beginning graduate school. At that point, grad school was his great hope. Now, it is not. He could not understand how year after year I continue to live in a country that is less developed than my homeland. He was my student when I had meningitis and had seen me in the hospital. I told him that I do have a purpose in my life and that I am where God wants me to be and encouraged him to search for God and real meaning in his life.

Anna, another former student, emails me occasionally and has said that last fall she had been depressed and was ready to choose a religion. For years I've known that she's had a spiritual interest in both Buddhism and Christianity but wasn't ready to make the choice. Since email wasn't the place to have the conversation, I told her that it was good to make a choice and to call me. I didn't hear from her for a long time, but then she showed up at my door the week before Christmas. When she came over, she cried and cried because she is empty. I called a Chinese Christian who is a friend and introduced them. They met the next day and Anna got introduced to a group of well-educated Chinese Christians.

She called me on New Year's Day and said that she had made the decision to become a Christian and wanted to know what was the ceremony to become one. We talked about how to become a Christian— in careful language—and I met her later that week at her apartment to see how she was doing. The best part is that she already has a group of Chinese Christians to meet with. She loves singing songs, and that night she wanted me to teach her *What a Friend We Have in Jesus*. We sang it over and over.

I know that God can, and will, reach both former students. It is a privilege to see the fruit of being in Chengdu for several years. I hope this encourages you that we are making a difference and that when you get to heaven, Anna will be there to share her story in more detail. You will love her as she has such an air of free-spiritedness about her. Maybe that's why she's my friend. ☺

From mouse eating, to baby killing, to resume reading, to chatting, that's what my life holds. Not all easy, yet I love my life. Again, thank you for faithfully praying for us, writing to us, and in general being a part of life in China.

Love,
Amy

March 2000—The threshold of spring

I was going to begin this letter by saying "the beginning of the end," meaning that this semester marks the official end to my tenure in Chengdu. I decided not to because I don't like the negative connotation. Instead, I feel like I'm at a threshold. I am drawn to this image because of the two sides and the idea of passing from one to the other. I'm not ready to say goodbye to Chengdu, and yet I'm quite aware that the doorway to change is before me and I can see through it from where I am.

Even though I can see it, I'm still here and busy with life. One big change to my schedule this semester is that I teach writing to sixty-six juniors . . . at one time. Oh my. These are students Shelley had last term, and many of them are new to me. On the first day they realized what a shock it could be to have a crazy foreigner teach such a large class. When they walked in, I gave each student a nametag to wear and took their picture to begin to put names and faces together. Ironically, the next week I was on an outing with the English Department teachers and one said she never learns her students' names and only refers to them by their clothing. "Will the girl in the red sweater please answer the question?" No wonder my class giggled and there was nervous tension in the air as they hung their nametags over their heads.

Of course, even after only two classes, I love them. Their first journal entry was about one of their favorite teachers. What came through loud and clear to me was that good teachers noticed them and said encouraging things, so I've committed myself to try to circle around this large class, making comments that are specific, more than the generic "good job." I look at their picture cards as I grade to personalize the mass of grading and remind myself that while I see a stack of papers, each paper is significant to the person who wrote it.

Isn't it great that, even though it's my last term, I've been put in a position to learn? As China struggles to educate a larger and larger portion of the population, classes across the board are expanding. I feel privileged to have learned to teach in different setups, most recently in a situation that's much closer to what my students face. They have repeatedly told me that while my teaching style is great, it would never work when they teach because their classes are much larger. Here I've been given a chance to model, showing both sides: we are right and we are wrong (wink).

Another area I'm learning about involves teaching foreigners— Americans and Canadians. TIC and Azusa Pacific University in California have a joint master's degree program. Last summer, I taught a class to about twenty-five of our people who are earning their MA in teaching. These TIC grad students handed in their homework to me in Thailand (oh my, I had assigned a lot!), and I'm about halfway through grading it. Not only have I been pushed to learn about larger classes, but also I'm navigating through the differences in teaching graduate classes of native English speakers. It's a bit awkward because I'm in TIC and they are in TIC, I grade their papers, they read my comments. It's that whole colleague and then the student/teacher dynamic. I guess I still have more to learn.

This month you can tell I have pondered teaching and modeling. When I think of the Great Teacher and how he too had students who didn't get his lessons on the first try, he too worked with large classes, and he too taught a variety of students, it encourages and challenges me to press on and grade with a grateful heart.

Teachably yours,
Amy

PS: I'm going to call this section "Ask Amy." In recent letters, some have asked questions about things I've written, letting me know that I didn't communicate as clearly as I could have. Here, I'll try to answer your questions.

Question: Are you excited about moving to Beijing? I couldn't tell.

Answer: Yes, I am excited. I don't always like change, that may be what you're picking up on. I was also surprised God asked to move to Beijing. Moving to Beijing is a little bit like moving from Denver to Los Angeles, where crowds and traffic come to mind, but I want to be willing to live where I'm supposed to be and that is Beijing. Knowing that, Beijing excites me.

Question: When you were called fat, didn't you know that Chinese think foreigners are fat?

Answer: Oh goodness, yes. You cannot be in China more than about seven minutes before you realize that. I had been asked if I ate too much beef as a child, and I repeatedly hear from the students that "Americans are fat because they love to eat butter, cheese, and sugar." Trying to point out that Americans don't eat butter all by itself and that I personally don't like cheese is futile, but that doesn't always stop me from trying. ☺ The surprise in being told I was fat was that it was done publicly—and even most Chinese would say that he was being rude by Chinese standards.

April 2000—"My vocabulary is lacking"

A common complaint from our students is that they lack the vocabulary to be able to express themselves clearly in English. Honestly, they do a fine job, and we rarely have difficulties understanding what they are trying to say. As I sit here and try to put words to these last months and the range of emotions and experiences I've had, the right words escape me. All that's coming to mind is, "I lack the vocabulary to express myself!"

The one word that keeps coming to me is extremes—in emotions and in experiences. On one end of the spectrum, I spent two weekends visiting middle schools and being the center of attention. On the other extreme, two people near and dear to me died. Then in the middle was a bunch of normal, keeping up with daily life in Chengdu. Up, down, up, down. When will my heart level out?

I went back to Zitong, the school I had visited last spring where I was the great Yang Laoshi (aka Teacher Young). Zitong is an exhausting place to visit because they see me as their savior. While that might be a tiny bit satisfying to my ego, it is completely overwhelming since I can never ever be all that they want or need. I will never be able to live up to the idol they have created me to be—I will disappoint at every turn.

To give you a little flavor of a visit to Zitong, I arrived and stayed with the mother and grandmother of my former student Wendy, who was unable to be there because she had given birth in January. Since I had visited last spring, it wasn't as awkward as it could have been that Wendy wasn't able to accompany me. The biggest concern of her mom and grandma was what to feed me for breakfast. I tried to stress that a normal Chinese breakfast was A-okay with me, but apparently I didn't eat enough last spring, so I was fed white bread and a huge bowl of hot powdered milk each morning. Ugh.

After breakfast, two teachers escorted me to the school where I taught junior middle school year one (first year of junior high). Some foreigner who has probably never been to the countryside where her textbook is used, created the book they were using. Good grief. It is far above the ability of these cuties who have been studying English for about seven months. Like last spring, the teachers from around the area and every teacher in their school came to watch me teach. There was a video camera on me allowing my teaching to be played on the TVs in all of the other classes. Surreal.

At meals, the school officials would sing the praises of the great Yang Laoshi (Man, I would like to meet this person). "Unlike other foreigners, the great Yang Laoshi doesn't work for money. She refuses our money while others demand more. The great Yang Laoshi is an excellent teacher. And so on and so on. Please come back to our school. We all love you." Near the front gate of the school is a permanent display documenting my entire last visit. My picture was taken hundreds of times with hundreds of people. My signature was in hot demand. The experience is difficult to capture, but I hope this helps you see a little bit of what that extreme felt like for me.

Now, to the other extreme. One of the people who died was Joe Brouwer, my dad's good buddy for the past ten years. He died after a battle with cancer. He was only sixty, and his death was a blow to our family. My sisters and I emailed back and forth what a hole we feel. I was in an emotional funk for a good two days and couldn't focus on anything.

Reeling from his death, my parents took off to Michigan to visit my grandparents. After their trip, while they were driving home, they were called by my grandparents' assisted living place and told that my grandma was throwing up and was taken to the hospital. Grandma died before they made it back to Michigan.

Those of you who have been reading these letters the last five years know that every summer I've made a point to visit my grandparents because they're important to me and are advanced in age (ninety-four and ninety-five). If one of them died while I was in China, I wanted to have lived without regrets in the way I spent my summers. Grandma's death wasn't a surprise, but the loss is still real. For me, the true loss was not being a part of the ritual of marking her life during the memorial service. While my family has wonderfully kept me in the loop, I still wasn't there, and that is the hard part of "dying to your family."

The Chinese handle grief in ways that seem the opposite of comfort to my bruised heart. Because she was old, I was comforted with, "It's natural." Oh, thank you. "Turn your sorrow into strength." I'm not sure she meant physical strength, but I had to fight the urge to hit her. "Don't cry. It doesn't help your mother or grandmother." Yes, but it helps me.

The weekend after my grandma died, Shelley and I went to the countryside again to teach at a middle school of some of our former students.

Up, down, savior, mourner, Yang Laoshi, just Amy. In the midst of the ups and downs, life is sprinkled with encouraging happenings with students. Anna, whom I mentioned earlier, has several friends asking her to tell them about the One who has changed her life. She keeps telling me, "Amy, I don't mean to tell them. They keep asking." We're also reading good stories weekly with two students, and it's exciting to see the stories through fresh eyes. Hopefully the two will decide they like the stories.

While I feel I can't adequately express all that's been going on in my life and in my heart, I have been comforted on a level that requires no words. The last month certainly hasn't been easy, but it has been worth it. I am being refined and taught and have the bonus of being used. Who could ask for more than that?

Simply,
Amy

May 2000—Living in small pieces

Last week, I read a book called *The God of Small Things: A Novel* by Arundhati Roy. While the beautifully written novel has nothing overtly to do with God, it does show how the little pieces of the lives of a family are woven together. Though none of the pieces look overly significant, in the end, each piece plays a part in the plot. This sums up the last month. Nothing inordinately large or interesting happened, and yet it is obvious that God has been present in the small things.

Piece #1: Those large classes! Who would have known what a joy to me those sixty-seven junior students would be?! Because it is a writing class, the students hand in journals weekly and I respond to them. This is a wonderful chance to get to know my students and be aware of what's going on in their lives. Topics run the gamut from birthdays to boyfriends to missing their husbands or wives who are back home, and may include worry about the future; even the movies they have seen have been written about. Reading and responding to the journals allows me to "rejoice with those who rejoice [and] weep with those who weep."[14] I encourage, offer hope, and sometimes even dole out advice. It's in these small ways that God is planting seeds and tending the hearts of the students.

Piece #2: One Sunday I woke up with swollen lymph nodes . . .

Well, it was April, which in recent years has translated into hospital visits, so I shouldn't have been all that surprised. The next day, there was shooting pain in my right ear, and then on Wednesday, the right side of my face was swollen—even my earlobe was swollen. Oh, dear. I had to go to the hospital. Sigh, again. Shelley and I prayed about it during our team prayer time. Xiao Yang—no way was Xiao Feng going anywhere medical with me—and I headed off to the hospital.

We had to wait a long time, but when the doctor finally saw me, he mentioned he had recently been to a seminar on this kind of problem. I had a mouth problem, not an ear one, and he sent us off to another hospital. I ended up seeing two more excellent doctors and was eventually diagnosed with an infected saliva gland. Go figure. I had no idea that part of the body could be infected. Xiao Yang kept saying how we were having good luck, and I was able to say that this was God at work answering our prayer. "Oh," she said, and another small piece (or in this case a seed) was placed.

Piece #3: I was in Changchun on an official TIC visit with two of our teachers. We had tickets to a Wang Fei concert. Wang Fei is the Ricky Martin of China—on Pepsi cans and billboards, for instance. We excitedly hopped in a cab and were driven to the concert. We were babbling away in the cab until we came over a hill, and there was the largest, most round, most spectacular sunset. Wow. Huge. Can the sun be that round? Can it be that vibrantly orange? That huge? Maybe because we were so far north. Maybe. But it was one of those moments. In a cab. In Changchun. On the way to a concert. As it turns out, the cab driver dropped us off in the totally wrong area of town, and the concert was still about a ten-minute drive from the TIC teachers' home; but had he not made a mistake, I wouldn't have that sun in my mind now. It wasn't a mistake—It was a piece of God at work.

Piece #4: As you know, we've been meeting on Fridays with two students reading Bible stories and being courted by the Son. Several weeks ago, one of them told us how the day before she had been out with another student and had been pickpocketed. Our student felt terrible because the stolen money was her friend's, and her friend told her not to worry, saying it was a little bit of money and the money wasn't important. Her friend's reaction spoke to our student. Her friend is a Christian. Clink. Another piece of God at work.

From my job as a teacher, to health issues, to sunsets and rock concerts, to reactions after being robbed—some of these pieces mundane, some breathtaking, all small—this month, it is the small things that God has been at work in. I have six weeks left before I leave

Chengdu, and I wonder how in the small ways He will sustain me, day by day, as I say goodbye. It won't be easy, and I don't know if I'll ever fully understand all of the pieces, but I'm hoping that the picture my life has made this past month and these five years has been one that glorifies the One who orchestrates the pieces.

Piecefully yours,
Amy

July 2000—And can it be . . . that five years have passed?!

Hard to believe, but yes, it can. Five years have come and gone, and the time came to say goodbye to Chengdu. As many of you know, I'm the kind of person who strongly attaches to places and people, but when the end finally came, it was easier than I expected. Why? There were several reasons with the key one being that God had been orchestrating this and it was time to go. Other things that helped—

• **Saying goodbye well.** I had been advised about intentionally saying goodbye and not letting the time come to an end. I made a point of meeting with people who were important to me and having a final meal, movie, or outing with them. Both Shelley and I had talks with our students who will be here next year about what they can do to speed up the process of getting to know their new foreign teachers. I've asked certain students to show the new teachers specific things I know they'll be interested in. Hopefully, the way has been prepared for as smooth of a transition as possible for the new teachers, so finishing well helped to ease the leaving for us.

• **Loose ends tied up.** The young women that we have been working with have been plugged into local groups, either at the Three-Self Church or in house churches. Knowing that they will be fed, challenged, and grown in Chinese is exciting. Miss M has become a Christian, and Miss S is still thinking about it. When we asked them if they would like to be introduced to another former student who attends a home church, they both enthusiastically said yes. I'm encouraged that Miss S can continue to learn and come to God on her own time schedule and not on ours. A final word on Anna—oh, I wish you could meet her—she's growing spiritually and last week gave the closing prayer at her Bible study group. So cool. Oh, but I will miss these women.

• **A reminder of who we are serving.** While this has been a hugely significant five-year period in my life, for the English Department we've been merely more foreigners to work with. The Monday before we left, the English Department gave us our goodbye present: a book in which they had written inside the front cover. Before they signed their message to us, they wanted us to proofread it in front of them: *"Now, Amy, you've been here since '97."* Um, no, '95. *"And, Shelley, you've been here since . . . '98."* Nope, 1997. *"Now, what are your family names?"* And so the book is given to Amy YONG for her great service. It was good to have a reminder this close to the end that we are serving God and not working for the praise of the English Department.

• **And the last reason** it wasn't as difficult to leave as I had anticipated involved flames. The room down the hall had a fire about a month before we left. The cause was either bad wiring in the walls or the TV melting down. In the end, the waibans decided to replace all of the wires in the rooms in our hall. Why they chose the last week we were here to do it, I'm not sure, but the constant banging, drilling, and construction workers in our hallway made it easier to leave.

This coming school year, my support need goes up significantly for two reasons. For five years, the school that I taught at as a regular TIC teacher provided for my housing and salary. When I move to Beijing, I will only be teaching part-time and will be renting an apartment. As a part-time teacher, I won't be earning a salary but will be "paid" by the school being willing to process the paperwork providing a visa to live in China. Due to this, I will need to pay rent and raise my own salary in one of the most expensive cities in China. The rent and salary will be about an additional $1,500 a month. My support has been much better this spring, and I'm not anticipating the extra funds being a major issue, but I am curious to see how God is going to provide.

I feel a little bit guilty about the extra support needed because I will be living in a nice apartment—the kitchen and bathrooms were built with Americans in mind. I'm not sure I'll know what to do with a kitchen sink that has hot running water . . . and four burners seems extravagant. The refrigerator is as tall as I am! The floors are wood and the best, best, best part? Well, as I've mentioned before, I have furniture fantasies, and the former resident is leaving me a soft green SOFA. My color and my degree of softness! I think it will be hard for me to live in such a nice place at the expense of others, but I know this is where I'm supposed to be and hope that my home can be used as a refreshing oasis for other TIC teachers.

I haven't said much about what I'll be doing next year, but this letter is getting a bit long and I don't want to push your patience. ☺ I'll give you more details next time. I'm happy to be home, recharging for a while because towards the end I could feel myself becoming worn down. China is a great place to live, but it can be draining. I'm looking forward to people, movies, reading, and thinking about my new sofa.

Love,
Amy

#5 If You Write Newsletters

Five Things Newsletter Writers Do Well

By Davita Freeman

After three years on the field, Davita Freeman returned to the US to work in the home office of her organization. She worked in the communications department and primarily with paper newsletters and mailing list support. Over the years, she read more than five thousands newsletters. I contacted her asking for *Five Common Newsletter Mistakes* and *Five Things Newsletter Writers Do Well* (after Chapter 5). The following is Davita's answer to "What common mistakes have you seen newsletter writers make?"

~ ~ ~

Again, based on my experience of reading thousands of newsletters, here are my top five things I've seen newsletter writers do well.

1. **Consistent Communication.** Set up a realistic schedule for consistent connection with supporters. Ideally, aim for monthly updates (using various mediums as is best for your supporters, i.e. blog, email newsletter, paper newsletter).

2. **A well-crafted short story.** Readers may not remember the city you're working in, but many remember the fruit seller who shared her extra mangos with your crying child or the beggar who invited your family to his home to share the little he had. Keep it to around five hundred words for a quick, fun read.

    a. Look around. Your stories may not seem exciting, but what moved your heart or the heart of someone around you in the last month? Tell us about it.

    b. Practice writing stories.

    c. Google "Flash Nonfiction" to learn tricks on writing short, powerful stories about your life

    d. Have fun!

3. **Play with a theme.** I'll never forget a letter I read several years ago that shared a brief story about an opportunity for a young father to go fishing with a local coworker that resulted in an encouraging conversation; no great conversion story but a building of relationship. This family stuck to the fishing theme as they moved into their prayer requests and a brief financial appeal as they prayed for nets they were casting to find fish, for the growth of baby fish, and their gratefulness for those who held the nets with them in prayer and with finances.

4. **Never forget the redemption aspect of your update.** A good newsletter should end with encouragement of what God is doing, or, if you're in trials, taking the reader back to who God is even in the midst of trials brings encouragement.

5. **A quiz or riddle.** There's one worker who always includes an opportunity for a prize in her newsletters, whether it's a challenge to caption a funny picture, identify a strange food, or correctly answer a quiz. The prize is just a postcard, but I'm always curious to read what she has each month . . . and she always gets responses..

Which tip will you try in your next newsletter?

Year Six in China

2000-2001

*A letter always seemed to me like immortality
because it is the mind alone without corporeal friend.*
—Emily Dickinson

August 2000—Past, present, and future

Being at a crossroad this summer between living in Chengdu and living in Beijing, it seemed a natural time to look at where I've been and where I'm going. Okay, I know that is a bit sappy. This line of thinking was actually kicked off by my sister Elizabeth, who has been storing many of my worldly possessions in her basement for the last five years. She noticed items I probably wasn't ready to part with five years ago about which I could now easily say, "What was I thinking?" and pitch or move on to someone else. So I spent time this summer sorting through a bit of my past. It was good to have a look at things and see what used to be important to me. Some I was not willing to part with because . . . because I like them, while other items sparked memories I hadn't thought of in years but weren't overly special and I could move them on to new homes.

A highlight of the project was going through all of the letters I had received throughout my childhood and college years. I had forgotten some of the people who faithfully wrote and encouraged me. What a powerful reminder that I am where I am because many have invested in me. Words of encouragement from my parents, cute letters from my sisters when we were children, the parents of my friends who wrote me at camp every summer, letters from my grandparents. I even rediscovered a letter from Grandma Young after I was baptized. As the firstborn child and first grandchild on both sides, I have joked that I came into this life royally celebrated. The truth is that I have led a celebrated life and I am thankful to God for the blessings I've been given through those words of love.

The *present* part of this summer involved a road trip with Elizabeth.

I wanted to drive out to Michigan and see my grandpa, and on the way stop in Chicago and see Aunt Bobbye and one of my college friends. Elizabeth and I have a history of fun road trips, so she took a week off from work and the two of us set off. I hadn't been on a road trip since before I went to China, and it was funny to see how my concept of a road trip has slowly shifted to more of a Chinese idea of a road trip.

When we got to the first motel, I asked Elizabeth if I should come in too when we registered. She gave me a weird look and said, "Just one of us is enough." I forgot, in America all guests do not have to register with their ID, give the reason for why they are visiting, how long they plan to stay, and their resident permit number and expiration. Each time someone visited us in Chengdu, we were required to fill out the paperwork for our guest; probably a quarter of the time something wasn't right with the way we did it and the school officials would call us. Here, it only took one person to get the room, and we didn't have to check which hours they had hot water because there's always hot water. ☺ During the present, I was reminded that parts of me have been rewired to how we do things in China and know the rewiring is good.

Looking to the *future* this year, I have two positive developments from this summer to share! My rent in Beijing has been reduced, and it looks like I'll be receiving a salary for the teaching I'll be doing. This reduces my monthly needs about $400. Happy, happy! I'll be teaching at Beijing University and will be working with either freshman oral-English students or teaching writing to graduate students. Another TIC teacher, who will also be teaching at Beijing University, and I haven't divided up the assignments yet. If I had my choice, I would much prefer to teach writing, but either one will be fine.

I am a little disappointed at the lack of enthusiasm I received this summer when I mentioned that I would be teaching at Beijing University. (Wink!) Most people gave me simple smiles and a little nod at the head as if to say, "How nice, dear." In June when I told my students which school I would be teaching at, classes would spontaneously break into applause. No kidding. It's a little daunting to be assigned to teach at one of the top universities in China, but the truth is that I'm going to miss my sweet Sichuan countryside teachers.

In addition to teaching, I'll be part of a team of five individuals who will provide the leadership for the University Teaching Program within TIC. I'll be the representative for the Curriculum Department, and others will represent other areas of importance within TIC. It's exciting to have a chance to invest in our teachers and to see them catch the vision for doing well within the classroom as a way of increasing the credibility of their witness.

Specific things to pray for in the upcoming year:

- The transition from knowing and being known in Chengdu to life in the big city.

- I won't specifically be assigned a teammate, but another single gal and I have committed to be unofficial teammates. Being part of the staff, it is easy to fall through the cracks in terms of having someone to pray with and eat meals with regularly, someone who knows what is going on in your life. Please pray for this small little team.

- Health-related request again. My last week at home has been spent with two beautifully swollen tonsils that have white sores all over them. You know it's bad when the doctor looks down your throat and says, "Eww!"

- Anna and I have emailed each other often this summer. Her house church is having trouble with the police, and they have stopped meeting for a while. Please pray for their protection and her continued growth. (Note: I can be more open here because this is written from the US.)

God gave me a chance to look back, look around, and look ahead this summer. This time of reflection has allowed me to see again how He has been providing for me throughout my life, helped me to recognize the ways I am being changed by China, and recharged me so that I am excited to get back into the foray of things. Thanks for continuing to support and lift me up; I am truly blessed. May my next newsletter be penned from the soft green sofa!

Love,
Amy

September 2000—So what is it you do?

Being a childless single woman, I haven't felt great solidarity with stay-at-home moms up to this point. This last month, I realized I get the same reaction, regardless of whom I'm talking to, when I explain what it is I do. Not fitting into a nice, easily understood box, people don't quite know where to mentally put me. I've had both fellow

TICers and my new students try to fit me into a pigeonhole that they can understand, and it doesn't work. Repeatedly I've been asked, "Now, what is it that you do?" or "Do you have enough to do all day?" Because I can't summarize my life in a nice sound bite, such as "I'm a teacher at Sichuan College of Education," my work doesn't seem to be valid.

I'll start with where the confusion lies with my students because it is a little easier to explain. Usually in China a foreign teacher works for a school and that school provides them housing. I'm working part-time at Beijing University and I am living in the TIC headquarters building. The building happens to be located on the property of a private K—12 school. Even as I write this, I can hear the sounds of little munchkins out at play. When my co-workers and I come and go, we often see rows of uniformed children march around the campus—they are cute! When I tell my students that I live at the 21st Century Experimental School, they respond, "So you teach at Beijing University and you teach middle school students." No mental box exists for me to be teaching them there but living here.

My students aren't the only ones who aren't sure what I do. My fellow *laowai* (foreigner) TIC teachers often don't get what I do. Their tone of voice and the looks on their faces imply they think that I must lie on my beautiful couch all day eating bonbons. I checked my email a few minutes ago and read a desperate plea from one of our teachers in Lhasa needing five more copies of books "immediately." This first month of the school year, much of my time has been filled with going on book runs, making friends at the post office, and taking frantic phone calls late at night. "Amy, what do I do in teaching a lesson about job applications?" I don't announce that I receive phone calls, respond to emails, and make book runs; subsequently people wonder what I do. (Ironically, the person who snidely asked if I had enough to fill my days with has already called twice, her teammate has called three times, and I've ordered them books from America as well as bought books for them here in Beijing.)

This is a season when I'm learning about living outside of a neat definition. At first I felt myself being defensive because the implied message is that I'm not doing enough. As an American, if you're not doing enough, you're nothing. Where was my identity? Was it in what people thought? Was it in the recognition I receive? Yet, I know I'm where I'm supposed to be and doing exactly what I should be doing. Oddly, I don't miss Chengdu and can't explain it other than to say God has changed my desires. Much to my surprise!

This first month has held a lot of learning, from getting around—

buses, subway, taxis, and not as much biking—to shopping, cooking on a gas stove that goes "boom" when you light it, and making new friends at the post office. I've taught my students for two weeks and feel blessed by my teaching situation. Erin Dittmer, the business manager for TIC, not to be confused with my first teammate, Erin, and I both teach in the Department of International Relations and work with graduate students. Our students are the future movers and shakers of China. I have a total of sixteen students, unbelievable after last term. I teach them reading, and then I teach half of the class oral English. Even for those who do not love math, you know that is a class of eight students—eight, wow. What you can do with eight is totally different from what you can do with seventy. I love them already. Four of the women are coming over for dinner on Sunday. Let the bonding begin.

Last week I was reading in Psalm 15. In part it says, "Lord, who may dwell in your sacred tent [or sanctuary]? . . . [He] who keeps an oath even when it hurts. . . . Whoever does these things will never be shaken." What do I do? I help TIC to keep our oath with the Chinese government. We are teachers and we want to give our utmost in that area, whether we have classes of eighty or eight, whether we have textbooks or not, whether we have taught American literature before or not.

I don't fit in a nice category, but I'm learning that doesn't matter, because the privilege of being here is bigger than categories. Thanks for being a part of something that defies definition.

Definitely yours,
Amy

October 2000—Same, same, but different

Moving to a new city brings the expected questions of comparison. For me, this move has been especially interesting because I moved from what is perceived as a poorer and less cultured part of China to the "big city"—one of the meccas of Chinese culture, history, and taxis. I always knew there was a strong pecking order in China, but having moved up in it, I am growing in my awareness of how deep-seated it is. Even the first day of class this term, the students said how glad I must be to be here in Beijing teaching "real students." I had to smile with that one.

What are these real students like? In many ways they are a different breed. Part of it is that my students are younger than the students I worked with in Sichuan. Another part of it is that they are a bit more worldly-wise because they're from all over China and have traveled to school in Beijing. They simply have been exposed to more; for example, many own computers and have easy access to email and Western movies. Combine knowledge with a bit of immaturity, and you come up with some interesting results. One of my classrooms was "decorated" with three giant penises drawn on the walls in white chalk. In another class we had to make a "no cussing" rule during a game. I don't think we are in Sichuan anymore, Dorothy!

The students are also a bit more bold and direct. In trying to build relationships, I've started bringing baked goods to my students on Monday. This Monday they had a suggestion for me. China can be the land of a lot of suggestions for foreign teachers, so you kind of always brace yourself and wonder what is coming. They have suggested that I start bringing them juice as well. Cheeky monkeys. ☺ Having chili at my house one night, a male student informed me that it didn't have enough salt because Chinese food always has salt; well, thank you. When I announced that Erin and I would like to invite them to dinner this Saturday for meatloaf, mashed potatoes, and salad, we were informed that wasn't enough and given the suggestion of adding cake to our menu.

Yet they still possess a sweetness like my Sichuan students. In an email thanking me for the chili dinner, a student wrote, "First I want to thank you for giving us an access to typical American food, although I am not completely compatible with it. Here I want to tell you a secret: all of the four boys of our class had a pack of noodles when we got back for we felt kind of hungry when we were back." How precious.

Two nice surprises: God in the unexpected

Because my class is small, my students are able to speak out and share their opinions. Weekly I assign two of them to call me on the phone for homework. Our class is Thursday morning, and invariably they wait until Wednesday night to call. At the beginning of class recently, I told the class not to wait until Wednesday night because I'm involved in a women's Bible study on that night and I unplug my phone.

"Bible study! We want to study the Bible." "Yeah, the words are simple, but there is deep meaning that we can't understand." "Hey, there's a church near here and we could all go, buy English/Chinese Bibles for about twenty-five yuan!" "We aren't Christians, why would you want to study the Bible?" I was caught off guard at their enthusiasm toward the subject, especially since the point I was trying to make was not to call me the night before class. This is an oral English class, and it would be both illegal and unethical for us to read the Bible during class, but I'm going to be in class telling them a parable or some other story and use it as a listening practice.

The second nice surprise started off not so nice. This past Sunday, as Erin, Liesl, and I were getting into the backseat of a taxi, Dae got into the front to give directions to the taxi driver—the taxi driver started to make harrumphing fat noises and gestured that three large fat people were getting into the backseat of his taxi. He even went so far as to say in Chinese, "Fat, fat, fat." I was a bit overly excited to use my new vocabulary of "impolite" and let him know what I thought of his noises and actions. He apologized profusely, but I was less than thrilled with taxi drivers.

Later in the day when Erin, Liesl, and I took another taxi, I sat in the front seat to better distribute our weight. Just kidding. I did it in order to give the driver directions of where to drop Liesl off and how to take Erin and me home. He was friendly and wondered where we were from, what our salary was, where we were teaching, and if we were married. I went into my whole spiel about having lived in Sichuan where the men are short and how being a little tall and fat, I hadn't had any luck in finding a husband. He wondered when I plan to get married now that I've moved to Beijing. I told him my parents were wondering the same thing. Ha—it's a joke. When your language skills are poor, you have to go for cheap laughs.

He looked at me and said that I seemed happy anyway. I told him that I was a Christian and that God gave me love and happiness, so I didn't have to worry about not having a husband. He wondered if the one in the back (Erin) was a Christian. Yes, she is. This was my first time to share my faith with a taxi driver, and it was unexpected coming right after the rudest taxi driver I've encountered. God in a taxi.

Same, same, but different. The location may be different, the students may be different, the traffic may be quite different, but God is the same. He is faithful and continues to meet and surprise me in little ways. I was surprised in a taxi. Where were you surprised this week?

Surprisingly yours,
Amy

November 2000—Home sweet home

This month I returned to Sichuan to visit two TIC teams. One of the teams is at my former school, so in many ways it was more like a homecoming than my return trips to the US. I haven't lived in Denver since my last year of high school, but it's only been a few months since I left Chengdu. A strong sense of "Oh, that's my home, my classroom, the market. This is where I killed a mouse, and that was where I cried over a student. Oh, there's the phone I spent hours on" pervaded.

Xiao Yang, one of the waiban staff, and Driver Luo picked me up at the airport. When we got to the campus, Driver Luo rolled down his window as we passed people I knew. He laughed out loud shouting several times, "*Amy Laowai hui lai le!*" ("Foreigner Amy has returned!"). At the guesthouse my Chinese mama, Shen Yang, hugged and hugged me. The new teachers have gotten a cat to fight the mice, and I spent part of the evening petting the cat and enjoying catching up with the new teachers.

The next morning I boarded a four-hour train ride to Nanchong to visit the teachers at the Southwest Petroleum University. When I first came to Sichuan, there was no train to Nanchong and we had to ride a ten-hour bus on a windy road. The train sure is more convenient! The visit wasn't an easy one because the team is having some rough spots, but it was good to see them in person and get a fuller picture. Up to this point I had been relying mainly on phone contact. Team relations can often be the most challenging part of living cross-culturally. We can understand the cultural bumps of students not following directions, or being served chicken's feet, freezing in the heat, and even having to kill mice. But how can people from our own culture be so darn annoying?! This unexpected stress can push a person over the edge, and I went to minister to some people living on the edge.

Forty-eight hours later I boarded a train back to Chengdu. It is a rare privilege to get to return to your former life and see how wonderfully things go on without you. I know I am missed and loved, but it is liberating to be expendable. I saw again how I am free to move on and live without worrying unduly that those I love will be cared for. God is faithful. One of the students with whom Shelley had been working was baptized this summer and has grown much. I was proud to see how she has allowed God to work in her life. Toni and Abigail, the teachers who replaced us, are busy loving on the students and getting involved in Sichuan College of Education. While Shelley and I may have been more familiar with life in China and further along in our professional development, we lacked the enthusiasm of a newbie. It was fun to see a mirror of where I was five years ago.

But you know what? Sichuan is not my home now. So it was with joy that I boarded the plane to Beijing. It's fun to travel, but coming home has a special feeling all its own. One of the reasons I was eager to get home was that my sister and brother-in-law were about to come for a visit; they've been here now for a week and a half. Elizabeth has been to China before, but this was Del's first trip. Many people in TIC have families who won't come and visit them . . . and here I was getting a repeat visitor.

While in China, Del and Elizabeth came and spoke to my class. The highlight for me was that my students could see a real American couple, as opposed to the images they get from Hollywood. The students asked a lot of questions about how they had a good marriage and about how they communicate. The students were genuinely shocked that Del and Elizabeth would put their marriage over their jobs. After class we went out to lunch, and I think the highlight for Del was seeing the price—maybe now they understand a little better why I have a fit over the ridiculous prices in America. Ha-ha. So we had our own little cross-cultural shock there.

This is a completely unrelated story to the theme of family, but it's fun and I want to share it.

Erin and I invited our students over for Thanksgiving dinner. In preparing for the meal I had taken in sets of silverware and napkins to practice setting the table, putting the napkins on their laps while eating, and learning how to use forks and knives to cut food. All of the students set their places, and I asked them what we should do first. I was looking for the answer, "Put your napkin in your lap," but from the back of the room I heard "Pray!" Right you are.

In this holiday season I'm reminded how truly blessed I am. Thanks to all of you who faithfully support me with prayer, letters, email, finances, and love. It helps me to be home wherever I am.

Love,
Amy

PS: For the US presidential election my friends Joann and Dae rented a hotel room to be able to watch the presidential results on CNN. We joined them at 8:00 a.m. and stayed until checkout time at 3:00 p.m. We kept meaning to make a McDonald's run, but the results were too close and kept changing. By checkout we were starving and still didn't know who the next president would be, Republican George W. Bush or Democrat Al Gore. We didn't realize it would be unknown for a long time.

December 2000—The following is a true story

At the beginning of December I traveled to Harbin, a city in northwest China, to visit two of our teams and see how life was going.

I had a 5:00 p.m. flight and arrived at the airport at 3:30 p.m., with plenty of time to spare. At the check-in counter the flight was listed to leave at 5:30, but there was a cardboard sign taped below it saying it was delayed until 7:30. I asked the woman working the counter, and sure enough the flight was delayed.

Even though delayed, I went to gate 32. You might wonder if I have made up a gate number for the sake of the story. No. When one hears a gate number repeated by a less than enthusiastic gate worker as many times as I heard it that night, one is not quick to forget. I parked myself near the gate within eye contact of the aforementioned gate worker and befriended the man next to me. (One can never have too many friends when one doesn't speak the language all that well and the flight is still listed as leaving at 5:30 and there are no cardboard signs suggesting otherwise.) New Friend, as he shall lovingly be called from here on out, worried that the TIC teachers in Harbin wouldn't know that my flight was delayed, so he lent me his cell phone to contact them. At 5:00 p.m. sharp a man with a cart showed up with a box meal for each passenger, and he was swamped. I will say this, the Chinese are serious when it comes to mealtimes.

At 7:00 p.m. a woman asked the gate worker when the flight would leave. A curious crowd gathered and started heckling the gate worker, who made a call and two airline representatives showed up. The woman started to cry, and the crowd got a bit worked up. Then something happened, I'm not sure what: either one of the representatives took her ticket or hit her. He turned and took off running, and three people started chasing him. At this point six policemen were called in, and a photographer from the newspaper showed up. The airport workers were able to board the plane in the midst of this mini-riot, and the boarding area finally settled down after we were all served bottles of water.

Finally at 9:30 p.m. we boarded our plane and took off for Harbin. The whole time New Friend made me walk in front of him and would not let me out of his sight. When we arrived in Harbin at 11:30 p.m., he wondered if anyone was going to pick me up since the airport is about forty-five minutes outside of town. I said that the school had arranged for me to be met and he didn't need to wait for me, but thank you. Well, he didn't listen, instead insisting on waiting for me to claim my bag and meet the car waiting for me.

When I walked out, guess what? I was greeted by no car, no school officials, no TIC teachers. Nobody but a bunch of taxi drivers vying for my business. New Friend lent me his cell phone again, and I called a TIC teacher who said that because it was late, the school hadn't sent a car and I could take the public bus. Whatever. New Friend took over and told me to follow him. He took me in his taxi to the school, got me checked in to the hotel, waited until I had contacted a TIC teacher, and then he left. What a blessing.

I do so enjoy being with our teachers! One of the teams gets along great but hasn't been meeting regularly for prayer. As a team they agreed to start meeting twice a week. The other team wasn't talking to each other. When we had our team meeting, I told them that they did not need to be best friends, but they did need to pray at least twice a week. Though agreeable, they spoke to each other through me as they were setting up the time for prayer. Please don't think these are horrible people. They're not. I firmly believe that Satan is happiest when teams don't get along and don't pray together. Hopefully, this challenges you to pray for those you support and ask them how team issues are going.

And then the other bizarre bookend of my trip happened. In the meeting with the school officials, a vice dean told me that the TIC teachers are completely unprofessional. In addition, he doesn't like the way TIC handles contracts and a variety of other things. His opinions weren't based on much, as he didn't know the names of the teachers and hadn't observed any of their classes. But I was quite taken aback by his attitude. A few other people talked, then somehow the ball was back in his court. He started to yell at me. This simply doesn't happen in China. I have never heard of anyone being yelled at during a meeting, never. My heart was pounding, and I couldn't think clearly. I told him that he needed to stop yelling at me. He said he wasn't yelling but raising his voice. "That's fine," I told him. "But if you don't lower your voice, I am going to walk out of the meeting because I can't think clearly when I am talked to at this volume." He suddenly was able to control his volume, and the other officials had glowing reports for our teachers.

I think this particular man's outburst had nothing to do with TIC but with other parts of his life. At the end of the meeting he and I were alone together and he asked me how I was able to think clearly and respond quickly to his attacks. We all know that it was God who put words in my mouth. The man ended up inviting me to teach at that school. Tempting—ha!

I returned home to Beijing and my nice riot-free, yell-free life and caught up on grading. For Thanksgiving I had asked the students to write about what they had to be thankful for in the past year. Here is one student's response:

> I have never thought about something that I have to be grateful for. Once in a while I would remember someone who had helped me before and I hardly spent time in thinking about that . . . Moreover, I met

Amy and Erin, who are my first foreign teachers. Amy is active and Erin is gentle. Though I have learned English for years and communicate with a culture completely different from Chinese culture, I have not so many good chances to understand it before. They give me knowledge not only in class but also out of class. They often invite us to their quarters and have dinner together. They cook American food for us and make us feel American culture by eating. It's a great environment for me to learn English.

My favorite line is that he feels American culture by eating. As this semester ends and we prepare for the break, would you pray that more and more chances will come up for us to share with students? Up to this point Erin and I have done most of the initiating. Our prayer would be that the students would start to take some initiative and that there would be chances for deeper conversations.

From a riot at gate 32 to being led to my hotel, from teams that haven't been praying together to school officials who yell, from touching journals to students who discover culture via eating—this is true life. I'm glad it's ours.

Love,
Amy

January 2001—A Christmas fish

"Which of you fathers, if your son asks for a fish, will give him a snake instead? Or if he asks for an egg, will give him a scorpion? If you then, though you are evil, know how to give good gifts to your children, how much more will your Father in heaven give the Holy Spirit to those who ask him!"[15]

In November I heard about a United Airlines deal for people flying to the US on Christmas Day. I called to ask if it was true, and sure enough, for $525 I could fly from Beijing to Denver and arrive at about 8:00 p.m. on Christmas night. Talk about visions of sugarplums dancing in my head. Christmas at home! Even if only for a few hours. Wow. I hadn't spent Christmas with my family since 1994, so I booked the ticket.

A few days later I heard that United backed out and claimed it was only an internet deal. I called to see what was up and found out that sure enough, because I haven't paid for the ticket yet, the ticket was considerably more money. Several of us who live here in Beijing had booked on the same deal.

Oh, we were mad. No cultural wrath exists like a foreigner scorned, but there was nothing to be done. I thought I was trying to force the issue and decided it wasn't meant for me to be home for Christmas. Maybe next year.

The first week of December I was restless and edgy. I was cranky, I was irritable, I was . . . wanting to be home. Since there weren't any traditions for me in Beijing, it was Denver and my family I wanted. On December 8th I called TIC's travel agent and frantically asked if there were any seats left on a plane to Denver. He told me that the twenty-second and twenty-third were all booked, but there was one seat left on the twenty-first. Book it!

Ever since I came to China, I've wanted to surprise my family by going home unexpectedly. I dreamed of surprising my parents by walking into their Bible study with all of the people I have known and loved for years, but that didn't seem likely. I decided to tell only my sister Elizabeth that I was coming home, because I needed someone to pick me up at the airport.

On the twenty-first, Elizabeth and Del picked me up at the airport. Driving home, Elizabeth called Mom and Dad and found out that Bible study was meeting at their house. When we got home, Elizabeth and Del knocked and walked in. By this time, Dad had gotten up to see who was coming into the house. When he saw me, he simply repeated, "You, you."

"Tom, who is it?" my mom asked.

I said, "Hi Mom," and stepped out where she could see me. Grabbing her face with her hands, speechless, surrounded by lifelong friends, it was the kind of welcome anyone would want, like a little taste of the welcome I'll get in heaven.

A few days later, we went to get Laura and Sue at the airport. Again, they didn't know I was coming. Mom and Dad greeted them, and as they were walking down the hall, I walked up and said, "Hi Laura," who replied, "Hi Amy . . . Amy, what are you doing here?!" She grabbed me in a bear hug with tears in her eyes.

Remember that at the start of all of this, I was willing to settle for a few hours on Christmas night, but God had a wonderful gift for my family and me. I surprised them like I had always dreamed of, and we got to spend several days ahead of time together. I was given a fish for Christmas, a wonderful Christmas fish beyond anything I could ask or imagine.

"My screw is stripped. Do you have a small bit?"

While in the US, I bought some additional RAM to add to my computer. When I got home to Beijing, I carefully read my manual and figured out how to add the chip to my computer. I needed to remove three small screws. No problem, except that I don't own a screwdriver, so I borrowed one. It was too big. I borrowed another one. It was also too big. I borrowed a glass repair kit and broke the small screwdriver. This was beginning to read like a bad Dr. Seuss book. I went out and bought a set of small screwdrivers. Sadly, by this point, one of the screws was stripped. One of the itsy bitsy teeny weeny little screws went way down inside. Ugh.

I called my dad, and he said that I needed to have it drilled out. Oh bother, said Pooh. I ignored the problem. The next week, in my language class, my teacher asked if I had any problems. He laughed when he heard my problem, and the advice he gave me was the same my dad had given me. After laughing, he taught me how to say, "My screw is stripped. Do you have a small bit?" Two days later, armed with my computer and phrase, I went into my neighborhood and accosted four unsuspecting workers with, "My screw is stripped. Do you have a small bit?" I'm sure more than a few thought there was a stripped screw in my head.

One of the men worked outside of a car wash and was repairing a motor. I went over and squatted next to him and said my mantra, "My screw is . . ." His coworkers quickly came to his aid, and a small crowd gathered. When they understood what I wanted, they said that it would be no problem and ushered me inside their workshop. Four people worked on the project—a boss and three workers. They were precious! It was like they were performing an important operation. While I stood with knots in my stomach, these four men were as gentle as possible using a big drill on my fragile computer. One used the drill, another held the flashlight, the third man blew the dust away while the boss asked me about myself. Finally, three bits and a lot of nervous twitching later, they got it out. I almost floated home.

I share this as an example of the little victories I get to celebrate. I am faithfully provided for—even to the smallest screws.

Love,
Amy

February 2001—It's in the cards

I'm often teased at the building where I live because I get many letters. A few of my former students have e-mail, but not many of them do, so much of the way I keep up with people is through writing letters. My former students were English teachers, and some of their students write to me as well. A handful of my correspondents I have been writing to for several years and have never actually met. In this newsletter, I thought I would share some of the correspondence I have received this fall. I'll make comments or explanations in italics; enjoy reading the sweet words of some dear friends and some people I only know through the pen.

From former students:

> . . . In addition, dear Amy! During the two years I got on with you, what I most regretted is that I haven't taken photos with you. Can you answer my such a request: I would like keep a photo of you taking in Beijing University Campus (in front of the library of gate of campus, or anywhere, only in the campus) okay? I sent a photo of me in Wang Jian park in Chengdu. I wish you'll love it. Looking forward to your letter or photos. Yours, Pearl.

I love the specific request of a photo with the words Beijing University in the background.

For some background, the first day that I taught this next student, I had the class do a get-to-know-you activity where we each selected an adjective that began with the same letter as our English name. For example, I was Amiable Amy.

> Dear Amy, it's three years since I left Sichuan College of Education (SCE). I hope you can still remember me. My English name is Sober Stephen. I have been missing all of my teachers and classmates since I came back to teach in my school, but I miss you the most. Whenever I recall my life in SCE, I think of you, you are so good a teacher. I often talk of you in my class to my students. I tell them that you are an excellent teacher, you are responsible very much. You always try to make every class vivid, and all of us liked you very much. Though after three years, I can still remember every minute I spent with you. You're my example. I teach my students as you taught me .
> . . .

He asked me if I would write to his students, and a new correspondence relationship has begun. I think what got me about this letter was that I do remember him, and choosing "sober" was a great adjective for him. I don't think my teaching was, or should be, that memorable. Wow. This letter challenges me to be a person of integrity, because people are watching and remembering and retelling, and years later, you may hear about it.

My precious Anna, whom I cooked dinner with on Tuesday nights last spring, sent me two different kinds of dried mushrooms for Christmas. She handwrote the following instructions for them:

> This is named Chicken Mushroom. Usually, it's cooked for soup with chicken, or jam, or—oh, I don't know—anyhow, more water for soup, some salt, not soy oil, the legs can be kept. The second mushroom had these directions: sink the mushroom in the water for about 40 minutes, then wash it clean. Throw off the root part. Cook with chicken or pork and garlic, about 100kg, salt, and a little water. This isn't for soup, so water can't be too much.

Isn't that endearing? I haven't cooked them yet, but this is truly where it's the thought that counts.

From my students' students:

> Dear Amy, How are you? I'm Margaret. We haven't written each other for a long time, so I miss you very much ... Amy, I miss you so much that I want you to write me back as quickly as you can, and, do you tell Alice your address? I think she is also worried because she misses you very much too. Best wishes, yours, Margaret.

Margaret is one of the girls I have been writing to for years. She is so direct and bossy in her letters that it cracks me up. We went through a phase last year of me giving English names to most of her classmates. She would send me a description of their personality, and I'd name the students. Margaret is a college student now. Alice is my former student whom I haven't heard from in years, so it's doubtful that she misses me very much.

> I heard of you have some stamps. I very like stamp, I hope I get some stamps from you. This is my first letter in English, so I write is not good. I say sorry to you. I hope to hear from you quickly.

Obviously, I sent the dear boy some stamps. Those of you who faithfully send them, they are truly loved, so thanks.

> Dear Amy, how time flies. I am writing to you about my idea. Would you give me your suggestion? I have graduated from senior middle school. In July, I made great progress by hard study. I was very happy. Nanchong teacher's training college sent admission notice to me. To be an English teacher is my dream, however, my parents can't afford me to go to university, and I have to abandon the chance, I am very sad. Would you help me? Please tell me what I should do. Now I stay at home. Sometimes I go to sell vegetables. Actually, I want to go on with my lessons. Do you know that Zhou Jun Ying has left school? She works in Guangdong. I hope I have a job, too, and I will find much money to get further study. I am looking forward to your help. Best wishes to you. Yours, Luo Ying Xia.

Oh, this kind of letter tugs at my heart. What do you say to an eighteen-year-old who thinks she might have missed her one big chance? I wrote back to encourage her to keep studying, because with the rapid changes that China is experiencing, it's likely she will have some kind of chance in the future.

The letters remind me that I need to focus on the little as well as the big things. I must admit that some of the letters I don't want to respond to because I'm asked the same questions over and over—how to improve English, how to speak in English more, how to . . . and so on. But occasionally, among the mundane, there will be a jewel. God is good to me, because He throws in enough jewels to keep me faithful, with that which He has asked me do (correspond with students), even though I sometimes don't want to.

As many of my students say . . .

> Yours,
> Amy

March 2001—Did Amy become tired of China and become a telemarketer?

[I included a photo of me looking like a telemarketer, with a telephone headset over my head sitting behind a desk.]

No, no, no. I am as surprised to find myself in this position as you are. About a week and a half after I returned home from our conference in Thailand, the president of TIC blazed past me one Saturday morning and said, "Hey, Amy, could you go to California on Tuesday and work in the office for two weeks?" What? Can I what? Where? Why? It turns out the number of new personnel for next year is running low while our need for teachers is greater than ever. The president hoped that if someone who lives in China and knows what it's like to raise support called people who have applied, it might help them and increase their excitement. Why me? Well, two reasons. The first is that with the administrative work I do, I'm not in the classroom full-time and it would be easier to find people to cover my classes. The second reason is my . . . um . . . bubbly personality.

I was in shock for a few hours and went around muttering repeatedly, "I can't believe I'm going to the States. I can't believe I'm going to the States." I had to apologize to my friends, asking them to bear with me until the shock wore off. When it did, I jumped into action and planned two weeks' worth of lessons, packed, ate all of the food I had bought, got the paperwork done for a reentry visa, and said a few more times, "I can't believe I'm going to the States."

This is written now from the other side of the two weeks, and my new mantra is, "I can't believe I get to go to Denver tomorrow." Actually this has been a wonderful time, and even though I didn't see it coming, I can see that Somebody else did. As it turns out, there were two main tasks that my coworker Brooke (who also came from Beijing) and I had while we were in California. Since I work in the University Teaching Program, I called all of the people who have already committed to go to China next year, the people who have been accepted to go but haven't committed yet, and those who are in the application process. In addition, we helped interview applicants.

Brooke and I worked in a conference room with a long table. It could be comical when we were both on the phone at the same time and had to turn our backs to each other, plug an ear, and focus on the conversation. At one point we were both leaving a message and said in unison, "My number is 1-800-366-3333 and I'm at extension . . ." We about lost it.

It is a privilege to talk with people and answer their questions. We have wonderfully qualified people here in the office, but somehow being able to say that I live in China carried much weight. When they would ask how long I have lived in China and I would tell them that it has already been five and a half years, I would usually get some reaction like, "You must really like it," or "You seem so normal."

Talking to me demystified the whole "China thing." I talked with one woman who worried about schooling options for her children and got her in contact with a mom I know in Beijing. Another woman spent a long time agonizing over what to do with the cats that she desperately wants to take. I talked to a man who said that he changed his mind and didn't want to come to China anymore. That was fine and I didn't push him to reconsider. I did wonder what had drawn him to China in the first place. He said that he had wanted out of the US. I had to agree this is not the motivation we are looking for.

The interviewing process took about four hours per person. In preparation I would review the application, read the applicant's essay answers to ten questions, and look at their recommendations. Next came the phone interview, lasting about two hours, followed by another hour writing up a report. I don't know how to put into words, without sounding cheesy, what a blessing interviewing potential co-laborers was. There are amazing people in our world—all of whom were born in 1977 or 1978. I only talked to one person who was anywhere near my age. In talking with the young pups and asking them what they might like in a teammate, most said that they would like someone near their age (not a problem, thought I). But if someone was old, say forty, that might be okay, if that person was cool.

Not to paint my time in only rose color because it was also some of the most draining work I have ever done. One day I hit a wall and knew that I was in no frame of mind to call people because my tolerance level was nil. If God told you to go overseas and you saw what to do with your sofa as an insurmountable wall, I had no sympathy. None. And so I worked on typing up reports that day and avoiding the public.

I leave after these two weeks with a new appreciation for all that goes on in our office here in California. The people who work here are wonderful, and their focus is on those of us who serve overseas—our pictures are all around the office. The staff talks about us, prays for us, and loves us more than we give them credit for. In helping with the phone calls and the interviews, I am much more aware of the effort it takes to get someone from point A to point B and eventually to point C in Asia.

I'm excited for next August when I'll get to meet these people I spent hours talking with on the phone. God has blessed me with a little peek into the bigger picture. I kind of wonder where next month will find me.

Love,
Amy

April 2001—Spring-cleaning

The building I live in has been a flurry of activity recently with the arrival of spring. Yesterday all of the rugs were hauled outside and professional cleaners washed them in the courtyard. I took a picture of it, but the film hasn't been developed yet, and you'll have to use your imagination to see four large rugs being washed one at a time, with a crew of men scurrying around each rug. Afterwards, wet rugs were draped around the courtyard. The roof will be repaired today, so in preparation scaffolding was put up. As I look out of my window, I see a man directly outside of it. *Hi there!* I took pictures because this violates every safety code, and pounding and laughing and pending accidents are in my sight. ☺

With spring-cleaning all around, I've decided to write a letter of odds and ends, kind of to clean up the clutter in my mind. This letter doesn't have any pictures because for the last two weeks my friend Deborah from Scotland visited. Something was wrong with her camera, and she borrowed mine, allowing you the chance to use your imagination in this newsletter.

A recurring question

In trying to be more tourist accessible, Beijing has decided that all taxi drivers need to learn one hundred English phrases. Several taxis that I've been in recently have played their practice tapes for me and complained about how hard it is to learn English. We practiced the words "right," "left," and "go straight." In one taxi the driver launched into the usual questions of where am I from, what is my job, am I married. Well, that one stopped him. Do I have a boyfriend? No. He looked at me in the rearview mirror and asked if I had *ever* had a boyfriend. Cheeky driver (smiley face). That was a new twist on an old conversation.

The other morning I was out on my morning walk and saw an old man I see about twice a week. I've never seen him in the same spot, and he was confused about where I live. We've chatted briefly before, but on that morning we stopped to have a real conversation because he wanted to clarify where I live. He also wondered where I work, how much my salary was, how much my rent was (all perfectly acceptable questions to ask in China). Then he wondered who watches my child when I'm out on my morning walks. Well, you can guess where this line of questioning was going. When he realized that I'm over thirty, not married, and with no prospects on the horizon, I was given a big lecture with the basic theme of "who will take care of you when you're old" and "who will feed you or clothe you." The poor man left, visibly shaken.

Relationships are important in China. They define you as normal. They provide security for you when you're old. So this month, over and over in conversations I have had with people this theme has come up, and I'm reminded that my security isn't in earthly relationships. Praise be.

The cats in our lives

In the last newsletter I wrote about a woman I had talked with while working at TIC office in the States who was fixated on bringing her cats with her to Asia. While a real concern to her, the whole issue seemed out of proportion when you think of people needing to hear *good news*. When I returned to China, one of the teams under my supervision called me with a problem they were having at their school. A foreign teacher, who isn't associated with TIC, had taken possession of the printer from the TIC library. One of the TIC teachers wanted it back because her printer had broken. But this other teacher was refusing to give it back unless TIC could show proof of ownership via a serial number. The non-TIC teacher is a believer, and again it seems like a little issue has been blown totally out of proportion.

But I was convicted that we all have "cats" in our lives, things that are inordinately important to us and take the focus off of where it should be. Recently the weather has been my "cat." I'm obsessed with wanting to be warm and can't stop fussing about the cold. Another good reminder to me to watch out for the specks in my eye and instead focus on the prize.

The international scene

Well, well, well, there has been no lack of interesting things going on between the US and China recently. This is when it's interesting — or unnerving, as the case may be — to be teaching international relations majors. Pertaining to world events (the Iraq war was on the horizon) things have only begun to heat up, so by the time you read this, everything may have blown over. As I wrote this, I was interrupted by a phone call from Toni, who teaches in my old school, asking if it was still a good idea to have her parents visit. The issue is quite real here. Please pray that our students can continue to differentiate between what governments do and what we, as their teachers and friends, do.

Receiving the newsletter

The last order of spring-cleaning business is that I never seem to hear from some of you on my mailing list. This doesn't bother me, but if you would rather not receive the newsletters, I don't want to be filling your mailbox with junk mail. It costs about $600 a year for me to write newsletters, and I love doing them, but I also want to be fiscally responsible. You can easily be removed from my mailing list by calling TIC at 1-800-366-3333 and asking to speak to the Communications Department.

~~~

That about covers it. Now that life is tidied up, it's time to dive in and get dirty again with living. Next week Erin and I will have the students over for an Easter egg dying party and then an Easter egg hunt. We are hoping that it will stimulate some thoughts and questions. I'll let you know how it goes.

> Glad to be clean,
> Amy

May 2001—International Teacher Brag Month

[I'm not actually going to share this newsletter because it was mostly excerpts from students' work. In class, we read Walter Wangerin's "The Ragman" and discussed allegories; then I assigned them to write allegories related to Easter. A student wrote an allegory about a taxi driver that was simply fantastic. I also shared drawings from a vocabulary quiz where they had to draw a picture to illustrate that they understood the meaning of vocabulary words.]

> Proudly yours,
> Amy

July 2001—Crash!

Usually when I make that sound, I take my two fists and hit them together saying, "That would be the sound of two cultures clashing." However, the sound that you hear is not two cultures clashing but a few of the balls I have been juggling, as they hit the floor. May and June ended up being the two busiest months of this year. I'm sorry that I haven't gotten a newsletter out to you earlier—there's been plenty to share with you, simply not enough time to share.

The reason that I've been busy is that in March, I was offered, and I accepted, another position within TIC. This spring has been a juggling act between teaching, still being TIC's curriculum director, and transitioning to the new job. In a nutshell, the new position is to head up our Member Care Department. I realized what I've enjoyed the most this year is interaction with the teachers on a personal level—helping them adjust to life in China, working with team quirks, and meeting with school officials—basically all the elements that my new job will focus on. I will continue to teach part-time (Yippee! Things worked out for Erin and me to continue at Beijing University!), but I will be traveling more to visit teams, seeing how life is going and encouraging them.

Because much has happened since I last wrote, I've decided to share a few snapshots from this spring.

Snapshot #1: In preparation for the new position, I attended a conference hosted by the State Administration of Foreign Expert Affairs (SAFEA)—say that quickly! The purpose was for the various organizations that have foreign teachers in China and for the government to get together and have a wee chat over regulation changes, projects the government would like foreigner involvement in, and an introduction to the province the meeting was held in. Oh my, but it was a long three days. For me, the most interesting part was when we divided into subgroups. I was part of the "foreigners teaching English" subgroup. The government representatives said that moral education has become a huge problem for society and wanted our suggestions in how best to teach morals. Well, we have plenty of ideas . . . but few of them were voiced!

Snapshot #2: In determining whether Erin and I would be teaching at Beijing University next year, we had lunch with Mr. Fan, the head of the Foreign Affairs Office, and Mr. Xu, the department head. I had met Mr. Xu one time before and had talked to Mr. Fan several times on the phone but hadn't met him face to face. After we ordered, they said to Erin and me, "We are old friends. Please speak freely. What do you think of the Communist Party?" Oh my goodness! We hardly knew these men. We hemmed and hawed and said something innocuous. "No, no," they said. "What do you really think? Don't be so diplomatic." I finally said, "We're going to be discussing our future employment with you in a while. We can't help but be diplomatic." They laughed at that and thought that the US government should have more women involved in diplomacy.

Later in the meal they asked us which country had the best-looking men. What? I have never been asked that question. Again, we took turns saying silly things like "Beauty is in the eye of the beholder"; "The more you like someone, the better they look"; and "In the US, we have men from all over the world, so we're not used to attractiveness being associated with one particular race." Well, you could almost see them rolling their eyes at our answers. "No, no, which country?" "China must be the answer," I ventured. "No," I was told. "Yugoslavia has the best-looking men." Who knew? I'm ready for the next time I'm asked this question.

Snapshot #3: Moving to Beijing I hadn't fully anticipated how long it takes to feel normal in a place. In my head, I knew that I hadn't instantly made friends in Chengdu. My most fulfilling relationships last year were at least two years old and some went five years back. As you know from previous letters, Erin and I have done a lot with our students, but they haven't reciprocated. There hasn't been a sense of friendship with any of them. Early in this semester I got a phone call from a former student of another TIC teacher. Madeline, the former student, had moved to Beijing and her foreign teacher had no desire to do things with students outside of class. She knew that TIC teachers did and wondered if I wanted to be her friend. It was around that time that I was whisked back to the US to do the phoning for TIC.

When I returned, we met for dinner and she brought one of her roommates whose English name is Helen. Madeline and Helen brought two of their other roommates over to my house to make banana bread. I've started regularly emailing with one of them. Helen and I hit it off, and we now meet weekly for lunch. Last night as we met to have a goodbye dinner, she told me that the first time she saw me, she had this sense that she liked me. When she went home and told her husband, she said it wasn't because I was a foreigner. We had a connection. One of her husband's cousins has divorced and since become a Christian. Helen said that her cousin is simply not the same person and wants to know about the power behind the change. Now we talk about that, among other things.

It's a relief to be at the end of this crazy semester, finally able to hand off some of the balls I have been juggling to the new curriculum director, Mike Packevicz, and not worry about them crashing down. When you read this, I will be *crashing* somewhere in the US getting some needed rest.

> Tired but happy,
> Amy

August 2001

Two things struck me this summer. The first is that body piercing has become quite prevalent in the US. The second is that everyone is older. For some reason, this summer it hit me more than it has in past years . . . people look older. People on TV. People in my life. People in my home. The person in my mirror. People I know are getting joints replaced. Joints!

On almost the opposite end of the aging spectrum, our family was blessed with the birth of Elizabeth's first baby. Emily joined the family in June. Miss Em is what you would want in a baby—she is wonderfully made, has a pleasant disposition, and cries mostly at night with her parents! I was holding her the other day, looking into that sweet face, and asked myself how I could leave her for another year. When I next see her, she'll be toddling around and getting into things. She will have heard of her Aunt Amy, but I will be a stranger to her. She'll be wearing outfits with cute little split pants from China, but she won't know my voice.

What is all of this for? These aging bodies? This living far away from loved ones? The answer is both simple and complex. You know the answer as well as I do. We were not created to live only this earthly life. We will live forever—either with God or apart from him. Our bodies will age, our families will move, and we will not always understand what happens in our lives. This summer reminded me of the importance of holding on to what is true and choosing to keep my focus on what is important.

Below is the testimony of one of my Chinese friends. She said I could share it to encourage others. It has been a wonderful summer—spending time with my family and friends and reevaluating where and how I will invest my life.

In the upcoming year, as I begin my new job, I would especially like to ask that you would pray for me to have some discernment as I work with TIC teachers and school officials. 1 Kings 3:9 captures this request perfectly, "So give your student a discerning heart to govern your people and to distinguish between right and wrong. For who is able to govern this great people of yours?"

Love,
Amy

[I shared her testimony in the rest of the letter.]

#6 If You Write Newsletters

Ideas for Supporters Reading Your Newsletters

1. Have a family member read the letter (or selected paragraphs) out loud during dinner. If you have children, have an age-appropriate discussion. What surprised you in the letter? What did you learn about either the cross-cultural servant or the country they serve in? What touched you? What did you learn about God from this letter? End the meal with a short prayer for the author(s) of the letter and their work.

2. On a regular basis, read a paragraph or story out loud during a church service. This allows for safety if security issues exist as you can control what is shared; but it also keeps the person you support in the hearts and minds of congregants. As an act of service to the cross-cultural servant, have a table in the lobby/narthex where congregants can read the rest of the letter and sign up for newsletters if interested.

3. Assign small groups or Sunday School classes to adopt a cross-cultural servant. Introduce the leader (or teacher) to the person on the field. A common fear on the side of supporters is they don't want to say anything that could cause problems for the cross-cultural servant. If this is a concern, having a point person who can answer questions or be the primary person to communicate with those on the field frees the class up not to be overly anxious. Too often people don't communicate out of fear of saying the wrong thing when this is a solvable problem! So let's solve it. Taking a picture of the class with the letter and sending it to your person on the field can foster connection. Knowing people truly read the letters written is one of the best gifts to receive.

4. In your family, if you support several individuals and families, assign each one a different night. For instance, Mondays pray

for Michelle in Honduras; on Tuesdays pray for the Jacksons in the Middle East; on Wednesdays you pray for Bill and Stacy in Russia. When you get a letter, read or review it on "their" night.

5. As one who wrote letters, I loved hearing about people's routines with my newsletters. Do you make a cup of coffee before you read? Do you have a certain place where you always read? Even if you don't have a routine, technology now makes it easy to snap a picture of yourself and say, "I just read your letter while waiting to pick up my kid at school." Or "Great food for thought as I ate my lunch at work. Thinking of you, buddy!"

Which idea can you implement this week?

Year Seven in China

2001-2002

*I am a little pencil in the hand of a writing God
who is sending a love letter to the world.*
—*Mother Teresa*

September 2001—You asked for it!

This summer a frequent request was, "Tell us mouse stories!" I tried to explain that the days of mouse stories had gone once I moved to Beijing. I can thank all of you for willing a mouse into my life. Ugh. The other night, I went up to the fourth floor of the building I live in to help a babysitter with two disobedient children and a screaming baby. In the middle of looking for a lost toothbrush and trying to herd the little ones towards bed, the phone rang. I answered it. Erin said in a confused voice, "Amy, is that you? Where's Mike." I explained that Mike and Anne were out and wondered if I could help. Erin explained that a rat was running around the fourth floor, and she wanted Mike to kill it. No way I was going to hunt a rat without sticky paper! Erin got a sixteen-year-old boy to chase it and he used two brooms to try to catch it. Needless to say, the rat is still on the loose.

All aboard—it's time for training

In the past, TIC has done most of our pre-field training for new teachers in California. This year, we broke out of the mold and split the time 50/50 between California and Beijing. It was great finally to be able to talk about what life in China was like, when new teachers could walk out the door, and then . . . experience life in China. I think our teachers are more comfortable with the idea of eating in a restaurant without a Chinese friend or of going shopping alone because, by golly, they have done it on their own already.

We waited to do the team training until all of the teachers were together, allowing each team to go through the training as a group. I was in charge, and I don't want to brag too much, but due to much vertical help, the teams are going forth as units who sort of know each other, rather than as strangers. One of the focuses of the training was on the importance of prayer time as a team. Keeping me humble, I will share one of the comments from the evaluations. The person said that the team building felt like forced relationships. Well, no duh. As I've said before, being assigned to a team is a bit like being part of an arranged marriage. Please be praying for our teams.

The theme of the year: what's mine is yours. Literally.

My predecessor as the head of Member Care said that each year seemed to have a theme. One of the emerging themes for this year involves our teachers returning to their possessions being gone. One guy opened the door to his apartment, only to find it completely cleaned out. Oh yes, everything was gone. The girls in charge of cleaning the rooms had been told that the foreigner wasn't coming back, so they got rid of all his possessions. Imagine returning to your clothing, household items, and decorations gone. Another gal had put her stuff in boxes, and three days before she got back, the school officials opened her boxes and either took the stuff or put it out in the hall where a little old man walked off with it. The school officials have at least returned all of the things that they took. At a third school, the apartments were redone, but the teachers didn't find out until they returned to the campus. The three returning teachers, all women, found their belongings thrown into a communal room.

It's amazing how few areas can feel as violating to us Americans as someone messing with our stuff. Granted, in all of these situations, the teachers are not wrong for feeling annoyed or angry. The challenge is to be gracious in the midst of being distraught. In the first case, early today I wrote a letter to the school asking for financial compensation. The second case has pretty much taken care of itself. In the third situation, according to email contact I have had with the team (since the phones haven't yet been hooked up), this is bonding them in a way that only a crisis can.

Classes start next week, and the working out of our schedules is another story! I'll fill you in when I write next. Needless to say, some themes never change. ☺

Happily home,
Amy

October 2001—Where were you when you heard?

I'm sure since September 11th, this has become one of the most commonly asked questions. For me, I was in bed, asleep . . . or trying to sleep. My phone kept ringing; I didn't answer it because I have a Chinese friend who calls consistently late, even though I have explained that I'm in bed by that time. Then I heard someone in the hallway calling my name, and my neighbor entered my locked apartment. She had gotten the master key and let herself into my apartment, since I wasn't answering her calls. Joann told me that her mom called to say that terrorists had flown into the World Trade Center. I said, "That's so shocking, so terrible," because I knew that that's what one should say in that circumstance, but I had no idea what it meant or what had happened.

Joann decided to go to a hotel where she could get CNN and watch what was happening, and asked me to go with her. It was only when I saw the second plane fly into the building that I began to grasp the magnitude of the attacks. We stayed up until 1:30 a.m., and then got up at 6:00 a.m. to begin calling teachers. We didn't want the first time that they heard about the attacks to be in the classroom in front of a group of students.

I don't know what you have heard about the Chinese reaction to this tragedy. At first, it was in line with the government response: how sorry that the Chinese were that something awful had happened to the US. But the tide is beginning to change. Because America is more developed, many think it only fitting that we were brought down a notch or two. This is not a new reaction or all that surprising; just look back at the Chinese history over the past century. But when historical facts and current emotional reality hit you, it's a bit too close.

Some TIC teachers are struggling to stay when they perceive that they aren't wanted. Yesterday I was talking with a teacher who was told by a like-minded student that to his face, that the students were sorry; but behind his back, they had cheered when they watched the news on TV. Some teachers are already talking about whether they will return to the US next year or stay here. I understand their feelings of wanting to be closer to family and to what is happening. I am reminded again and again how deep my allegiance to the US goes. At times, I feel a stronger bond with the US than with the Kingdom of God. It is hard to sort through where my loyalty should be. Remember us as we wrestle daily with these tugs. Who knows, by the time you are reading this, potentially even more will have happened.

On a different note, my schedule has worked out as the following: I am teaching on Mondays and Tuesdays and will be traveling much of the rest of the week. I'll share my travel schedule with you so you can follow me on a map and with your thoughts. [Then, I shared the travel schedule of October through December.]

On yet another note, the following is an email from a former student that Shelley and I taught. I shared her autobiography with you earlier this year and hope you will be as encouraged by this next installment as I have been.

> Hello, friends. My mom accepted Him this evening! Yes! You have a new sister now. A couple gave a clear and gentle speech to my parents. My mom accepted right away. My father said he still needed time to think. Oh well, at least he doesn't deny dad now. He agreed that to let ego control himself wasn't right. That was a great improvement.

Back to Amy. Truly good news, eh? I know I haven't said much about my students . . . That is because I have only seen one class once, and the other twice. We are getting off to a slow start when it comes to teaching, but other areas of life have kept me plenty busy. For example, Liesl was to fly out the eleventh of September but obviously didn't. I have been teaching her classes until flying resumes and she can get to Beijing. I realized that this is the second newsletter in a row without any pictures, and I will rectify that in the next newsletter. ☺

It's a hard time to be away from the US, but a good time to be right where I should be.

> Blessings,
> Amy

October 2001

[I wrote another newsletter at the end of October about a road trip several friends and I took to a walled city in China. Train trips are common, so I compared a Chinese road trip to an American one.]

November 2001

Having finished three of my trips to visit TIC teams, I have seen ten different apartments, four schools, nine classes, four planes, four trains, countless taxis, and eleven teachers. The range in housing provided, classes taught, food available, and team relations was—um, how to say—large. Seeing the variety of situations reminds me that it isn't what you have or don't have that matters, as much as a person's attitude. The psalmist invites us to "enter his gates with thanksgiving .

. . For the L ORD is good and his love endures forever."[16] As the holiday season approaches, I can get a bit sappier than normal. I know, know, know that I have much to be grateful for. This is a brief snapshot on this particular day.

I am thankful for

- Shower curtains! Most of the Chinese guesthouses I stayed in didn't have shower curtains and it was a challenge to shower without getting water all over. I appreciate my shower curtains much more.

- Coal heat—The heat was turned on last week. What a change from Chengdu.

- My students—This year they are much more eager to do things with me outside of class!

- In particular, a student named Jennifer. I've started going to her dorm room Mondays after class, and then we eat lunch together.

- My good health. Part of my job is to help/talk to our teachers with health problems. We've had a woman hospitalized and evacuated to Beijing for high blood pressure problems and another one hospitalized for dysentery.

- A HAND-KNIT sweater that my Chinese mama who lives in Chengdu made for me. The color has grown on me. ☺

- Dryers! When I come home from trips, laundry is laughably easy because we have dryers available.

- My VCR and taped TV shows!

- My fruit lady—The open market near us is "open season on foreigners," but I have found a woman I trust. I was buying oranges a few weeks ago, and her husband overheard the price she quoted me. He scolded her for not charging me more, but she looked at him and said that we were friends.

- Plants—I've nursed little spider plants along and now have them in several rooms. After living in gray, polluted cities, I crave color and the plants added to my home.

- Old friends—The student I went bungee jumping with in Chengdu several years ago called me last night out of the blue.

- Supporters—We all were a bit anxious/curious to see how our financial support would be for the month of September, but I am fine.

- Chocolate—A guy I only met only once at a TIC event in Kansas City years ago is on my mailing list; he moved to Switzerland, came back to Nebraska to marry a local woman, and they returned to Switzerland. Two weeks ago they sent me some Swiss chocolate. It's those little things that amaze me again and again and again. I am not doing this on my own. (Thanks, Tim and Mitzi!)

- Taxi drivers who laugh at my cheap humor—When they ask what country I'm from and I tell them America and then I basically ask, "And you?" invariably they say, "Me? Me? Ha-ha-ha, I'm Chinese!" Never fails to get a laugh.

- Not needing to wear long underwear every day like I did in Chengdu.

- Diet coke—I'm glad that the store near us stocks it. It is sold by the can; I usually only buy three or four cans at a time because they get cumbersome to carry home. But it is an option!!

- Kleenex brand toilet paper—Man is it a lot nicer than what used to be available.

- My students' unusual English names—Lempicka, Charles Barkley Gao shortened to Barkley Gao, and Skywalker.

- My coworkers—Erin, Liesl, Joann, Mike, Jon, and Charlie.

- My friend Wen Li who is as taken with my niece, Miss Emily, as I am. Wen Li has the second largest Miss Em photo collection in all of China. Elizabeth has started to send me doubles of cute pictures because Wen Li always asks for them, so I give them to her and then have to email Elizabeth asking for another copy for ME—the auntie!

- And the fact that I could go on and on and on.

I'm up early today because the electricity is going to be turned off at eight and won't come on again until five this afternoon. But when you have divided your day into electrical and non-electrical things to do, it doesn't matter because it is not the electricity that lights my life.

Alight with gratitude,
Amy

December 2001—Smile, You're on Candid Camera!

I love to take pictures. Love it. Love it. When someone says, "I want to take your picture," I don't protest like I used to; instead I start grinning. Well, you can imagine my concern when my camera started making grinding noises as I'd zoom, not a good sign. At picture 20 the camera officially died. I walked my film down to the local Kodak store and had it developed, but alas, none of the pictures turned out. Thankfully, I am happy to tell you what was on it.

The main picture is entitled "Get into my car"

On Tuesdays I have Chinese lessons from 3:00 to 5:00 p.m. and then walk to the subway, ride to the closest station to my home, and take a taxi from there. As I was leaving the building last week, I pushed the door open and then held it until a woman behind me could catch up. It is the kind of entrance that has another door before you can get out, so I pulled the next one, held it, and gestured for the woman to go ahead of me. She protested, I insisted. I left the building and was walking down the sidewalk towards the subway station when I heard, "Get into my car," in English from the far side of the bicycle lane. I glanced around to see if this was directed at me and kept walking. "Get into my car" came through the air again. I looked over at the driver and had no idea who she was. I walked over to the partially rolled down window, and the driver said, "You held the door for me, I will drive you home."

I told her that she didn't know where I lived and that it was far away from there, but she said it didn't matter. I told her where I live, and she said she actually lives fairly near and could drop me off at a bus stop by her house. I got into her car. Her English is on par with my Chinese. As she drove home, she spoke in Chinese and I spoke in English and we both practiced our listening. The only scary thing is that we were driving down a busy road, like Kipling (in Denver) or 23rd Street (in Lawrence) during rush hour . . . in the middle lane. Because Wang Ting Ting was practicing her listening, she drove incredibly slowly. It wasn't scary getting into a stranger's car; it was a bit scary with cars passing us on both sides. She asked me to come over to her house that weekend, but I was going to be on my last member car trip and wouldn't be in town.

Well, this week during my lesson my cell phone rang and Wang Ting Ting wondered if I was at my lesson because she was at hers and wanted me to wait for her after my lesson. And I got another slow ride home in the middle lane. At one point she asked me if I was scared ☺; I tried to be as casual as possible and assure her I wasn't. Next week when she drives us home I'm going to go to her house for dinner and will meet her policeman husband. This picture began with a simple gesture of opening a door I was going to go through anyway and being willing to get into a car. China is a great place for the totally unexpected if you're willing to go along for the ride—even if it's a slow ride in the middle lane.

A few snapshots from the roll: Handel's Messiah

This year for the first time since 1949 Handel's *Messiah* was performed in Beijing in Chinese. I invited a Chinese friend, her husband, and another friend to attend with me. The performance was set to begin at 7:15 p.m. When 7:40 rolled around and it still had not started, we began to get antsy—okay, mostly I was getting antsy and the others were getting hot in too many layers. A man came on stage and said that they would begin soon and . . . they did. It was a FABULOUS performance. The program was in English and Chinese, allowing me to follow the different movements flipping back and forth and piecing together the Chinese I knew. When it came time for the Hallelujah chorus, tears ran down my face knowing that while this song hadn't been sung for over fifty years publicly, The Power behind the gap in performances couldn't be banished.

Guo Laoshi and Amy

Guo Laoshi is Teacher Guo, my Chinese teacher for the last year and a half. He is nearing retirement age and has taught foreigners Chinese for years. He has never been overly interested in spiritual things other than criticizing Fa Lun Gong (a cult that has recently been banned by the government and which is one of his pet topics and he can go on and on about it). Last week, I have no idea how the subject came up, but we spent an hour and fifteen minutes talking about false beliefs and true ones (the whole conversation was in English). At the end, he said that even though he has many friends and has known many people, he had never had a conversation like that and thanked me for talking about the subject. This week I took him a book written by a Chinese intellectual who has similar beliefs to ours. Guo Laoshi was thrilled to have something written in Chinese by a Chinese author and even started reading it during our break. I would have never guessed that I could have a conversation with him like that.

~~~

Erin and I have been in the midst of having Christmas parties for our students; I was desperate to take pictures of the parties that I went out and bought a new camera to have while I figure out where to get mine fixed. I am back to my happy self and clicking away!

Love,
Amy

January 2002—It's party time!

When I look back at the Christmas parties that Erin DeRoos (my first teammate) and I gave our first year in Chengdu, I laugh to think of what a flop they were. Okay, they weren't a total flop because our hearts were in the right place, but we were new to the culture we didn't understand what constitutes a party through Chinese eyes. We had been told the "rules" and thought that we understood them. Stating the obvious, head knowledge and experience are two different things. We basically threw American parties with Chinese characteristics.

It was when Shelley (my second teammate) and I were working on a culture lecture about all of the different types of parties a person would have throughout their life that we began to grasp the difference. In China, traditionally people lived and worked at the same place—a work unit—so when they had a party, they wanted to DO something: sing songs, play games, or go on an outing. In the United States, our circles don't overlap to this degree, often when we get together socially we'd rather talk about what has been happening outside of that social circle. Shelley and I summarized a good party as one where you get to eat and talk.

I'm glad to say that the learning curve might be long, but I've finally been part of giving a good party in China. Erin Dittmer and I teach some of the same students at Beijing University and decided to have them over in groups of eight students for a total of six Christmas parties. The first cultural hurdle we had to jump was to convince them that it was okay to have parties before Christmas. For the Chinese Spring Festival, the festival is celebrated after the Lunar New Year, not before the actual day.

We succeeded and convinced them to come to a Christmas party before Christmas day! Because we live in Beijing, we have the option to order Domino's pizza and have it delivered. Our parties started with chitchat until the pizza arrived. Then I would give them a brief introduction to the four pizzas—an American pizza (pepperoni), a Mexican pizza (pepperoni, jalapenos, and onions), a supreme pizza, and a kung pao chicken pizza. A moment of hesitation occurred when they realized that they would use their hands to eat the pizza ☺—my sanity saver when it came to dishes. We also had veggies and dip. "Um, Amy, those vegetables don't look cooked." Well, they're not. "Um, we Chinese don't eat raw vegetables." I know, still, have a try. And usually not much was left by the end of the feeding frenzy.

Knowing that we couldn't only eat and talk and call it a party, we moved on to the next activity. While Erin set up to make cutout Christmas cookies, I read them *Wombat Divine*—a precious children's story with great pictures. Because the Chinese roll out dough for making jiaozi (dumplings), they were able to dive right in to cookie making. From the chaos of cookie-land, as the cookies baked, we moved back into the living room and Erin and I would teach them the ever-famous gestures for the "Twelve Days of Christmas." Maybe you've never heard of these gestures (smile), but they are a hoot. Shelley and I came up with the gestures one year, and they have been a hit ever since.

After the exhausting twelfth verse, we sat down to cookies and a Veggie Tales Christmas video. Having watched it six times, I hear it in my head as I type this! After cookies and the video, we chitchatted a bit more and then we announced the party was over. Even though the event was formulaic, each party was fun and allowed us to get to know the students a little better. For example, we found out at a party that one of our students majored in the language of Myanmar as an undergrad! Erin and I are seeing a difference in class, as students are much more likely to come up and chat with us.

I've already begun planning the Easter Egg hunt/hot dog roast we want to have in the spring. Party on!

Love,
Amy

February 2002

[In February I had my teammate Erin write my newsletter. She received two humorous emails from students who are "in love" and had done poorly on the final. They explained how their love factored into failing the exam and asked for another chance.]

Valentine Culture Quiz[17]

1. T / F   It is common to see married people hug in China.
2. T / F   Couples almost never hold hands in public.
3. T / F   The words "I love you" are the three most common words in a Chinese family.
4. T / F   Two men can be seen holding hands, grabbing knees, leaning on each other, or touching in general.
5. T / F   To get a room at a hotel a couple must show their marriage certificate.
6. T / F   College campuses have married housing.

Valentine Culture Quiz Answers

1. False. I hugged a student once, and she was stiff as a board and said she wasn't used to hugging. I asked, "Don't you hug your husband?" Mortified, she replied, "I can't talk about it!"
2. True. It is becoming more popular with younger people in big cities for couples to hold hands, but on the whole it is not seen much.
3. False. I asked two students if they told their husbands they loved them. They both said, "No!" I asked them if they would like their husbands to tell them they loved them. "Yes." I challenged them to tell their husbands they loved them. One came back and said her husband was happy and said it back to her. She has since told me that her marriage has gotten a lot better. The other student told her husband, "My foreign teacher told me to tell you I love you." He replied, "She's weird."
4. True. The same for two women. In China, men and women touching in public is not acceptable, but touching of the same gender is common and a sign of friendship. Nothing more.
5. True. Chinese married couples have a small form of a marriage ID, similar to a passport that shows names and a photo.
6. False. Chinese college students are not allowed to be married.

Love, Amy

The greatest Valentine gift of all has already been given to us. "For God so loved the world that he gave his one and only Son, that whoever believes in him shall not perish but have eternal life."[18]

Love,
Amy

March 2002—You say helping, I say cheating, let's call the whole thing off!

I imagine some of you have read in recent years about the China copyright issues and all the pirated items now available from soundtracks and movies to North Face jackets. On the education front, we often have to address this issue as well. What I might call *cheating* is often classified as *helping* or *good writing*. I used to see this issue in black and white, saying that either helping or good writing were clearly cheating. But the longer I'm in China, the more I understand this line of thinking.

In a society where relationships are incredibly important, if your friend asks for help and you refuse them, you have no idea what future door you have closed. Maybe that friend's father's sister's husband could have helped you move your mom to Beijing. Maybe not. But without helping, that person is not indebted to you.

In terms of copying being good writing, this used to be where I, as an American, would roll my eyes and say, "Whatever! A good writer is one who can use their own words." But in China, a good writer is one who has read extensively and is able to incorporate others' words into their own writing. Chinese writing is laden with proverbs and set phrases. Everyone knows that a good writer uses others' words; it is not considered cheating, but a sign of being educated.

Because I've grown in my understanding of both reasons, I am able to be a better teacher and explain that when writing in Chinese, using other people's words is exactly what the students should do. But when writing in English, they need to operate under different cultural norms. My students are consistently surprised when I can tell they haven't written something themselves and want to know how I know. Well, if you read enough students' papers, you know! This past semester I had two students hand in the exact same paper on the topic of forgiveness. I couldn't tell who had copied whom so I gave them both a zero.

To make the point that copying wasn't going to get by me and that I do read and remember what students write, I had a student stand at the front of the class and begin to read from one of the homework papers. As she was reading, I joined in reading the other paper. Of course, the class noticed they were . . . exactly the same. Point made. Since it was the first time plagiarism had occurred, I told the class the two students could rewrite their papers, but they had now all been warned and any future copying would receive a zero. The last laugh was on me because neither student copied off of the other; instead they both chose the same paper from the Internet to copy! Ha.

I am thankful I have the same students that I had in the fall. This semester I teach them on Monday and Wednesday mornings from 8:00 to 10:00 a.m. When they heard the time, you would have thought I poked them all in the eye. Grad students usually have classes start at 10:00 a.m., and now they have two early classes!

Teaching them twice a week is already a great answer to prayer, and I'm looking forward to more opportunities to stimulate thought.

Honestly grateful,
Amy

PS: This letter was hand-carried out of China. It also included the rewritten paper by one of the dear "cheaters." I do love the students!

April 2002—Three lessons

The semester is definitely underway, and I know that if I don't sit down and write you today it won't happen for about two weeks. Spring tends to go fast in China anyway because the academic semester is about four weeks shorter than the fall. Even though I'm moving at a breakneck pace, three teachable moments stand out from this past month.

Di Yi Ke—The first lesson

Part of my job is to help with emergencies or unusual situations. What has influenced the tornado feel of the month is the sense that something is happening to everyone. ☺ We've had a teacher have a heart attack requiring evacuation to Hong Kong, several grandparents dying, a grown son back home being depressed and his mom wanting to be with him, schools not wanting teachers back, one team in particular having troubles. And on and on.

A teacher who lives here in Beijing had a minor bicycle accident in which a fifty-year-old woman caught her sleeve on his backpack, lost her balance, and fell over. The woman wasn't hurt and was able to walk around. The bike lanes are crowded, and it's more amazing if you *don't* bump into someone than if you do. But this wasn't a normal bump; this was a bump with a foreigner. The police were summoned, the woman was taken to the hospital (where it was determined that she had a sprained ankle but nothing was broken), and the next day the TIC teacher was questioned by the police.

Later that week I found myself, along with my boss, the teacher, his school official, and a Chinese lawyer in a meeting. The lawyer said that if the teacher had not been a foreigner, there would be no case. It was solely because he was not in a position of social power and is perceived to be wealthy. I don't want to sound whiny, but it was unfair. However, going into the meeting, my boss encouraged us to "focus on being righteous instead of being right." And that struck a chord with me. There is much in life that isn't right, pure and simple, but ultimately, being righteous is more important than being right.

Di Er Ke—The second lesson

This lesson is cultural—and was a big aha moment for me. This semester about nine students aren't registered in my class but attend faithfully. One of them is a doctoral student named Xiao Hong Yu. She invited me out to lunch to chat and to thank me for letting her attend the class (I guess Chinese professors don't allow auditing, I didn't know). A little cultural background information will make the next part more understandable. China is a country of comparing— who is older, richer, fatter, smarter, slower, more beautiful. All of life is ranked: students in a class, universities within a province, if your mother's family has more money than your father's, foreign teachers and their teaching ability. It is one of the areas that can be hard for foreigners to adjust to when they come to China.

Xiao Hong Yu was telling me that her sister lives with her and helps take care of her five-year-old daughter when her husband goes on business trips. This is where the aha moment comes in: the other night her daughter was teasing the aunt that her mother's school is better ranked than the aunt's. What five-year-old in America would know whether KU is ranked better than CSU?? The daughter consoled her aunt by saying that at least she earned more than her mother. I knew that adults openly talk about their salary, but it hadn't occurred to me that they don't magically start talking about salaries at the age of eighteen. ☺ The whole comparison aspect of life, like anything else cultural, starts young!

On a side note, I attend a Sunday School class where we study some Chinese phrases. When Erin asked me about the ability of the people in the class, I said that of the nine students, my Chinese ability is probably third from the bottom. And the culture rubs off on more than the young.

Di San Ke—The third lesson

This lesson involves my job as the head of Member Care. I sometimes have to confront difficult people and situations. I understand that it is often easiest to lash out at the messenger or to try to turn a situation to make it my fault. Sometimes the situations are rather humorous and don't hurt my feelings. For example, a teacher explained to me the other week that the problem with the school was that the waiban (school official) was reacting hysterically because she was female and females have a tendency to be hysterical. Whatever! But other times the frustrations will be directed at me personally. I've been reading *The Celebration of Discipline*, and the chapter on the discipline of silence says that a person doesn't always need to justify him or herself, that sometimes we should be silent and let the True Justifier justify us.[19]

Honestly, in the situations with a person who doesn't believe that I have handled things properly, it is a challenge not to want to justify myself right away. When I have to make tough phone calls, I have started writing on a piece of paper "He is my justifier." I look at it as I talk as a reminder to myself of ultimately whom I need to please on that phone call.

I have a feeling this is going to be a lifelong lesson. This month when you chat about me around your dinner table, you could mention the following quote from Ken Gire: "Help me to surrender to the daily crosses in my life. Give me the strength to shoulder the beam, to submit to the nails, to be silent before the abuse. Help me to bear antagonism without anger, insult without indignation, ridicule without retaliation."[20]

Still learning!
Amy

May 2002—Lunch with Iron Baby

In other newsletters I've mentioned my student with the English name Jennifer. Her Chinese name is Liu Tie Wa—Liu is the family name and Tie Wa means "Iron Baby." She's told me it's an unusual name in Chinese and people often laugh when they hear it, but I quite like it because it is easy for me to remember. We have lunch weekly after class, and she is a great cultural informant, keeping me connected to what is going on at BeiDa (Beijing University) and in the lives of the students. Our class is from 8:00 to 10:00 a.m., and after that we usually go and hang out in a restaurant until a decent time to order lunch. Through our routine we have found out that most restaurants don't open until 11:00, but some will let us sit until they open.

Last week several interesting cultural tidbits came up, and I thought you'd enjoy them too. First of all, let me say that I enjoy eating with Tie Wa because she likes to try new food and knows that I am game for about anything. She enjoys *doufu* (tofu) as much as I do and likes to try vegetables she's never heard of. I sit back and enjoy the ride, and we take turns paying. On a side note, she seems to have much more disposable income than my students in Chengdu did. I feel a little awkward having this twenty-two-year-old take me out to lunch. But she says that her parents give her money each month and she spends a lot less in graduate school than she did as an undergrad on going out to eat with her friends.

During this lunch she told me about recent problems in her life and how nice it is to talk to me because I don't know any of the people; she can honestly say how she feels. She went on to talk about weight that she has gained (I couldn't tell) and how she plans to start exercising but the problem was taking a shower afterwards.

It is typical for dorms in China to have one central shower house for all of the students with set hours that the students can bathe. Each student at Beijing University can have sixty shower tickets per semester at the price of one yuan per shower (about twelve cents). After you have used your allotted tickets, showers start costing four yuan or about fifty cents. At the beginning of the term students who live off campus will sell or give away their tickets. When I first heard this, I was shocked at how few showers students are allotted, but in reality it is about fifteen a month—about every other day—which is slightly more frequently than I bathe, so not a big deal. As I was in my shower this morning, I was reminded of the convenience of having a bathroom connected to my living quarters and the freedom that I can bathe pretty much whenever I want.

Tie Wa recently got a part-time job at Siemens, a German company, working half a day on Thursday and all day Friday. This is her first contact with foreigners who are not teaching her. What cracked me up was that she kept saying, "Amy, there is no free lunch!" and was truly appalled by this. I don't think she knows that this is an idiom.

She repeated again and again, "The salary is high but there are many things they don't provide for their employees—they don't provide housing! And there is no free lunch." That lunch thing stuck with her.

This bright young woman has come of age when China has been making rapid changes from all that the state provides. If she is having a hard time wrapping her brain around the changes, I can only imagine some of the struggles that others are going through as they realize all of the "lunches" that are not provided. Yes, the salaries are higher, but what your company provides is less than before. I think that China is moving in a healthy direction, don't get me wrong, but it is a huge shift in thinking. Huge.

The restaurants also don't provide free lunches ☺, and we asked for the bill, bringing another enjoyable meal to a close. Next week we are going to one of our favorite jiaozi (dumpling) restaurants, and I'll continue to learn and enjoy the company of this colorful young woman.

Enjoying the tidbits of life,
Amy

June 2002—What have I been doing?

I am embarrassed that I haven't written recently. May and June are the craziest months for me, and I've pretty much been working seven days a week. I will head back to the US soon, and I'm ready for a few movies, bagels, phone conversations, and not having to grade, plan lessons, answer contract questions, place new teachers at schools, answer e-mails . . . you know, work.

I have mentioned before that part of my job involves visiting several of our teams to see how they're doing. A trip begins with me writing a slightly sappy letter to the waiban letting them know when I will arrive and asking them to set up a meeting both with their office and the English Department. I say that the letter is slightly sappy because the Chinese are sappier in their communication style than Americans—in a nice, innocent kind of way. I had to turn in a report to TIC, and my boss made a comment that I kind of went over the top in my praise for one person. I guess sappy can be catching!

Before I go on the trip, I e-mail questions to all adult teammates to help them reflect on how the semester has gone up to that point. I ask them to fill out the reflection questions before we meet. Also in preparation, I bake cookies to take to the teachers. I have a nice big Western-sized oven, and I do "oven ministry." About thirty minutes before I leave, I whip out my suitcase and pack. This last-minute packing causes stress for my friends living in the same building. I think I have more pre-trip drop-by visitor saying goodbye because they just want to see how long I wait before I start packing!

The next phase of the trip is to take a taxi either to the train station or to the airport. When I arrive at the destination, I'm greeted by a school official and escorted back to the school. I'm usually at a school for two or three days, depending on the number of teachers. During my visit I meet with each teacher individually—often it's nice for them to have someone from the outside to talk about life with. I mainly listen and, at the end of our chat, lift up any special requests that they have.

At some point I meet with the school officials. The reason I always have this meeting is that in China problems are often not directly addressed; instead they're handled through a middle person. I am the middle person for both the teachers and school officials. Usually the meetings are a big lovefest with both sides expressing how much they appreciate each other. I am pleased that our teachers, for the most part, are culturally sensitive and take teaching seriously. If problems do exist, both sides will wait until the end of the meeting and, after much mutual appreciation has been expressed, slip in a few small areas that might be changed or addressed.

We have a banquet together, after the meeting, with the school officials, the teachers, and me. I enjoy the schmoozing and getting to see another side of the officials that goes on at the banquet. And it's at the banquet that some of the school politicking comes out as the various departments talk with each other. Quite insightful as the team and I become more aware of the broader picture of school life.

Before I leave, I spend time with the team. Since this is after meeting with the school officials, and if anything needs to be passed on, I can convey it then. I try to have an encouraging word—frequently I'm amazed that what I read in the Bible applies to their situation. At some point on the trip I take the team out for a fun dinner. When I was last in Chengdu, the team decided they wanted to go out for Beijing Duck. I thought it was funny that in the land of good Sichuan food, they wanted to eat Beijing Duck. Funnier still, we went to the restaurant Erin, Mark, and I went to for my first Thanksgiving in China.

I enjoy visiting the teachers and seeing a small slice of what life is like for them on their campus, in their city, on their team. To see the joys and the frustrations. To know small details, like what their bathrooms look like. I don't always do a perfect job and am kept humble by comments like the one I received on a recent trip, "Has TIC ever considered doing pastoral visits?" Um, this is kind of what that's supposed to be . . . sorry you could not tell.

Still, I count it a privilege that I'm allowed to see a larger part of the work, that I am allowed into people's lives and hearts, and that I can professionally and personally provide input. Sometimes I wonder why many strange things have happened to me in China, but three days ago I was reminded of how all parts of life can be used. A teacher had her passport stolen, and from my experience ten years ago in Hefei, Anhui Province, when my passport was stolen, I knew what she needed to do. And that is just one small example.

A school trip ends with me heading home, being greeted by food that my teammates have put in my fridge, and closely followed by a shower and doing laundry. In the upcoming days I fill out a feedback form for each adult, letting them know what is going well and maybe one or two areas to address. Most of our teachers have the voice of "I am not doing enough" in their heads. I am glad that TIC values documenting all they are doing. Next fall I will visit four of our schools and supervise the nine people who have visited the rest. While I'm ready for a break, I am sure glad this is my job. I love what I do—thank you again for your continued love and support. I know I don't travel alone.

Happily employed,
Amy

August 2002—The six-and-under crowd

I wasn't in the US long this summer because my boss and I take turns staying in China through the process of placing the teachers for the next year. He stayed last summer, and this summer it was my turn to stay. I'm becoming a small "visa expert" through this part of my job. It cracks me up when I get an email from our home office with a visa question. When did *I* become the one with the answers? Yet often I do know the answer or whom to ask.

Since I wasn't going to be in the US as long as usual, I kept my plans short and simple: spend time with my family and go to Texas to visit my college buddy Amy Lester and her family. Amy and Bill have three kids, so between them and Ms. Em, my niece, I had plenty of opportunities to interact with the under-six-year-old section of our society. From James (six) and Aaron (four), I learned a lot about lightsabers (and marketing!) from Star Wars—blue, purple, and green are for good guys, and red are for bad ones. None of us wanted a red one! Here are a few highlights from my interactions with the Lester boys and Ms. Em.

Love, Amy

Aaron: Once, twice, or even three times a day I'd hear, "Auntie Amy, tell me something about Chi—na" with "China" being almost two words. I'd tell him about the traffic, the food, what kids his age are doing, about the one-child policy and the lack of siblings, about . . . oh goodness, but it became harder and harder to think of things that would be of interest to a four-year-old. I loved hearing that little voice from his car seat, from the kitchen table, from the couch, asking about China and learning a little bit about another culture—even though he wasn't about to eat the jiaozi (dumplings) Amy and I made together. Kids will be kids!

James: James has an insatiable curiosity when it comes to learning. We played a state game, and I'm embarrassed to admit that a six-year-old is more familiar with capitols, state flowers, and various industries than I am! Amy and I took the three kids to the aquarium, and James was excited to see the exhibits. In the most enthusiastic voice he would say, "Mom! Look at that!" while Aaron leapt into my arms and insisted I carry him (Amy called me "Aunt Sucker" for buying into it . . . I didn't care! Color me a sucker.) The otter exhibit had buttons you could push and learn about the habitat, eating habits, and the like. The boys had fun pushing several and we were almost done when I noticed that one of the buttons said "reproduction." Well, being the cheeky aunt, you can guess which button I wanted them to push. Amy began to herd us on and James enthusiastically said, "Republicans? I love republicans!"

Emily: This is a list of what I observed from Ms. Em since she speaks point-and-grunt.

- Someone can be adorable twenty-four hours a day—even when screeching in a restaurant.

- Contrary to what the Chinese, and many Americans, think, people (even adorable people) have a natural bent towards disobeying. "Emily, don't touch that book." She removes her hand and looks at me. Looks at me a little longer. Continues looking at me while extending her hand towards the book.

- Someone else in our family also has boundless energy. She's often referred to as "the Gerbil." I enjoy having another mover-and-shaker in the family—I'm glad that she's not called "the mouse" or I might have to hit her with a frying pan! Just kidding!

- Ms. Em is the only person who can turn me into a blathering idiot. I could go on and on but will spare you, realizing that only a few will still actually read if I continue.

Ten-Year Anniversary

It is hard to believe that ten years ago this summer I went to China for the first time. I was on a summer teaching team with TIC in Hefei, Anhui. How can it be that long ago? And yet it was. While visiting Amy and Bill they asked me how my support has been recently. When I went on full-time support seven years ago, I could not have imagined that some day in the future (let alone SEVEN years later!) I would be this well taken care of. Only four of the original monthly financial supporters have been led to stop financial support; and they contacted me asking to remain on my mailing list. In the past seven years I've had several opportunities to speak and have been able to grow my mailing list and add a few supporters each year. I am not in debt with TIC! Praise be!

And when I talk about support, I'm not only talking about money. I have been well supported, and I know I'm covered daily in prayer. I am not forgotten, somewhere over there on the other side of the world. You talk about me at the dinner table, you drop me a postcard, or you write an e-mail. Basically, you love me. I've been asked how it is that I have been able to be overseas this long and am still doing well. Simply put, because God has shown favor and blessed me through you.

This is a simple thank-you. I am truly blessed. It is hard to leave that cutie Ms. Em, and yet I have the assurance that this is what I'm supposed to do. As I return to China, please be praying for my students. I hope to teach the same students from last year, please ask for spiritual interest. In terms of my job in personnel, we are opening eight new schools. This means potential blips exist with the eight schools since they have never had TIC teachers. May the blips be few!

Again, humbly, thanks,
Amy

#7 If You Write Newsletters

Questions to Help You Develop a Theology of Newsletter Writing

Theology is the study of the nature of God. I can get lost in big words, nodding as if I am tracking without truly tracking what is being said. "Yes, yes, the study of the nature of God. I see." But at times, when asked by a local friend what I mean by a word like "theology," I fumble because I cannot simply express the idea. In cross-cultural work, it is important to have a theology of suffering and a theology of stewardship. However, a theology of newsletter writing is often overlooked. If I asked you why you write newsletters and I caught you in a raw moment when the truth popped out, I bet many reading this would say, "Because I have to." While true, this is a sad reason to do anything. Thankfully, you are not doomed to drudgery and can nurture this part of your ministry. C.S. Lewis said, "Theology is like a map . . . if you want to get any further you must use the map."[21] The following questions about your theology of newsletter writing are not meant to help you land on an exact answer, but they may help you start your journey.

1. What is the purpose of communicating with supporters?

2. What biblical examples can you think of where people communicated with supporters? What types of messages did they share?

3. What have you learned about God through writing newsletters?

4. How does writing newsletters help you in your own spiritual development?

5. How can your newsletters show the nature of God?

6. What overarching message are you hoping to communicate letter after letter?

7. What do you believe God desires for your supporters? How can your newsletters be used in the lives of your supporters?

Which question will you think about today?

Year Eight in China

2002-2003

What a lot we lost when we stopped writing letters.
You can't reread a phone call.
—Liz Carpenter

September 2002—Bits and pieces

I have wanted to write a newsletter for a while now, but a clear theme to my thoughts and what I wanted to say hasn't emerged. Instead, my head's been full of random parts of life. Typically, the way I write these letters is that my subconscious works on one and then when it is finished I just sit down and type it out. Maybe that sounds weird, but it works for me. Usually. The past week, nothing has surfaced, just bits and pieces. And I don't know how this is going to turn out, yet I want to communicate with you to help you remember me . . . maybe more than ever in the midst of my randomness.

- Most of the month of August was devoted to training the new teachers. For the first time, we did a majority of the training in Beijing instead of California realizing that it is better to talk about life in China . . . IN China! ☺ It was beneficial to have the training here even though it came with extra work and responsibilities. A couple was to do the team-building part of training, but the wife's mother died in early August, leaving the team training in my lap. I can see now how it all worked out as it should, and I enjoyed getting to do it, but it was another chance to practice dying to MY plan and living THE plan.

- I've mentioned before how we will have a theme surface each year for the types of problems we face. The theme this year, sadly, seems to be "death of a family member"—in addition to the mother who died, we've had an uncle murdered, a father die of a heart attack unexpectedly, a grandpa die while his grandchild was at new teacher orientation, and a cousin who died a week after being diagnosed with cancer. I have been in close contact with two of the teachers and counseled them to spend time with their families in the US, as we discuss when/if they will return to China. It is a privilege to be a part of these hard discussions, but it is emotionally taxing.

- This year TIC has about 170 teachers in China. I work with nine people who will help me in visiting the schools—we are switching from this being a part-time job to the primary focus of their work. Of the nine, four are full-time. Recently I've been busy answering a lot of questions about the contract—not sexy, but important!

- Teammates Gabe (age four) and Nate (age two) live in the same building that I do; before the summer break Gabe asked for a Broncos jersey and helmet. I was able to get him the jersey. His mother is both happy and sad about the jersey—happy that he can have a team to cheer for, if only he didn't insist on wearing it daily, making it hard to clean! I discovered KOA radio live broadcast of the Broncos game one Monday morning, as I was zooming around getting ready for class!! It was amazing and a little depressing. When I get a Broncos video, it doesn't depress me missing it because the game was usually at least two weeks before, but something about hearing it live and hearing the crowds and the announcers and knowing that it was going on RIGHT THEN was a bit much.

- My students! Where to start? Well, I am back at Beijing University (BeiDa) teaching the same type of students that I taught last year—first year graduate students majoring in international politics—and I teach them twice a week. The course is called 'disciplined English'. Any guesses as to what that is? Me neither at first! Take a guess and I'll put the answer at the end. The class is an elective and has the potential to be small. Unfortunately (or fortunately!) I have a group of fifty-two eager beavers and some PhD students who are sitting in for English practice. This year, housing at BeiDa is so crowded that my students can't live on campus; they live five kilometers away and take a bus to class. Poor dears. But it has only scared two students into dropping since the first day. I have two students from Taiwan and two from Hong Kong. The English name of one of the Hong Kong guys is "Holy" and his email address is HolyHolyHoly, leaving me wondering about what he believes. But when I asked the students what they hope to get out of the class, he mentioned FIVE times how wonderful it is to get to talk to the "beautiful girls" in class. Not that you can't like deep things and beautiful ones at the same time; it made me laugh!

- You may or may not remember that for the last two years Erin Dittmer was teaching at BeiDa with me. This year she is teaching at another school in town and I'm the only TICer at BeiDa. In general it doesn't matter, but with the amount of traveling I do, it is nice to have someone who can cover classes occasionally. Our business manager this year is new to Beijing—Lisa was in Myanmar last year—and isn't teaching! This past week she came to my class to get a sense of what a Chinese class is like, what goes on in my class, and to be introduced to the students. She is THRILLED (her words!) to sub for me on the Wednesdays that I'll be out of town. Last June I wouldn't have foreseen this solution, seeing as I didn't know Lisa and was grieving losing Erin as a coworker, but this is ideal! Praise be!

So there you have it, some of the different pieces of the puzzle that make up my life. By the time you get this, I'll be in the midst of traveling, returning to Beijing to teach, and heading out again with cookies I've baked for the teachers I visit. Even though I have been random lately, I have sensed a call to be more systematic in my knee time and more proactive in being in touch with the teachers I supervise. Please be asking for consistency in these areas.

Fortunately, in the midst of my randomness there is a Great Constant!

Both randomly
and constantly yours,
Amy

PS: "Disciplined English" means that we will be doing things related to their areas of study (their disciplines) while working on the four skills of reading, writing, speaking, and listening. Right now we are working on a unit concerning reparations and the role of government. Wish you could pop in!

October 2002—What's in a name?

In class we read an article that talked about Bulgarians forced to change their names in the middle of the night. To prep the students for the article, I asked them under what circumstances they would be willing to change their names. They said for things like the Internet or a pen name. I asked if they'd be willing to change to a French name? Japanese? African? Would they be willing to change for money? Oh yeah, that got people laughing. Chinese names carry a lot more meaning than the average American name; often each character will have a meaning of what the parents hope for their child's future. I think most of you know this, but as a brief review, the order of Chinese names is family name first and then the given name. People usually tend to have three characters in their names, but two is not unheard of. For their homework, I asked my students to tell me something about their names, and I found the following interesting:

> My name is Zhou Jia Li. I am proud of my name because my name has special meaning. Zhou is my father's surname and Li is my mother's surname. What makes my name interesting is that Jia means "plus." So, the meaning of my name is that my father plus my mother equals to me. The meaning of my name is clear, allowing anyone who sees my name the first time can tell the meaning of my name. Moreover, it is no doubt that my parents love each other deeply. In short, I love my name very much.

[I originally included four more entries explaining their names.]

When students choose English names, they usually want to know the meaning. Now you can see why! Meaning is significant. After living here, reading what the students wrote, and thinking about other famous names that were given to convey meaning, it makes me like my name all the more. And, wonderfully enough, my English name and Chinese name have the same meaning! Amy means beloved. I have the character "ai" in my Chinese name, meaning "love." When people hear my Chinese name, I'm consistently told it is a good Chinese name. I think this name suits me because I am, indeed, beloved. Thank you for all you do to make me feel loved. Your love enables me to love others!

The beloved one,
Amy

November 2002—'Tis time to be thankful

This letter is penned between travels. I was in Hohhot, Inner Mongolia, last week and returned home late Friday evening and will take off early tomorrow (Tuesday) morning on another trip. I zipped off to class this morning, zipped home to see if the TIC server was working (when did my life become this attached to email?), ran a few last-minute errands, filled out the paperwork for each teacher I visited last week, and now want to get a short note off to you.

I planned to write something different this month, but I don't have the time to get it fleshed out. Still, in the midst of the craziness, I am conscious that I truly have much to be thankful for! Limiting myself to this past week, I am thankful for the following:

- Mutton! I am thankful that I don't live in a place where the main meat option is mutton (um, like Inner Mongolia). Man, but that is meat with an attitude!

- The hand-knit sweater my Chinese mama made me—it weighs about five pounds (not an exaggeration!) but on cold days like today, it warms me outside and in.

- Popcorn. Okay, that was my lunch today! On days like today I love being an adult without children so I can eat what I want without having to set a nutritional example. ☺

- Chocolate, stain remover stick, and commentary on British Lit. Isn't that a great list? It is what the team I'm visiting tomorrow asked me to bring them. Doesn't it just about sum up what's important in life?

- [The list continues and ends:] My next newsletter . . . because I didn't get to use my newsletter idea this time I have something I want to say next time. Yippee!

During a rough period this fall, a friend gave me this promise: "Don't hold back Your tender mercies from me. My only hope is in your unfailing love and faithfulness."[22] And He hasn't. Even in just this past week, my cup runs over—He has been faithful over and over!

Indeed, 'tis time to be thankful!
Amy

December 2002 —Not since 1841 . . .

Isn't a phrase you hear often! But here in Beijing, we have just finished our longest continuous snow since 1841. And what made it delightful is that it was a light, fairly dry snow that fell day after day. I kept saying that I felt like I was in a poem.

The only time I didn't like the snow was early one morning waiting for a cab to take me to Beijing University for my 8:00 a.m. class. Literally no cabs appeared because they all stayed in for safety's sake—I can't say that I blame them in a city with no snow removal and lots of first-time drivers in these conditions. Loads of us were out trying to get any form of transportation we could! I finally went out to the main street and started waving at private cars. I thought to myself, "This is called hitchhiking in America and I'd never do it!" But this isn't America and I was desperate. Finally a small white van (called in Chinese a "bread-loaf vehicle" because they look like a loaf of bread) pulled over and I climbed in. I asked how much it would cost to take me to BeiDa, and his price was the same as a taxi—frankly, I was prepared to pay a lot more!—and off we went. I was only ten minutes late to class! Yippee!

The snow put us all in quite the festive holiday mood. Now that the holidays have come and gone, let me share some of the highlights. In class for Thanksgiving we read Abraham Lincoln's *Thanksgiving Day Proclamation*. Lincoln discusses the fact that even though the country was in the midst of the Civil War, there was still much to be thankful for and still Someone in particular to thank. On Thanksgiving Day, I received the following email from a student:

> Dear Amy,
> It is Thanksgiving Day today and I want to say something to you. Frankly speaking, I have never celebrated this holiday before, and haven't thought seriously to thank someone. Yes, I am busy with my study and with my friends that I am tired to think about anything else. While reading the article you gave us, I looked into myself and wanted to find what I wanted, why I wanted them and who gave all of these things to me. I need such a time to make a deeper thinking.
> I am lucky to be a student of yours and I should thank you about what you have done to me and to all my classmates. To tell you the truth, I am too sleepy

to get up every Monday and Wednesday morning. But whenever I remember your quiz,[23] I at once get enough energy to leave my warm bed. Haha! Because I have taught Chinese for half a year when I was a senior, I can understand how hard for you to arrive at class on time while everything is ready to teach a lesson. Thank you again for your hard work and all your effort for this class!! Wish you enjoyed your life in China~~~~~ And I will thank someone else today. Woo~woo~~

What she said is true: "Thank you" isn't a commonly heard phrase or idea in China. It is certainly becoming more common, especially among more educated urban types. But the traditional idea has been "Why would you thank someone for doing what they are supposed to do?" In a restaurant, why thank the waitress for bringing your food? She *should bring it,* it's her duty. Why thank your mother for cooking? Or your dad for dropping you off at school? These are tasks they are supposed to do. And you know what, when explained that way, I can see their point. But this is one of those times when "You can take the girl out of America, but you can't take the American totally out of the girl." And so I often sound like a silly bobbing-head "xie-xie" (thank-you) doll, but that's okay. I do have much to be thankful for.

After the first week in December I finished with my traveling for the semester (and the people rejoiced—both students and Amy alike!). Because I was going to be in town for a while, I scheduled Christmas parties like last year. For a brief recap, I had six parties with basically eight students per party. We ate pizza, read Christmas books, made Christmas cookies, sang and acted out the "Twelve Days of Christmas," and watched *How the Grinch Stole Christmas* while eating the cookies we made. Thankfully, Lisa, my friend who subs for me when I travel, hosted them with me! It is a two-person production to keep things flowing and gives more opportunity for us to get to know the students a bit better.

Two highlights

1. Having an opportunity to break the class of fifty-two into small chunks and interacting with the students more. At each party I felt like I knew the students a little better than I did before the party. It was interesting to see the different conversations that would come up! ☺

2. The second highlight was that at 7:00 p.m. at each party Isabel (age seven) and Gabe (age four) would come and help make cookies, sing the song, watch the video, and eat the cookies. They had also come last year and since then have wondered when we would "Have more parties!" Before the last party, Gabe wondered if we could postpone it and save it for later! Afterwards, Isabel would discuss conversations she heard with her mom. One conversation that bothered her involved a student who was *adamant* that Nature made the Creator. Isabel and I talked about how the conversation had made us feel. It's a privilege to get to minister with and involve the kids. And they sure brought an energy level to the party that Lisa and I simply couldn't have! ☺

Finals will be this week and then my focus will turn towards the conference in Thailand. In truth, my mind has already been there—we are getting about twenty-five new teachers. I've been working on finding schools for the new teachers and organizing plane tickets and preparing training material. But more attention is still required.

While it might not have been since 1841 that there has been such a long continuous snow in Beijing, I continue to be covered by you. Thanks. The Christmas cards helped make my season—and made me the envy of the building I live in. Keep the love coming, it pours out to others.

Continuously,
Amy

January 2003—On top of the world

My last trip of the semester was to visit our teachers in Tibet. Even though I had lived in Chengdu for five years, which is considered the stepping-stone into Tibet for most of China, I had never visited. The main reason is that I'm lazy. ☺ While Tibet is part of China, for obvious reasons it has some special rules, and one of them is that you need a travel permit to visit. I could have gotten one, but I never got around to it, and then, well, I moved to Beijing and life just had a way of moving on. So when a chance arose to visit and the TIC people in Tibet agreed to arrange for my travel permit, it seemed like the time had come to visit "the top of the world."

As with any good adventure, part of the story is getting there. A direct flight from Beijing to Lhasa with a brief layover in Chengdu exists, and the plan was for me to fly Monday morning, December 2nd. I contacted our travel agent near the end of November to arrange a ticket and let him know that the travel permit was coming. He got back to me saying that because I wanted to go in a different month, the airline hadn't posted the travel schedule and he wouldn't be able to issue the ticket until the last day of the month. He then commented, "I don't know how they can be in business," which made me happy since he is Chinese and I had wondered the same thing!

Imagine my surprise on Friday, November 29th at 4:30 p.m. when the travel agent called to say that December marked the beginning of the winter travel schedule and there was no longer any direct flights to Lhasa. ☺ To make a long story short, I would now need to overnight in Chengdu, taking my beloved travel permit, and get my own ticket into Lhasa. Off I flew on Sunday to my Chinese hometown, happy to have more time than just a layover. I was able to get my ticket to Lhasa purchased after three young women, who looked no more than twenty years old, scrutinized the dear travel permit for quite a while and sent me upstairs to have it photocopied. A woman had approached me while the three were examining the permit and asked me to stay in her "hotel"—they even had a "shuttle"—I guess that's what you'd call a dude with a cheap white van. Hey, why not, this was an adventure, after all! Ticket in hand and checked in to a hotel near the airport, I headed off to visit my former school.

The highlight was getting to see Shen Yang, my Chinese mama. I knew that she had knit me some long underwear because it is "so cold in Beijing." I am now the proud owner of itchy wool long underwear that fit well but must be worn with something on underneath.

After eating dinner with the teachers, I returned to my hotel to go to bed early. Awoken by the hotel staff sometime before 10:00 p.m., they asked me to come down and translate for a foreigner who had just arrived. "We can't understand her and she can't understand us, please come now." What?! Can I at least throw a coat on? Oh my word, this was going to be an adventure from start to finish!

Finally, on Monday morning I flew to Lhasa. The airport is one to two hours away from the city, depending on whether you go by bus or taxi. Because of the quick change of plans, the school wasn't able to come out and pick me up, requiring me to take the public bus, complete with a Tibetan woman next to me who kept blowing her nose on the ground and nearly hitting my shoe.

While getting to Tibet *was* quite an adventure, it was worth the effort. Here are some highlights and random observations:

- China functions on one time zone—"Beijing time"—thus, life in Tibet has its own rhythm. It is pitch dark until 8:00 a.m. at this time of year and people don't tend to wake up until 8:00

a.m. Classes begin at 9:30 and run until 1:30. The lunch break is from 1:30 to 3:30, and dinner is never before 6:30.

- Effects of the altitude: The first day I just felt a little light-headed when I walked. As long as I was seated, I was fine. In general, people need about an hour more sleep than they do at lower altitudes. We were also much closer to the sun! Wow, the blue, blue skies. The warmth of sun. In many ways I felt like I was in Colorado. It is shocking that Chengdu is close physically, because the weather is almost the complete opposite.

- In many ways, I found life in Tibet to be similar to that for TIC teachers in other parts of China. Teaching, spending time with students, shopping for food. The main area in which I, as a total outsider, noticed a significant difference was around the practice of Tibetan Buddhism. I have to say that it was depressing to see people prostrating themselves over and over for merit. I even saw a sheep being led around to earn merit. I can't go into it here, but Tibetan Buddhism is a much darker evil than the media in the West portrays it.

Right now, only non-Americans are permitted by the government to work in Tibet. After getting a taste of life in Tibet, I could see myself working there. It truly is an amazing place. After my visit and seeing many in active bondage, I am humbled by the free gift we have— there is nothing we have to do to earn merit. I am thankful that I was "permitted" to go on this external and internal journey! ☺

"Permittedly" yours,
Amy

February 2003—Please wait in line

I've just returned to China after about three weeks of pre-conference meetings, the TIC conference, and then a week of vacation. Why is it, I ask myself, that returning to China from Thailand is more difficult than returning from America? I'm sure that part of it is the time of year. Aesthetically speaking, Thailand is colorful with beautiful flowers, blue skies, and warm weather, while Beijing at this time of year looks a bit washed out. But I also think that in going from America to China my head has an internal switch I flip because the two cultures are different. In going from Thailand to China I forget to flip the switch and think,

"Oh, it's Asia, same-same." When it's not!

As Liesl and I boarded the plane in Bangkok with mostly Chinese fellow passengers, we felt ourselves getting cranky. Why is everyone shoving? Hello ma'am, could you please remove your nose from my back? I felt this surge of aggressiveness rising in me. After being in the "land of smiles," as Thailand is known, it was a shock to be returning to the "land of elbows." The boarding experience reminded me of a paper my student wrote last spring. In the spring semester we study the values and beliefs of Americans since my students are international relations students. Their knee-jerk reaction is often, "Why is the US government always doing XYZ to us?" (Just as ours can be about the Chinese government.) I try to point out that it often isn't the person, but that the behavior is a result of values and beliefs.

We read an article entitled "The Waiting Game," which gave an insightful look at what helps Americans to wait more patiently.[24] The article argued that certain factors, such as having information on how long the wait will be, whether or not there is a delay and the reason for it, or having something to do during the wait (like read), all help with waiting. It talked about how Disneyland has perfected the art of waiting by snaking lines and providing entertainment while people wait.

At the tail end of the article it briefly mentioned that part of waiting is merely cultural conditioning and gave examples of different cultures. Well, there was one sentence about China, and good golly if it didn't push buttons. As we neared the end of discussing the article, I asked if anyone had any more questions. Pretty much the whole class wanted to know if I agreed with the perceptions of the author. Yikes. I delicately explained that I could understand what the author was saying but that she had probably been traveling during Spring Festival and we all know that is the craziest time.

I did say that when I board busses I don't like it that I have to use my elbows to shove on and off. And with the subway I didn't fully understand why people didn't let passengers get off before those who are waiting get on the subway. Of course I heard from the students about the large population in China. True, but I lovingly tried to point out that Seoul, Korea, also has a large population and it isn't a shove fest to board the subway. Hong Kong, New York City, Paris, London—all of these cities have large populations. Oh, sigh, you're right.

Of all the articles and subjects we looked at—women in the military, husbands and wives and household chores, plagiarism, how to love your country but disagree with the government, and other topics—it was the waiting article that stayed with them. At the end of the term students each chose one of the areas we had looked at and wrote a paper.

As an arts student, I am quite interested in learning different culture. However, after reading "The waiting game", I am shocked by the sentence in the article "In China, though it is sometimes not a line but mass hysteria. At some train stations, people don't just push to the front of the line—they actually climb over the people in front of them." Amy, you are right, as a Chinese, I do not agree with the description in the article at first, I often think the author do not understand China much, and even never come to China, she is exaggerated and has some prejudice to east countries. So these days, I always observe the people around, chat with my foreign friends and discuss in our group, in order to find something that can change the description in the article strongly, but I failed. It makes me think deeply, and feel terribly uncomfortable. Maybe this article is not a perfect paper, but it is all the true feeling of my deep heart.

Scenes of waiting in China appear in front of my eyes: There are no clear lines in the dining room in my school, everyone try to push ahead. When I ask the boy who is cutting in front of me to wait in line, he looks at me surprised, "why are you so fussy?" Oh my, I want to curse him never get a girlfriend. When I draw cash from ATM machine, the person waiting behind me is closed! When we are waiting for the subway, no line preparing for the door open, no one remember "out first and get on later", everyone use elbows, (oh, Amy's poor elbows come in my mind again). The worst place is railway station, everyone seems to be crazy, and there are a lot of policeman who are shouting and trying to keep people in order. It always like finish a fight when I finally get my seat. People seldom bring books or something else when they are waiting, and I never see a place as smart as Disney that give you enough information to dispel the sense of waiting, no one will tell you how long you will need to be in line.

How about America? My American friend Eric

tells me frankly that he can't get use to the Chinese behavior of waiting. He is wondering why people still push to each other even when they get off the train and head to the exit, "why are people so hurry?" Just as Amy mentioned, people always waiting in a "/\" when the subway open the door and no one will get on until all the people inside get out. People are more patient, they wait for the bus; draw cash in the bank, buy the tickets, and etc in line self-consciously. My supervisor who backs from America recently tells me that it seems more comfortable in America, because you needn't to use your elbows frequently and no one will take away the things that belong to you.

Yes, above are just some simple examples of waiting in China and America. I agree that waiting is a trivial think in our daily life. However, is it too small to pay attention? Or can it be ignore? NO, I don't think so, it is why I feel strong in my bottom of heart. Sometimes people always ascribe it to the big population of China, however, it's only an excuse, and actually the population density of New York and Beijing is quite similar. In fact, it reflects some big problems in Chinese culture in my mind.

(Back to Amy now) Her paper went on to analyze where this mindset came by looking at history, social consciousness, the legal system, and the need to add this as a new virtue and not to "sleep on old virtues." She ended her paper with, "Yes, it is an order age, just like the Chinese saying, 'no order, no success.' As a confident and cultured Chinese student, I appeal to all Chinese people '**Please wait in line!**'"

I will teach the same unit this spring and have added a few new topics. Please be asking that as we look at values and culture, we will have some discussions that transcend all cultures.

Patiently waiting—ha-ha!
Amy

March 2003—Who said that?

During the TIC conference in Thailand I led a workshop called "How to Be a Successful Failure" in which I talked about learning from failure in teaching. Failure could come from a variety of areas, and one of them might be our refusal, as teachers, to change with the reality of the situation we find ourselves in.

Well, would someone please put a sock in the speaker? Oh my word, this is a perfect example of famous last words as I returned to the second semester. Last semester I taught fifty students on Monday and Wednesday mornings. I was told this semester I would teach the same students on Monday and Thursday. I went to the first day of class, but there were no students. Strange. I contacted the department but never heard back from anyone. I went to class on Thursday and the students wanted to know where I was on Tuesday. Tuesday? Ugh, the schedule had been changed and no one told/asked me. Tuesday/Thursday classes are the worst combination with the amount of traveling I do. Grrrrrr. In addition, we were moved to a much larger classroom, which would have been nice except that enrollment plummeted to about eighteen students.

Enrollment is down for a variety of reasons. First of all, my class is an elective and the students that didn't have high enough English scores are required to take another English class. That class is on Monday and Wednesday mornings (thus mine got bumped); an unspoken rule of grad students in China is that they don't have to take 8:00 a.m. classes. So, since they already have two days of early classes they simply are not going to "suffer through" four in a row.

It took me until the third week not to come home grumbling and refusing to adapt to the reality. With the room being large and the number small, it just felt . . . well, it felt pathetic. Like we were a bunch of losers up early huddled together in this huge room. The words of my workshop kept coming to mind as I grumbled, knowing full well that I needed to adapt.

It took a while, but I have. While the room still feels cavernous, we are working towards being a nicely knit group that is able to have more class discussion and jokes because of our size. Be asking that with the smaller numbers relationships can go deeper.

Crash!

Normally the crashes I hear are the sound of two cultures clashing. Unfortunately, last Monday the sound was an actual car crash in which I was in the third car of a four-car pileup. I was in the backseat of a cab coming home from my language lesson when the driver slammed on his brakes. I looked up from the book I was reading with just enough time to realize we were going to hit the car in front of us . . . and hard! Then we were slammed into from the rear. The trunk of my cab was totally squished, forcing the backseat to buckle in the middle and crash into my left kidney/lung/back area. The wind was knocked out of me and I couldn't breathe. The cab driver glanced back at me and then got out to start loudly discussing with the other drivers who was responsible to pay for what. No one came to check if I was okay, and after a few minutes I decided I would have to be the one to get myself out of the cab. After shoving the door open (it was slightly jammed due to structural damage) and hauling myself out, the driver just said, "Sorry," and went back to arguing with the other drivers.

We were in the middle of rush-hour traffic, and none of the drivers would stop to let me cross the five lanes of traffic to get to the curb and get another cab home. Finally I did cross, get home, and have friends say I needed to go the hospital. I was still in shock. It was hard to get back in traffic, wincing in pain, to go to a more Western hospital with "Western prices." Since I was in the emergency room, they let Liesl fill out the paperwork but wouldn't see me until I had given them my credit card. ☺ It turns out I have no broken ribs or internal bleeding. Yay! It has been five days since the accident and I am still in a good deal of pain, though wonderfully provided for. Lisa subbed for both of my classes, food has been pouring in like someone died, and people keep stopping by to check on me.

As usual, there are always a few good stories. On the first day that I missed class I got a call from a student seven minutes after class had ended; he was a new student and wondered if I would accept him as a student (oh and by the way, sorry to hear about your accident). Another student got on the line and in a heartfelt voice said, "Amy, I just want to say . . . congratulations! . . . No, no, that's not it. I mean, I'm sorry!"

One of my friends emailed, "Amy, I get more medical messages from you than from any of my friends." Well, here is another one! I certainly hope by the time you are reading this that most of the pain is gone and I'm able to move without the muscle soreness I have now. The accident could have been much worse. Praise be that I wasn't directly behind the driver, that it was my left side that was hit and not my right, and that my lung wasn't punctured!

> With either a sock in my mouth
> Or a pain pill, ☺
> Amy

April 2003—A little bit of everything

Greetings from the land of craziness—I'm referring to my life! I leave in about two hours for a trip to visit teachers in Henan. I still need to pack and Lisa is going to stop by and pick up the lesson plan for the class she *may* teach on Thursday for me. After class ended this morning and I let the students know Lisa will be there on Thursday, most of the class hung out talking about something—they don't usually do this, and I wondered what was up. Well, there is a sports meet on Friday, and they have *heard* that there won't be class on Thursday either, but it isn't clear if graduate students have the days off as well or if it is only for undergrads. Um, how could we find out, since I'll need to tell Lisa something? Check the website was the answer. I asked a student to check and give Lisa a call. But this seems indicative of how life is right now—things are happening, but it's not clear what or when or whom it involves. ☺ Here are updates on various aspects of my life this last month . . . take it all with a grain of salt!

- Brief follow-up to car accident: I am practically back to my old bouncy self! Through this experience I have discovered that we have a blind masseuse place[4] in the neighborhood and went to Dr. Wang for "treatment"—initially I went too close to the accident and it did more damage than help. But if I bought a card for ten visits, they'd throw one in for free; sucker that I am, I still have seven visits to go. Since I'm mostly recovered and not needing the back muscles worked on, Dr. Wang is doing general massages and giving me a chance to practice my Chinese.

- The war in the Middle East: I think it sounds like things here are fairly similar to the US—the war is covered on the news all the time, but people don't talk about it much. I have not experienced any negative reaction personally, but we have been asked by TIC not to discuss it because it is a rather volatile topic.

- SARS: For me personally, there isn't anything to say other than I know SARS exists and it's not clear what the situation is. My students were given a "disinfectant" and a pamphlet by Beijing University. The boarding school that I live at has used some sort of vinegar spray to clean the kids' desks and rooms, and that seems to be fairly standard around China.

---

4 "Massage parlor" has the wrong context, so I'm not sure what to call it. The massage therapists are "doctors" who have studied anatomy and massage for medicinal reasons. If you are thinking spa treatment, you would be wrong.

Love, Amy

Everyone is talking about "the vinegar spray." My students are split between those who are concerned and those who aren't. I think their parents are more concerned than they are, which is typical—I think mine are too. Mom was telling me the other day that my dad "comforted" her with a statistical analysis of the likeliness of me catching SARS. Frankly, I'm a lot more likely to be in another car accident!

But on an organizational level, following the news and being in contact with fellow TIC teachers has consumed a lot of time. We receive phone calls and emails—more than daily, but not hourly—from teachers who have heard rumors that SARS is in their cities. Because SARS tends to be localized, we are following it on a case-by-case basis and tracking some cities rather closely. I have been a part of a phone call with the home office and many meetings here about SARS. The subject certainly doesn't have an easy answer when you consider that it involves real people, some liabilities, the influence on the schools if we were to decide to remove teachers, and just wanting to be wise stewards of what we have been entrusted with —certainly an area we need discernment in!

The overriding reminder of the spring has been that life is going to happen and there is going to be a whole bunch of unexpected things— the war, SARS, my car accident, KU's great tournament (they made it to the NCAA championship). A lot of people have been asking me how I'm doing. While it is true that these things *do* affect me—and they should, they are big—they haven't rocked me. The question is, what is my foundation? Is it in political rest? Being national champions? Physical health? While none of these are bad things and I think we'd all like to have them, none is able to bear the weight of being my foundation. I have Psalm 15 hanging on my mirror to remind me: "Lord, who may dwell in your sanctuary? Who may live on your holy hill?"[25]

I'll let you look up the answer, but the final phrase of Psalm 15 is what captures me: *She who does these things will never be shaken.* I might be rattled, but I am not shaken. I might have statistical probability on my side, but I'm not counting on it. And while I hope that I have peace, health, and victory, they are not guaranteed. What is guaranteed is that I won't be shaken. Thanks for your thoughts; when I think of all that has happened this semester, I know that on paper it looks overwhelming. But I haven't been shaken. Keep the coverage coming!

Foundationally,
Amy

June 2003—My month with SARS

No, I did not have SARS, but SARS did seem to take over my life! I felt like I was in a movie, only I couldn't figure out if it was a comedy, horror, or drama. And in reality it was a bit of all three. I jokingly told people that I was going to call my next newsletter "My month with SARS, too bad it wasn't Lars ☺." But as I sat down the last three days to write this newsletter, nothing will come. I'm finally going to just make myself write because it won't get easier with time (the last three days have proved that!).

Why is this hard to write? Well put simply, the last month has been a season that I will look back on and see as a defining time in my life—because of the monumental size and seriousness. I read in a book last fall about using examples in teaching, and the author says, "I was reminded of a phrase I often use when guiding students in the writing of case studies or stories that teach: the material you use must be close enough to be immediate, distant enough to be safe! Until today, this event has not been distant enough for me to discuss."[26f]

I know that this is not distant enough to have sifted through, so this is a frontline report. I also know that this subject and experience have been multifaceted that one newsletter won't begin to capture it. I'm feeling more reflective now and plan to write about the experience in general and then in my next newsletter have some pictures and stories about what day-to-day life has been like.

At the end of my last newsletter I was on a trip and had just gotten word that classes at Beijing University (where I teach) were cancelled due to someone in a different department being rumored to have SARS. Well, let me tell you, the Beijing I returned to was not the one I left. Almost overnight the atmosphere changed radically. We weren't allowed in the airport and were bused to baggage claim. There was a rush on food in the grocery store, and the lines were twenty deep with people buying ridiculous amounts of food. The campus I live on closed down, and all of the students were sent home.

In terms of work, the Emergency Management Team (EMT) was formed and suddenly my life was devoted to SARS and serving the teachers as we guided them through this crisis. Two tangible lessons have emerged that I am walking away with. The first is the *absolute truth* in the fact that we will not be given more than we can handle![27] I was telling a friend yesterday that if SARS had to happen in China, I am thankful that after hitting Guangdong Province it hit Beijing as hard as it did. Literally overnight all other distractions and responsibilities were removed from those of us on staff in Beijing. We were able to focus and pour ourselves into the hours of holding meetings, making phone calls, coordinating with our home office, answering emails, and making tough decisions as to whether or not different teams should be removed due to their proximity to SARS.

All distractions gone.

Can you imagine that in one fell swoop, teaching responsibilities had been removed indefinitely? The campus that we live on sent students home and became a "locked campus," meaning that only those who live on campus could enter. Visitors/distractions were removed in an hour. Thankfully, we were given the freedom to come and go! Not all TIC schools have had that freedom and I don't take it lightly. As you know, part of my job is to travel around and visit teachers. Well, Beijing is the new Samaria! You tell people you're from Beijing and they take two steps away from you with the look of "*LEPER*" in their eye. I was denied a travel permit for my trip to Tibet. All of the people I supervise who are member care providers were denied the ability to travel—either their schools didn't want them to go, or the schools they were visiting didn't want them to come. Teachers in general were not allowed to travel, which meant we didn't have a steady stream of visitors in the building. Praise be.

But you know what, if even one of those three things hadn't happened—if I had been teaching, having visitors, or having to travel—I tell you the truth, it would have been too much. As is, it was one of the most emotionally draining times. We have all been under a low-grade stress since mid-April. I cannot fathom what it would have been like if SARS hadn't come to Beijing. As the crisis began to slow down and life edged towards normal, pieces of life were returned to us. I am back to teaching after five weeks being away from the classroom, and repair workers are allowed back on campus. We will not be given more than we can handle. Those words ring true to me like never before.

The second lesson has to do with being in leadership and needing to make tough calls. I've been reading material by John Maxwell about leadership, and one of the articles was about the subject of tough calls. He said that if many agreed with you, it wasn't a tough call. One of the tough decisions we had to make involved whether or not to end the school year early. We eventually decided to end it two weeks early—for many, many reasons that I won't go into here—overall, it was well received and most felt a psychological lift (somehow just having a definite end date made a huge difference), but not all applauded it. We were challenged on our commitment to The Call by a few. And that hurt because we are in this for the long haul and know that rest is needed by all if we are to come back and "do it all over again" starting in August. It challenges me as to whom I am listening to for approval—my fellow workers or just One.

On an issue unrelated to SARS, this is being written with a smile of déja-vu. One of the hardest times for me while I was living in Sichuan was the winter when the pipes were replaced in the building that Shelley and I lived in. We had no hot water for three months, and dust and noise were all around. Guess what is going on around me? Ah, that smile of déja-vu, that pound like no other, that hint of dust everywhere. Yes, the building that I live in is undergoing a major pipe project. I kid you not, I told you, it's like a movie around here! I'm in the process of packing up and storing all that I own in the bedroom and office of my apartment. The project is supposed to be done before I return in August. The water will be turned off on June 15th, so I shall be flying out of here on the 14th.

I know that many of you have been praying for us here in Beijing. We have seen amazing answers and been aware of the need for your backing in an intimate way. Why I have been allowed to experience such a time as this, I don't know. But as I walk forward from this, I feel like I am coming out of a holy and refining time. I am tired and in need of rest, but I rejoice in the undying faithfulness I have experienced up close.

From the front lines,
Amy

August 2003—Post SARS drama

When we left off last time, it sounded like our heroine was close to melt down. Several people told my parents, "I had no idea it was like *that* for Amy with the whole SARS situation." Having been back in Denver now for almost a month and having said daily that I need to get a newsletter written, but not quite having the energy or the focus or the physical strength (oh, the drama of it all . . . keep reading!), I am finally writing to you.

The physical strength part refers to my wrists. For the past two years I have experienced severe pain on and off in my left forearm when I type too much. But one of the advantages of my job is that I travel, with built in breaks from typing, allowing the pain to go away; and I would forget about it for long stretches. But this spring with SARS, I wasn't able to travel and the pain got worse by the day. At the beginning of May I started wearing a brace on my left wrist all the time (which helped with my sleeping!—one of the symptoms is that your arm feels asleep and it is hard to sleep). I need to stop here because the pain is getting a bit much . . . I say this only to give you a sense of how much I can type before needing a break. This letter is going to have to be written in installments.

Well rested, I return. I am calling this "the summer of shock treatment." Thus far I have been to the doctor three times, the occupational therapist six times, a neurologist once, and I will be seeing a hand surgeon later this week. It has been determined that I have no nerve damage, meaning it is not carpal tunnel syndrome. Instead I have quite bad tendonitis in my left wrist and just bad tendonitis in my right wrist. My occupational therapist has tried two different forms of electrical types of therapy and is ordering this "shocking" glove thing for me to take back to China. For the last few weeks we weren't sure if I was going to need surgery. Thankfully, I don't!

Even though my wrists have kind of dominated my life this last month, I still wanted to tell you a little bit about what led up to this—living in a SARS city. Here are a few snippets:

- **Are you hot?** While this question can be answered in several ways (hee-hee), it refers to your temperature being taken. Because one of the symptoms of SARS is having a fever, I have never had my temperature taken this many times or in such a variety of ways: from a laser pen on my forehead to a laser beam I walked under to an ear thermometer to the old-fashioned mercury thermometer. As I've mentioned previously, the campus I live on was closed during SARS and only those who lived on campus could come and go. But when we came back, we had to have our temperature taken and recorded. Most of the time it was with a mercury thermometer under the old armpit for five minutes . . . that will make you think twice about running out for some milk. Sometimes they would have the thermometer that you put in your ear. I think they must have been calibrated quite low because no one I know of even came close to normal—and twice it said that my temperature was too low to register.

- **How hot do you think you are?** ☺ Once classes started at Beijing University after five weeks of being cancelled, each class had to record and submit the temperature of each student and the teacher and the teacher had to sign the form. Again, it was to prevent SARS from being spread. The kicker is that no one actually had or used a thermometer in my class!

We all just wrote down a temperature that was below having a fever. (I could go into why this is an excellent way of saving face and not as nutty as it may look to you, but for the sake of time I'm not going to.)

- **The windblown look is IN!** One way to prevent SARS is to breathe fresh air and not be too close to others so as not to breathe in any airborne particles that may be infected. Because of this, during the height of the crisis people did not ride public transportation much. The buses and subway were eerily empty, and there were many empty cabs driving around. Those who did go out made sure that they were near an open window; I haven't ridden in a cab with the windows up in ages! (The lack of traffic was one of the very nice effects on society.)

- **Won't you be my neighbor? Oh, um, you already are . . . my mistake!** One of the highlights of SARS was the pace of life on our campus. You know that the students were sent home for over a month, which meant that the Chinese teachers suddenly had little to do. Lisa had already started playing soccer (football in British English) with anyone who wanted to play. It had mostly been other TIC teachers and the guards for our campus, but with SARS a lot of the teachers started coming out for it. I have never played soccer before, and I started for the sake of getting to know people and practicing my Chinese. I've learned some soccer vocab now and can shout "just missed it" with the best of them. I try to run around and avoid the ball and smile a lot.

But through this and the extra time people had (people either had nothing to do or were CRAZY busy), we have gotten to know many people on campus! For the first time I feel like it **is** a small community and not just a housing unit. One of the women is the gym teacher and had traveled internationally on the Chinese gymnastics team; she has such a tender heart. And guess what, she teaches aerobics! Several evenings she would teach an aerobics class on the school track. One of the benefits/curses for me of having a simple name is that she was able to remember it quite well. "Amy, straighten your knees," she sweetly commanded. How embarrassing! Anne, a fellow TICer, has started a seeker study with another of the women.

It is exciting to see breakthroughs in our relationships. Pray that we don't all slip back into the busyness of life and miss out on these relationships. It was good to be forced to slow down.

- **Hey, haven't I been here before?** One of the interesting aspects was the slogan-filled language that came out. It was representative of campaigns that would have been seen thirty years ago. Interesting to be reminded that for all of us, while things might change on the surface and the context may be different, our culture—whatever the culture may be—runs deep.

I am glad to be home, but frankly I am even gladder to be at the end of this newsletter and done with typing (smile). Those of you who know about my wrists have been wonderfully interested—thanks! I am blessed by your concern and prayers for everything from something small like my wrists to the great things God is doing in China. I am humbled.

Hot but not too bothered, ☺
Amy

#8 If You Write Newsletters

The Joys of Newsletter Writing

As you read, my hope is that you think, "I can do this. Yeah, she has her Amy take on life, but I have my own take. I don't need to over-think how others will receive my newsletters; my part is to write a good enough letter. And I can actually have fun in the process." Over the years, four great newsletter-writing joys have emerged from my experience:

3. I get to share my life with the readers! If you feel like writing newsletters is more like hustling for your worth, try a twelve-month experiment. For twelve months, type (or write) across the top of the page, "The reader cares about me. This is an opportunity to share my life and story. What one or two parts of this month can I share?" And then simply share.

4. Knowing I was going to communicate, writing newsletters has helped me to pay attention to my life and what is going on around me. The discipline of regular communication has freed me up to notice the small (and often humorous) parts of living and serving overseas. It has freed me up to trust in the long haul. No one letter bears so much weight I have to live up to the weight of the world; instead, my role is to be engaged and notice what God is up to. Phew, I can do that!

5. One summer in high school I was a volunteer tour guide at the state capitol. Best summer job ever. In essence, writing newsletters is being a bit of tour guide for one corner of the kingdom of God. I love that I got to introduce people to China, the Chinese, and how God was at work. I now get to share about what God is doing in and through Velvet Ashes. Through my newsletters, people get to see and taste God at work in the world! If I didn't write the letters, my supporters wouldn't know as much as they do.

6. I am humbled that through my newsletters, God allows me to spiritually help my supporters by providing them with opportunities to give, to pray, and to be a part of the Great Commission. Just think of how "less" their world could be without you, your letters, and your ministry. Not because you are great, but because through you they experience God at work too.

Which of these joys resonate with you?

Year Nine in China

2003-2004

How wonderful it is to be able to write someone a letter!
To feel like conveying your thoughts to a person,
to sit at your desk and pick up a pen,
to put your thoughts into words like this
is truly marvelous.
—Haruki Murakami

End of August 2003—Summer update

I'm sitting here trying to think of how to greet you in Californian since I am in Palm Springs helping out with the new teacher training. But I can't think of Californian greetings—do people say "Yo" anymore? "Hang ten"? "Dude"? Being here with the new teachers I mostly hear greetings about the temperature or meal times.

As to be expected, people have asked how my summer was. Well, honestly, it wasn't what I had expected (surprise, surprise!). I hadn't foreseen that my wrists would end up taking this much time, keeping me rooted in Denver because of the medical appointments. I thought I'd spend more time in Kansas and go on a road trip with a friend. But I didn't. I drove up and down Kipling Street on "my commute" to the doctors. And yet, in looking back, this was exactly the summer I needed. After my stressful spring, my soul needed time to recharge and spend with family. Again I am reminded that there is a plan and that the plan is good (who would have thought that tendonitis would be considered good?). And the plan often involves the stuff of daily life. I am still wearing wrist braces, doing exercises, using a galvanized hand stimulator, and trying not to type too much. I feel considerably better than I did at the beginning of the summer!

"My Reign Is Coming to an End"

One of the highlights of the summer was getting to spend time with my family and especially my niece, Ms. Emily (or Ms. Hoot). From my time with her I have learned that the words "no" and "mine" can be used much more liberally than I use them. The reason I say her reign is coming to an end is because in late August either a brother or sister will join her. But for now she is the queen bee and it was quite hard to say goodbye to the one who rode on my back, pointed, and commanded me to "RIDE."

An old woman and insurance

I received the following email in July from my former waibans at Sichuan College of Education where I had taught for five years. They were writing to let me know that my Chinese mama—Shen Yang— will no longer be able to be hired by the school to take care of the foreign teachers. This is hard for me to fully grasp in my heart as an outsider to Chinese culture, though my head logically can process the information. While I was crushed to receive the email, it highlights the continual changes that China is going through. The waibans wrote:

> One thing we want to tell you Shen Yang will leave her work because the college must sign the contract with each worker at campus also have an insurance for each. The insurance company will not give insurance to the older person. We feel so bad Shen Yang's leave. It was uneasy for us to explain this thing to Shen Yang but she is kind that she could understand the situation. For these days, we're busy in doing something for her leave. This Wednesday noon she has moved to her rented house, she is planning to run a small restaurant with her son Wang Peng.
>
> Since you've been kind to Shen Yang we think we need to tell you this, also she wants us to let you know that she'll be ok. We've done as much as we can. We hope she'll lead a good life even she isn't at the college. We've told her she could keep contacting with us if she has any difficulties. We will do our best to help her as she is considered as our mother.
>
> Ok, we have to stop here. You're welcome to be at our college at any time. We hope to see you someday.

I know that insurance is a good thing . . . but it grieves me that some company wouldn't give insurance to this "old" (sixty-five-ish) woman who is precious and probably only sees her as a disposable peasant.

Change comes with difficult choices. I am not sure how I'll be able to keep up with her now that I won't be able to write to her at Sichuan College of Education, but I hope we will stay in contact.

I'm eager to leave with the new teachers tomorrow and return to China. I've heard that the construction in the building I live in has gone well and we have running water! Yay! So as I am busy with helping in orienting all of the new teachers, I'll also be unpacking the gazillion boxes and trying to bring order to my home. It is fun to be with the new teachers and be around their energy and be reminded afresh of what an exciting journey we have been called on.

> See you in Beijing, dude!
> Amy

September 2003—By the numbers

Before reading any further, take a stab at these three brief questions:

1. How many TIC teachers do you think teach at universities or colleges in China?

2. How many new TIC teachers do you guess we had this August?

3. How many universities or colleges do you think have TIC teachers in China?

Okay, here's the deal. In talking with my mom this summer she made some reference to the 80 teachers with TIC teaching in the University Teaching Program in China (the program I work with). I just kind of looked at her with a quizzical look and said, "Ma, there are about two hundred teachers and that doesn't include spouses or children." Really? I had no idea it was that big. Knowing that if my own mother—who finds me fascinating!—didn't know the lowdown, I'm guessing you don't either. Here in a nutshell is what I do in August:

I fly out to California to meet the approximately **60** (this year) new teachers and spend six days with them in California before flying to Beijing to spend another two weeks preparing them for life and work in China. During this time I am mostly hanging out and getting to know people, so as I hear from them throughout the year or a problem arises or a decision has to be made, I have a frame of reference for who they are. The last three days the returning **140** teachers arrive and we start team training for the roughly **55** different teams/schools we are at. I am responsible for the material used in the team-building part.

Now, seeing as I can't actually know and visit all **200** teachers, there are nine Member Care Specialists (MCSs) who work with and under me to be in contact with teachers, do school visits, and keep me abreast of their teams. For six of those people, being an MCS is their full-time job/ministry and they teach four hours a week, whereas three of the MCSs do it on a part-time basis and are full-time teachers.

Are you surprised? Is it bigger than you thought? Smaller? Last year was a huge growth year for us. At this same point in the year we had **150** teachers and were at **50** campuses. Let me tell you, from this end, it does feel like we have grown!

The rest of the story

- In my last newsletter I told you about Shen Yang and how she had been let go by my school in Chengdu because they weren't able to obtain insurance for her. She was supposed to work at a restaurant her son was opening. When the waibans came to pick up the teachers in August, I found out that for some reason that plan has fallen through and Shen Yang returned to the countryside to live with her husband. I'm not totally clear on details, but the reason she left to work in the city was because he was a "bad" man. But the waibans assured me he has mellowed with age. I don't find that overly comforting! Remember her, please.

- Emily is a big sister! — in late August she was joined by Katy! I have received a video, and the Packevicz children find Emily and Katy as riveting as I do ☺ — whenever I babysit, they yell, "Do we get to see the Emily Movie?!" I have recently requested more "Emily Episodes." It is a crack-up to hear Gabe (age five) say, "Oh, the baby Katy episode is my favorite one."

- My wrists . . . well, I can say that they aren't worse, but I can't say that they are healed. It was depressing to see how the pain returned when new teacher orientation was over and I was back to typing more. I have started going to a blind masseuse in the neighborhood for an hour a day (the same one I went to after my car accident). My doctors this summer recommended acupuncture once I returned to China. Asking around in the neighborhood I found out we don't have acupuncture, but that the masseuse would be able to get the same results. It seems counterintuitive (and bordering on torture) to rub on swollen tendons for an hour, but it is helping. As I practice Lamaze-like breathing, I remind myself that no one dies from massages.

- This summer James and Aaron Lester had given me their tithe money to take the Packevicz kids to McDonald's since it is something the Lester boys like to do. Isabel, Gabe, Nate, and I went and had a great time and then stopped by the park on the way home to play for a while, until someone had to go to the bathroom . . .

Classes have begun and it seems like another good crew. Many of the MCSs have reported that the new teachers seem more serious about why we are here than we have seen in recent years. Though this has been the busiest September I have had, in the aftermath of the spring, we are in position to see great things happen.

> Knowing what the real deal is!
> Amy

October 2003—In which I smile for ten days straight

In September my parents visited for ten days. This was their second trip to visit me while living in China, the last time they were here was in 1997. Because they had been here before, we didn't have to go to the "famous" places. Instead we got to spend the time getting to know what normal daily life is like for me: where I shop, eat, and teach and whom I hang out with. Now when I talk about life in "the Mac" (the building where I live), Mom and Dad can picture the wonderful community it is—and yet it is a bit like being a resident of a funny farm. Do normal people see their coworkers in their pajamas? Do they fold their coworkers' underwear in the laundry room? Do they know when their neighbors are using the bathroom because they can hear through the walls? On the flip side, how many people know everyone in their apartment building? Or come home from a business trip and find that someone put milk in the refrigerator to welcome them home?

I have been in China long enough to know that I have lost that fresh edge of what sticks out to someone who isn't accustomed to living in China. I asked my parents if they would be willing to share a few of their impressions. My dad blessed me by getting out paper and writing without any prodding from me!

Dad wrote:

Beijing—the city of buses, taxis, private cars, trucks, bicycles, and pedestrians. It seems to have 20 percent of the population on the move at any one time. Move means in the streets, bicycle lanes, or on the subway. Move also means to "keep moving" because every moving powered vehicle, peddled vehicle, or ambulatory body around you is "calculating and executing" its course based on all the combined movements around it. Sometimes the cars and buses become gridlocked. This usually happens almost continuously at some intersections between 7:00 a.m. and 7:00 p.m. In the US it is common to call these crowded periods "rush hours"; here in Beijing you could call them "free parking." It is during these times when the bicyclers and pedestrians make faster progress.

Marsha and I walked so much the first couple of days that I said we would either go home in better condition or in a pine box. I didn't know which. As I write this, I think we will be able to fly home in equal or better condition. You don't need a Stair Master. Amy lives on the third floor, forty-nine stairs up, and you make the trip many times a day.

We were talking to Lisa, one of Amy's American friends here, about white-water rafting and motorcycling (Amy's sister has a motorcycle), and Lisa said she couldn't do either because of the risk. I said to her that she crosses major streets here in Beijing twenty times a day and is at more risk every time she is out in the intersection. How would you like to stand on a lane paint stripe in the middle of the road with cars turning in front of you and behind? From experience I can say it raises your level of anxiety. You can always thank the Protector when you get to the curb on the other side.

Mom's memories:

- Kind, friendly people; delicious food; always activity on the sidewalks (shoe repair, bicycle repair, card games, checker games, parked cars, people walking); streets teeming with crushes of cars, buses, bicycles, and pedestrians trying to cross without the help of traffic signals.

- A day spent encouraging moms as I talked three times with

different groups of mothers here at the Maclellan Center where Amy lives. They were appreciative as we shared mom to mom.

- We have gotten to see Amy in her Chinese environment—her class at BeiDa, her coworkers, her friends and family who mean so much to her, and the Chinese people for whom she came. What a blessing for us!

~~~

See what I mean about not noticing parts of life anymore? I had no idea the traffic would stand out.

On Sunday I invited a Chinese friend, Zhong Ying, over. I wanted my parents to hear her story and have the "joy" of learning how to play a Chinese card game. ☺ Learning is usually done from modeling, resulting in the Chinese not being overly good at giving clear instructions. Whenever I have tried to learn card games, usually several people are hovering over me pulling cards out of my hand and throwing them down without any explanation as to why they just made a move. I wanted my parents to have a tiny slice of what it is like to have to smile and be polite when most of you wants to snap, "You know, I'd be a better player if you were a better teacher!!!" Near the end, as I felt that my parents had learned the lesson, I said in Chinese, "You know, my parents are a little old, how embarrassing, but maybe they need a rest," and all ended well. Afterwards I received the sweetest email from Zhong Ying.

> Dear Amy:
> How are you these days since last time we meet? Do you enjoy the time with your parents? I hope your parents can enjoy their time in China.
> Thank you for your invitation of the lunch. and you are very patient in teaching me how to make the mexican taco. I think it's a quite good food. your parents are so nice that I feel they are very easy to get along with. and I love the story Koala Lou your mother told . your mother is a good story teller. and she has a heart full of love :)

While it was hard to see Dad and Mom go through the checkpoint and leave, I am humbled by how privileged I am that they got to come at all. Many teachers have parents who have no interest in coming, are financially unable to do it, or physically can't make an overseas trip. I have parents who not only came but they came and blessed our community!

With many happy memories,
Amy with help from Tom and
Marsha Young

November 2003—An encouraging word

I am in the midst of the busy travel schedule: three schools in three weeks! Normally I like to schedule a week home here and there, but due to important meetings I had to attend in October, this is the way it worked out.

Every week to ten days I write something encouraging or thought provoking to those I provide member care for and share it with the MCSs I work with—I do this to give them something to share or have a model for how to care for those they work with. I thought in this newsletter I'd include several of the emails to give you a feel for another part of my job. Thank you for all the ways you support me, allowing me to support and encourage others. A difference is being made in lives and hearts!

Love,
Amy

PS: Coming next newsletter another part of my job: a surreal banquet during a school visit where I had to slice a sheep's head during a ceremony! Oh yes, 'tis true. Just wait.

~~~

[I shared three of my emails to MCSs in the newsletter but only include one here.]

Abiding = Settling In

We are all familiar with John 15:5: "I am the vine; you are the branches. If you remain in me and I in you, you will bear much fruit; apart from me you can do nothing."

I'm doing a study now on what it means to be a person who loves, and in looking at the above verse, consider what Bruce Wilkinson says:

His purpose is not that you will do more for Him

but that you will choose to be more with Him. Only by abiding can you enjoy the most rewarding friendship with the Creator and experience the greatest abundance for His glory.

To abide means to remain, to stay closely connected, to settle in for the long term. With this picture the Son is showing the disciples how an ongoing, vital connection with Him will directly determine the amount of His supernatural power at work in their lives.[28]

I like that picture of settling in. Maybe it is because it is COLD and so I want to settle in with a warm blanket and a cup of something hot to drink. Maybe it is because I associate settling in with a fireplace and have determined that if I am ever allowed to live in the US long-term, by gum, I'm having a fireplace! Somehow, though, I think it has more to do with the idea of comfortableness and familiarity. I only settle in with people I can let my hair down and be "the real Amy" with, and this is the kind of relationship I want to have with my Father.

I want to be more than settled in for the winter; I want to be settled in with the One who is the sustaining vine. May this week be one in which we are found abiding.

Settled in,
Amy

December 2003—Highlights from the road

Well, this is long overdue, but after getting home from visiting the schools I supervise, my wrists started to act up, especially the left one. With all of the post-trip paperwork and email, I have begun to realize that I can't type the way that I would like to. Fortunately, I'm not in pain all of the time, but the main times are when I'm typing, chopping vegetables, and the tail end of sleeping. And honestly, the more I'm not at home (meaning away from my computer) the better I feel. I am in the process of trying to figure out what it means to have chronic tendonitis—my term, not a doctor's—and have a job that involves distant coworkers and email. All of that to say, I've had this letter composed a long time in my head and now will type it out so you can see a highlight from each of the three trips I made in November.

My first trip was to Zhengzhou, Henan. I have always enjoyed my time in Zhengzhou—the team is fun, the school officials involved and helpful, the city a good size, teaching is a priority, and the ministry is seeing lives changed. I look forward to my time there. What I do *not* relish about my visit is the paperwork that I have to do when I get home because it is a ten-person team! TEN people. That is a lot of classroom observations, one-on-one time, meeting with two different departments—all the while trying to get a sense of what is going well to help me encourage the team and maybe offer an outside perspective if there is anything that needs to be addressed.

But larger teams are becoming the norm for TIC. Granted, ten is a lot; we are not moving in the direction of having such large teams. But the days of two-person teams—like the one I was on for five years—are gone (out of our fifty-six teams, only four of them are two-person teams). As an organization, we are discovering what a four- or five-person team looks like. Many of the teachers in Zhengzhou had been on smaller teams and were a bit frustrated at the lack of team time and intimacy with all teammates. That's where it was nice for me to come beside them and say, "You are doing well! This is what a ten-person team looks and feels like. It doesn't feel the same as a three-person team, does it?" And there was a collective sigh of relief that they aren't doing a "bad" job.

Highlight: The reminder that life/team/teaching/society in China is changing. Am I staying abreast or trying to be a three-person team with nine other people?

Arriving home on Saturday, I was greeted by a stack of grading from the class that Lisa subbed for me. I taught on Monday and then Monday night Lisa and I boarded an overnight train for Hohhot, Inner Mongolia. Tuesday night, six school officials hosted a banquet for the six TIC teachers, Lisa, and me. We were taken to a restaurant and brought into a private room. So far all is going according to normal banquet scripts. Seated according to our level of importance in regard to that banquet, I was in the seat of honor, again, no surprise there. When an electric piano and a group of people dressed in traditional Mongolian costumes came into the room, things began to go off of the unwritten script. As they set up, one of the four or five waitresses carried in a l-a-r-g-e platter with a mock sheep's body on it. Picture this on a platter: a roasted head with a red bow on top, a pile of ribs and other hunks of meat for the body, and then a tail. The platter was set on the Lazy Susan with red candles on both sides of it and spun around to face me.

I made eye contact with one of the teachers, who had been at the school the longest, trying to figure out what was going on. She mouthed that she had never seen anything like this before and then the lights were turned off. Okay, so I have this sort of freaky sheep (with a lovely red bow) looking at me in the glow of the candlelight when the music started—at a volume loud enough to make a dog scratch its ears out. I focused on not grimacing because in the candlelight my face was the main one illuminated. When the song ended, one of the waitresses came to me (as the guest of honor) carrying a silver tray with a pair of chopsticks and a knife. It was obvious that I needed to do something with them. It was explained to me to use the chopsticks and remove the bow. All right, I can do that. Next, take the knife and cut the sheep's head. *Cut the sheep's head?* What does that mean in Mongolian culture? And am I supposed to cut it or just make a mark? And where am I supposed to cut it? I opted for the fake cut.

Next, I was told, cut it again so it looks like an "X." A small engraved bowl (more like a shot of Pepsi) was brought to me to drink. I did. Next the banquet's hosts went around the table and had all of the TIC teachers in the descending order of importance also empty a bowl—the same small bowl! Man was I glad I was first because one of the TIC teachers was quite sick. After we, the guests, had drunk from the bowl, all of the school officials each had a bowl of some kind of liquor. Finally, it was my turn to end the ceremony with one last bowl of Pepsi, so much for being the first in line! The sheep and candles were slowly moved around the Lazy Susan giving everyone a good look at the sheep (this was done for the sake of the foreigners), and then the banquet started.

Highlight: The reminder that life can take some delightful turns and one never knows when the opportunity to cut a sheep's head by candlelight might come up.

On my final trip I had three different appointments with school officials—usually the meetings are combined together to save my time and allow for all participants to hear from each other. I was a tad irritated at how the schedule worked out, but it was truly divine and I'm glad I kept my whining to myself. In the meeting with the head of the English Department, he shared how he had been taught a class called "The Bible" twenty years ago by a believing American. The class was an overview of the Good Book. He found it to be useful (he's not family . . . YET, but he's a marked man, my friends). Anyway, can you guess what class he has one of our teachers teaching? Yup—the Good Book to thirty-five graduate English majors. I observed the class and was impressed with the TIC teacher; she does some of the best note-taking EFL lectures I've ever seen. She is incredibly well prepared and professional, but man, when you are working with the Truth it is going to challenge some thinking. It was weird to be in a class where the teacher says, "Open your Bible and turn to 1 Samuel." The class read about when David took the spear and water pitcher while Saul was sleeping; she asked them if that was a wise decision or not.

Would they have done the same thing? The gal next to me said it was wise because Saul was the anointed of the Lord. Fun to hear the class discussion on this passage.

What encouraged me was the long-term chain of events. Due to the faithfulness of a man twenty years ago rightly handling what he had been entrusted, this school official was put in a place of position and influence, using it for far more than I could believe. The undergrads are now clamoring for the class and hopefully will get it next term.

Highlight: The man from twenty years ago will probably not know the ripple effects of his life until he gets to heaven. It was a great visual for me as I can be stuck in the small of now. Every so often I am zoomed up for a quick bird's-eye view, and then returned to my piece of the puzzle.

It is now the tail end of December and I have been home for a little over a month. These newsletters invite me to reflect on the lessons each month offers. In this case, adjusting with life and not against it can have unexpected delights. And the important reminder that there IS much beyond what I see. What legacy am I leaving that I will never know but others will?

Journeying on and learning lots,
Amy

January 2004—Expectations: They're everywhere

STOP. Before you read any further answer these questions:

1. Do you expect the **tone** of this newsletter to be complaining, bitter, humorous, or flippant?

2. Do you expect that I'll write **about** US history or life in China?

3. Do you expect that you will **enjoy** reading this or **dread** it? (Don't tell me!)

What are your expectations based on? I would bet that they are based on your past experience with reading newsletters in general and mine in particular. According to a little bit of Internet research, experience is the most common way that expectations are formed. You probably aren't even aware of the expectations you have in regard to reading this newsletter. However, if they aren't met, how would you feel? Disappointed? Relieved? Angry?

Before the TIC annual conference, all of the team leaders come to Chiang Mai, Thailand, for two days of additional training. As we, the leadership team, thought about the sessions that we wanted to include, it seemed that quite a few of the problems teachers have had this fall go back to the same root: unmet expectations. In preparation for the session, I have been amazed at how expectations influence many aspects of our lives. For example, according to some more Internet research, expectations influence the following factors:

- the effectiveness of medicine

- student performance

- voting behavior

- if you think you can hit a moving target (who pays for this research?)

- culture

- behavior within culture

- website quality expectations

During the session, I'm going to ask the team leaders in groups of three to think about expectations they have of the following:

- their waibans (school officials)

- their students

- teammates

- TIC

- their supporters

- their spouses/friends/kids

- Chinese food

- themselves

- our midyear conference

- the Creator

Later in the workshop I will mention that expectations go both ways and ask them what expectations they think the above have of them. We will discuss dealing with unmet expectations—a primary way to combat unrealistic expectations by becoming aware of them and then evaluating whether they are realistic or not. Because I have invested time in putting this workshop together, I have become aware of my own expectations much more than probably anyone attending the workshop will! Hopefully the workshop will not just be an academic exercise, but give the team leaders some tools for their teams as they live, work, and minister with their expectations.

On a different note, I told my students they could email me and ask for their semester grades a few days after I had given the final. I received the following from one student and share it with you because even though the Beijing Olympics are still four years off, they are a part of our reality here!

Dear Amy,

Happy New Year! Though it is late to say that, I'd like to send you my sincere regards. New Year is a new start, you will have new happy 365 days in China, and we are lucky to see you again in beautiful February. We're expecting it.

The Olympic Games will be held in Greece this year, if my memory is right. It's one of the most important things for our students. The competitions will be stirring. We will enjoy watching it. I think we will learn from it and prepare for the Olympic Games which will be held in Beijing, 2008. I cherish the chance to study English with you. If I can use English fluently, I will try my hard to do some contributions to the Olympic Games in 2008. So I will work hard next term.

Thank you for your great help. Your encouraging words always make me happy and confident. I'm sorry to say that I did a bad job in the final examination. I failed to remember some definitions, such as expediency. But because I failed, I remember them deeply now. ^_^ Thanks for the examination. I want to know my score, would you mind to tell me? No matter what it is, I will be happy. The most important is to master what you taught us, not the score I believe.

Have a good holiday! Don't miss to watch some traditional Chinese performances in Beijing. Send our good wishes to Lisa. She is so pretty, we like her.

sincerely, Yang Dan

Today the department head called and told me my schedule for next term. I've adjusted to the reality that I won't find out much ahead of time and now don't *expect* to. ☺ Thankfully I will get to teach the same students!

Expecting good things
in the spring,
Amy

PS: I was reminded this past week of how much protection I have. I was in another car accident! Very, very thankfully, I wasn't hurt . . . sadly, the same thing cannot be said for the car. We rear-ended the car in front of us, causing the hood of the cab I was in to be shoved to half of the normal length. I tell you, nobody else here in Beijing from TIC has been in a car accident and now I've had two! It looks like I'm trying to take the 1.2 RMB (the price per kilometer) cabs out one at a time! ☺ Praise be for the safety I walk in every day.

Late February 2004—Upcoming changes

For some of you this newsletter is going to be a big surprise, for others it will be a chance to fill in some blanks. Since I'm writing for a rather wide audience, humor me as I back up and provide background information. As you know, a major part of my job is to watch over and help TIC's field supervision. It has been a primary focus the last three years, and I love it! I can't believe that this is what I get to do with my time. This sort of job wasn't mentioned in ninth grade career day, so I had no idea such a fulfilling and eternally important "job" existed. I can see how my gifting, interests, and experiences come together to allow me to work with a wide variety of people.

Have I mentioned that I absolutely LOVE my job—I am humbled by how teachers invite me into their lives, their hearts, their joys, and their struggles. I am amazed at how the Creator has allowed me to be involved all over China in small ways. With the privilege of being allowed into people's lives, I am often invited into sticky situations. In these I describe myself as a "barefoot counselor."[5] Last spring I began sensing that after this academic year I was being led to come back to the US to receive training in this area. The training will enable me to lead the field supervisors more effectively and be in a position to train and equip them more effectively to serve. I am impressed with the historical commitment TIC has towards member care. Member care is not just a bullet on a mission statement, as you can tell from all my traveling. That being said, I can see how we could readily benefit from having a trained professional on the field. And while the thought of leaving China for a few years is hard even to type, let alone to do, I am the person whom He is raising up to lead this change.

Ironically, even though I have served overseas for almost nine years, my gifting does not lie with sharing the good news or even in follow-up. Often I felt embarrassed about this—why weren't more students coming to Him? Am I a failure as a Christ follower? But as I became more involved in leadership, I realized my gifting isn't to work with the Chinese students as with the TIC teachers and free them up to use their giftings. Don't get me wrong, I still do a lot with students and maintain relationships with former students, study the language with a tutor, and my heart sings to live in China—but in terms of my gifting, He has given me the type of personality that can be in relationship with almost any personality.

I have been in many situations that make me more approachable to our teachers. God is good at using the stuff from our lives—be they team, teaching, medical, or family situations. I am at a place in my life where I can look back and begin to see glimpses of how He is weaving parts of my life together for His glory and purpose and to feel surer of the gifts He has given me.

While the call on my life has been the same for the last thirteen years (serving in China), this has been a reflective season; seeing how He has been growing the call and adapting the journey as my knowledge and maturity develop. If you would have told me thirteen years ago that I would be pursuing a counseling degree, I probably would have scoffed, "Yeah, right." Yet here I am, and it is good. I have applied to and been accepted by a local seminary and will start studying in September for another MA, this one to become a licensed counselor.

---

5 The term "barefoot doctor" is from Chinese history, most recently the Cultural Revolution. In an attempt to provide medical care to the rural areas, farmers were trained in basic medical skills and viewed as a primary health care provider at the grassroots level.

~~~

And now for the answers to the questions I was asked over and over in Thailand as it became known I will be in the States next year. I bet you are wondering too.

1. **What about your furniture?** Okay, maybe that wasn't your first question, but through this process I have been reminded of how I tend to cling to certain things for control and security. For some reason, *furniture* has been a recurring theme in my China experience. Jenny Martin works as one of the field supervisors and has agreed to take over being Member Care Director and to live in my apartment! Which will become her apartment. But it is helpful not to have to deal with shipping all of my stuff to the US for two to three years, only to have to ship it all back later. Isn't that cool?!

2. **Are you, like, still with TIC or what?** Like, I am. I am blazing a "study trail," and while in Thailand I needed to work out a few details with the home office. TIC has traditionally been more of a short-term organization, without a mechanism for people to leave the field for more than a year without severing the work relationship. But as we are moving towards being a more long-term organization, we know that we need resources to support personnel. Thus, while my body will be in America, I will still be officially "with TIC."

3. **Not to be tacky, but, um, well, you know, money?** Not to be tacky, but, um, you know, that wasn't actually a question, wink. But I understand where you are coming from. I have found that money can be a touchy subject and people don't always feel comfortable discussing it. (Except for my Chinese friends who are FAR more comfortable than I am discussing salary!) I am still with TIC and will continue to be on support. I plan to live with my parents and house sit for anyone who asks as a way to avoid rent—thanks, Mom and Dad; we're going to have a great time! And by staying on support it will enable me to focus on my studies and continue to be involved with TIC (I'll tell you more later so that this letter doesn't get too long). I know that for some of you, this is the first time you have had someone you support return to the US for study and are not sure if this is how you should invest in the Kingdom. That is okay. I have been

given assurance that this is what I am to do and that I will be provided for. If you are led to shift where your support money goes, I understand.

4. **Two to three years is a long time. Um, well, what if you get married? Are you, really coming back?** Oh, for heaven's sake, can a single person not do something without the subject coming up? I even had one of the leaders in Beijing say to me (as we were discussing what to do with my furniture before I knew there was a home for my beloved dears), "You know you're going to fall in love and jiaozi is going right out the window." I wanted to throw him out the window! To compare the Call to meat dumplings got me boiling and fuming for a while. Yes, life is going to happen. I may be in a bad car accident or something terrible may happen to someone in my family, which would require a change of plans. *And* getting married doesn't preclude returning. That being said, no, I can't see all the way down the road to know exactly where it leads, but know that I am to start down it and just keep . . . um, well, living!

In some ways this isn't the most convenient of times to go (there is a huge field leadership change in TIC), but you know what, big life-altering decisions rarely come at convenient times. And convenience shouldn't be the standard for obedience. While there is much to be sad about if I choose to leave, I am choosing to focus on what I'm gaining, not losing. Of course the months ahead will be sprinkled with tough moments. Change is not easy. But then I think of the Broncos games I'll go to with my dad and the tea parties with my nieces and the movies I'll see on a BIG screen and the ticket(s) I might get for speeding—because you never know what may happen. ☺

Back to, um, well, living!
Amy

March 2004—A roll of film

I recently finished a roll of film on my camera. Several friends have digital cameras. When they whip them out, I'll ask them to take my picture and email it to me so I can use it in my newsletters. These pictures all came from one roll and give a nice snapshot of the last few months.

[Remember when we used to have rolls of film? The joy of picking up the developed pictures and seeing how well the pictures turned out . . . sometimes even being reminded what events were captured! I enjoy the convenience and immediate feedback of digital cameras, but I miss some of the routines related to film development. Obviously this newsletter was mostly photos and a few captions.]

Still clicking away,
Amy

April 2004—Things that make me smile

The quirkiness of life in the last few weeks has brought a smile to my face. Some moments because they are endearing, some because they capture what is uniquely China that I will miss, and others because they are uniquely China but that I won't miss! ☺

- While on my trip to Inner Mongolia this spring, I learned that the school is having an evaluation by the Ministry of Education in September. The evaluation will influence how much money the school will receive from the government. Understandably, the entire school is consumed by this upcoming inspection. What caught my interest is that there is to be no summer holiday. For anyone. No students will go home. All teachers will teach. All personnel will work. And I smiled. For several reasons. First (and selfishly), because it didn't affect me at all! Second, because I tried to project this onto the States. Can you imagine the uproar if a school announced that there would be no summer vacation? Oh, my cow.

But it works. And while the teachers and students aren't happy, they will stay all summer and hopefully the inspection will be a success. On a more important note, this has been a fruitful spring for the teachers. All of the teachers will be leaving for various reasons, please remember the new team that will have to teach students who have been in classes for months without a break. Think of them and smile.

- Knowing that I have had a special relationship to Beijing traffic, any article on the subject catches my eye. Here is a short excerpt from a recent article with a question from the driver's test. How would you answer the question?

Love, Amy

"Carnage on World's Deadliest Roads" (April 7, 2004, *AFP*)[29]

> The mainland's roads are fast becoming death traps as 11 million new drivers take to the streets each year without proper training—making the country's highways the world's deadliest. Accidents are so common that one question in the written driver's exam asks: "If you come across an accident and see an unconscious motorist with his internal organs lying on the road, should you pick up the organs and place them back inside the person?"

- One Sunday I was walking home from my friend Erin Dittmer's house and ran into an old man friend I have in the neighborhood. He hadn't seen me for a while and wondered if I had been in the US getting married. He keeps checking! I'll give him points for consistency! Nope, not married. *"Do you have a boyfriend?"* Nope. *"How old are you again?"* Hoping that I have been experiencing anti-aging! Um, thirty-six. He's still holding my hand from shaking it when we greeted. *"You HAVE to get married before you are forty. You have to!"* I tried to divert him by asking about his health. He gave me this disgusted look that implied, "We need to stay focused here." Still holding my hand and gently pumping it up and down, he said, *"You have to get married before you are forty or"* — he starts patting his stomach— *"your uterus won't be open!"* *As we parted, I continued on my way home, smiling.*

- Yesterday Lisa and I had the students over for a barbecue. The first week of May is a weeklong break. The class before the May holiday I told the students it would be fun to have them over and maybe we could cook outside. They said that they'd probably come over in small groups at their convenience and not have a class barbecue. I was a little disappointed, but hey, whatever. Wednesday night, during the holiday, at 9:30 p.m. a student called and said that a group would come the next day for the BBQ and would it be okay if some of them brought other friends. Um, well, given the fact that I had a meeting all Thursday morning working on August training for new teachers and the slight problem of food for a class BBQ for lunch the next day, no, it wouldn't work. We scheduled the cookout for Friday and had fun! About ten came (without friends). These comments made me smile:

"Amy, this is so interesting! Chinese grills are usually long rectangular and not convenient to have in your own home. Do most Americans have a grill like this? That must be wonderful." (The building I live in owns a round charcoal grill.)

The building has a lovely large flower garden, and while we were having our cookout a few of the TIC kids were playing near us. Two of the children have recently turned two, and this observation was made as they ran around: "Foreign children are not as stable as Chinese children." I wanted to ask how many Chinese two-year-olds run around without a parent holding them or hovering closely; but sometimes foreign tongues are not as stable as Chinese ones and it was a time for being quiet.

"Hey boy, come here." This was said numerous times to six-year-old Gabe. I repeatedly nudged, "His name is Gabe," and wanted to add that there was no way a six-year-old was going to come to a stranger saying, "Hey boy, come here."

In introducing the students how to put a hot dog together, we showed them ketchup, mustard, and onions and used bread instead of buns. Great confusion arose over what mustard was. The easiest way to explain mustard was to put a little on a plate and have them use their pinky to taste it for themselves. The verdict? "It tastes like Chinese medicine!"

And my favorite came when we were making s'mores: "It's like cooking and playing all in one! They are sweet to eat, but we were all talking and if we were children, we would have LOVED them."

What a delightful description, "cooking and playing all in one!" As my weeks are numbered, many reasons to smile exist with much to be thankful for. I am reminded of a quote from *The Pilgrim's Regress* by C.S. Lewis: "Be sure it is not for nothing that the Landlord has knit our hearts so closely to time and place—to one friend rather than another and to one shire more than all the land."[30] I am thankful for the knitting that has taken place and for the many opportunities to smile and rejoice.

Smilingly,
Amy

June 2004—The last hurrah: Going to Harbin

Traditionally on a Chinese train you could purchase four types of tickets. From cheapest to most expensive: hard seat, soft seat, hard sleeper (like a triple bunk bed and open compartment), and soft sleeper (closed compartments with bunk beds and four people per compartment). Most trains had all four; if they didn't it was because of distance, with shorter trains only having seats and some longer trains having a majority of sleepers. In April a new type of train started around China that only had soft sleeper compartments and something I call "super soft sleeper" compartments. The SSS—I've heard—only have two people per compartment and a sink! I'm not sure if they had a toilet or if that is still at the end of the compartment.

Two TIC teachers in Harbin have fallen in love and will marry this August. Because most of us will not be able to go to their wedding in the States, they had a "wedding party" (Chinese thing) for their students and friends to be able to attend. Lisa and I decided to take the train up to Harbin for the weekend and attend the party.

Before April it would not have been a problem to get hard sleepers, which are approximately half the cost of a soft sleeper ticket. Well, you guessed it, there are now few trains from Beijing to Harbin that have hard sleepers! The vast majority are these new fancy-schmancy trains. For the sake of adventure, I was happy to have the chance to ride on one of them; for the sake of economy and the fact that I didn't have a choice of the type of ticket I bought, I was a little irritated.

Boarding the train, the only difference I could see in the compartments was that a small TV screen had been built into the foot of each bed and once the train left the station movies were shown on three or four channels. Headphones were included so you wouldn't disturb others—I know that this would not even need to be stated regarding most public transportation in the States, but the fact that there wasn't news or music blaring over the PA system is quite a change!

Another nice change was the excrement collection system. Previously the squat toilets (and Western ones in soft sleepers) opened on to the track. When you were in a station, the bathrooms were locked in order for the tracks at the stations to remain excrement free. The only problem was that if you needed to go to the bathroom, some stops were longer than others. Yikes! The new trains have a lovely booklet outlining in Chinese and English the "service facilities on train" and gave the following description to the toilets: "Toilet: an excrement and urine vacuum collection equipment is adopted, the excrement and urine will be drawn to a sewage box by the vacuum for concentrated handling, the method may avoid pollute the environment along the railroad. Please press the rinsing switch after sh------." Oh yes, it does say sh--!

So far this final adventure had been worth the price of admission.

We arrived an hour late. The train was supposed to be a direct trip with no stops (so, one might argue, no need for the vacuum collecting system for excrement ☺), but for some reason the train stopped in the middle of the night for about an hour.

Our friends actually teach at two different schools in Harbin and were having a wedding party at each school to allow all of their students a chance to come. We decided to go to the morning party, giving us the rest of the day to explore and experience the "pearl under swan's neck" (that train brochure was coming in handy). Even though we were an hour late, we were not too late to see the hairstylist do Bridget's hair. Truly a sight to behold. I think every hair was sprayed into place and given an extra spray—why not? Final touch? Glitter. Lots of glitter. I have to admit I was a bit jealous about the glitter, though Lisa thought I was being ridiculous (Lisa is kind of an anti-glitter person).

Traditionally at Chinese weddings firecrackers are set off. Sort of like the glitter . . . lots and lots. But in the cities firecrackers are illegal. The modern solution? Balloons! In particular, a massive red-and-pink balloon arch at the wedding. The arch was mostly a photo op at the party. However, at the second party the aisle was lined with balloons. As Ben and Bridget walked, friends walked near them with pins popping balloons as they went. Voila! The noise you want at a fraction of the cost!

Harbin is famous for tigers. I admit I didn't know this before I went to Harbin (begging the question, how famous are the tigers? But literally every place is famous for something—wine, TVs, silk, soy sauce, why not tigers?). We had heard that at the Siberian Tiger Park you could buy food to feed the tigers ranging in price from strips of meat to dead chickens to live chickens—more expensive because more exciting to see the tigers chase them, we heard—to live deer. The deer were outrageously expensive and I think would mainly have been bought by a company that was entertaining employees.

The park is located outside of the town, and we got a taxi driver to take us out, wait for us, and then bring us back into the city. The roads near the park were under construction, resulting in parts that felt like we were four-wheeling on a dirt road; each bump seemed to raise the doubt of a real park existing this far out of town. Were we that near to tigers? And then, we were at the park.

Picture a safari park where you ride around in a van looking at the tigers and lions, driven from one locked and secure area to the next. Lisa and I were in a van with Japanese and Chinese tourists who kept opening their windows and banging on the side of the van to get the tigers' attention. There are times when I sense that I have adapted to China and do things in the Chinese way; there are others when I feel the American in me roaring to the surface. It took a lot not to remind everyone that these were WILD animals with sharp teeth who like to eat live chickens and having the windows open, while, yes, was a bit exciting, might not be the wisest move and that everybody should sit down (as we had been told) and keep their appendages in the van (as we had been told). The rules were not being followed and it was pushing internal buttons for this American.

Fortunately we visited the park around noon when it was rather hot, which helped the animals to be sluggish. And I suppose that we were probably the twentieth van that had driven by that day making such a ruckus. With countless vans banging through the day before. The tigers probably think that the vans just make that noise.

After riding around we were dropped off at the feeding area, and sure enough plenty of signs reminded us we could buy meat strips, dead chickens, live chickens and deer. But no one was around to sell the items. I'm guessing that since it was noon, the workers were having lunch. The tigers were lying around (due to the heat) and didn't look hungry. We walked past a place where you could hold a baby tiger and have your picture taken. Knowing we probably wouldn't get to hold a baby tiger in an American zoo, Lisa and I jumped at the chance! The baby tiger was a month old and was fine when I held him but was a little bit frisky when it was Lisa's turn.

We bounced our way back in to town and later that evening caught the train back to Beijing. With no stops, we arrived on time and were back at work by 8:30 a.m. What a way to end this phase of being in China. In a nutshell I was reminded that China is changing rapidly (that train would have only been a dream when I first arrived), some things will always be different (I don't foresee popping balloons becoming a wedding trend across the States), and being at a wedding party surrounded by students who love their teachers is a slice of the heart of TIC.

Yes, it is interesting to hold tigers and ride new trains, but there will always be new technology and interesting things to do. If we are not engaged in relationships and making a difference in people's lives, it is like we are just driving around banging the side of the van.

Enjoying the trip,
Amy

PS: My next letter will be written after I have returned to the US and started classes. Prayers welcome with the goodbyes, hellos, and adjusting from being a leader in China to a student in America.

#9 If You Write Newsletters
Three Final Practical Tips for Your Newsletters

These tips were modified from a blog post I wrote for Velvet Ashes.[31]

Make it easy for supporters—This first one is born out of my own personal experience this year *as a supporter*. I started supporting someone who moved to the field a few months ago . . . at least I think she did. I have not heard from her. Recently I was meeting with a friend who is in the process of raising support himself, and I told him this very tip: make it easy for supporters. "Take our mutual friend, I haven't heard from her." He looked at me confused and said, "But she blogs."

Clearly I am a fan of blogging, as this first appeared on a blog. A blog can be one tool in communicating with supporters, but here is why I believe it cannot be the primary tool: you are putting the responsibility for communication on your supporters. Now that I know the gal I support has a blog, guess who is a tad annoyed that I have to track down the info to hear about her? Yup, the person she wants not to be annoyed over something trivial, like tracking down a URL.

If you use blogs as your primary way of communicating, may I offer two additional recommendations? First, still have an email list and quarterly send out an email with links to the blogs. Deliver the news to them; put the onus for communication on you, not them. Second, blogs (unless password protected) are public, very public. This is a neutral fact. You can share more when you know the whole world or a random stranger is not going to be reading it.

Use strong verbs—Let's be honest, weak verbs are easier to write. They just are. So, instead of stressing over your verbs and getting all in your head, write your newsletter and then go back. Go back and look for two weak verbs and make them stronger. Don't strengthen every verb. How to kill the joy, right? But over time, slowly, your verbs will get stronger.

What am I talking about? Look for this phrase *"There was"*—or some form of it (there is, there were)—because it is a weak verb alert.

There was a man on the bus who was getting in my personal space.

Instead of "was" (a weaker verb), how about this:

#9 If You Write Newsletters

On the bus a man encroached on my personal space. It took every fiber in my being not to back away; I kept uttering the pre-field training mantra for personal space in this country: "my space is your space." In the battle between "was" vs. "encroached," it is not even close.

Consistency is more important than content—Let's be honest again: given how much time we can spend writing a newsletter, don't you kind of hope your supporters basically memorize them? Or at least do more than scan? When I met with the young man raising support last week, I stressed, "If you ask people a year later what you said in July, they probably will not remember. But if you asked them if they hear from you, that question they can answer." Do not overthink what you are going to write. Just write something and ship it. Get it in their hands. If you think the letter wasn't great, move on. Trust that the Holy Spirit will give you an idea for your next communication. Live, minister, write, rinse, repeat.

Which tip do you need to experiment with?

Conclusion

The one good thing about not seeing you
is that I can write you letters.
— Svetlana Alliluyeva

Dear Reader,

When I first set out to write this book, I thought it would contain all twenty years of my newsletters. I wanted to show what it could look like for the long haul to write newsletters. How they can morph over time as location, amount of experience, and roles change.

Obviously, my plan changed. I know the word count range most nonfiction books fall into, and I thought the twenty years would fall within the range. By year six I thought to myself, "Houston, we have a problem." Clearly I had no idea how many words twenty years of letters contain. Can you imagine if I had included all twenty years? Neither can I. Instead of cutting out parts of the story, I decided to focus on one leg of the journey.

Our world is one that loves big, change-the-world stories. I love them too. Part of me wishes my newsletters contained throngs and multitudes coming to Christ because of my work. I thought that is what a "real" cross-cultural worker would do. Don't we all want our lives to matter? I believed that mattering was measurable. By compiling and writing this book the lesson *Love, Amy* has taught me is that too often we confuse size with significance. I still hear the whisper that says, "Amy, really? You wrote about the cultural beliefs that influence standing in line and you think that is worth people giving of their prayer, money, and time?" I am tempted to downplay the importance of understanding culture or that culture is a doorway to connection and hearts. Part of me is reluctant even now to publish these letters because they are common. In truth, I am happy with my life and the contributions I have made. Of course I have regrets and wish I'd handled certain situations differently. But if all we hear are the spectacular stories, we can miss the gift our beautifully ordinary lives can be.

Who made it into the Gospels? A widow and her two mites. A boy and his few fish. She is described as offering out of her poverty. His common lunch was used to feed more than he could have imagined. Jesus did not tend to elevate those in power or those who seemed impressive.

"You're lucky you're still in your first year. Wait until your second year and you have told all your stories. You'll have nothing to say in your newsletters." Isn't that the heart of what we fear: that we will have nothing to say with our lives? The secret to combating this fear is not that secretive. Show up and be present. Taken individually, these letters don't add up to much; but put them together and to my surprise, month after month I wrote an accidental memoir.

Who knows, you may be baking in an accidental bakery or teaching in an accidental school, or feeding the hungry in an accidental soup kitchen, or reading books in an accidental library. The accidental life you are living isn't as accidental as it may seem. Show up and be present because your days are adding up and you, too, are feeding more than you can see.

Thanks for going on this journey with me. I'd love to hear how you are doing. Drop me a line at amy@messymiddle.com.

Love,
Amy

Glossary of Names

Alice—Alice is the English name for one of my Chinese students at Sichuan College of Education. We maintained contact after she graduated and I was able to visit and guest lecture at the school where she taught.

Anna—Anna is the English name for one of my Chinese students at Sichuan College of Education. She became a dear friend as I would bike over to her apartment on Tuesdays and we spent hours together as she taught me to cook.

Anne—Anne was my teammate in Beijing. If you read *Looming Transitions*, Anne is my friend who is a post-griever while I am a pre-griever. This is but one of many lessons I've learned from our friendship. Anne is the wife of Mike and mother of Isabel, Gabe, Nate, and Tommy.

Carrie—Carrie is the English name for one of my Chinese students at Sichuan College of Education. I cannot help but think of simple English played at loud volume when I think of her.

Cynthia—Cynthia joined TIC at the same time I did. We went through pre-field orientation together and Cynthia was assigned to teach in the city closest to Chengdu (where I was assigned). In a time before easy travel or connection via the Internet, people assigned to the same region have a special bond. To this day, Cynth is a dear friend.

Dae—Dae was only my teammate for one year in Beijing. Too short! But thanks to our mutual love of Jesus, a good laugh, and the NFL, one year was enough to establish eternal ties!

Deborah—After college my friend Kim worked for several years at a church in Scotland. At that time Deborah was ten-years-old. To this day I am friends with the Petrie clan and Debs is well into adulthood. If we do get palaces in heaven, I am going to live in Scone

Glossary of Names

Palace[6]—though it will be more like Scone Cabin. You are all welcome to visit; a cup of tea and a scone may not be needed in heaven the way they are now, but they will still be lovely all the same.

Del—Del is the best brother-in-law in the world.

Dr. Smith—Dr. Smith was a British neurologist who "happened" to be working in Chengdu when I was deathly ill. His conversations with my parents—who were in the US—left them wondering if he was real or an angel.

Elizabeth—Elizabeth is my sister, friend, and cheerleader. She is the family member who was able to visit me the most when I was in China. If you too have people who get passports, visas, buy expensive plane tickets, and rearrange their schedules just to be with you . . . You know how inadequate this sentence is to express the gratitude of being known in your "foreign" context.

Emily—My oldest niece, Emily turned me into a hypocrite in the best sense. After rolling my eyes at aunts and uncles who gushed about nieces and nephews, I got it. And then I lead the Gushing Parade. Nieces and nephews are amazing. They simply are. Emily, you opened my eyes to this universal truth.

Erin DeRoos—Erin and I were teammates my first two years in Chengdu. Erin was also new to the field, and those first two years were filled with many shared adventures!

Erin Dittmer—Though "Erin" is not an overly common name, I had two significant Erins in my life! Erin Dittmer and I were teammates in Beijing for several years, taught at Beida together, and remained friends throughout the years.

Gabe— Now a grown man, at the time of these letters, Gabe was a child. But more than that, he was my teammate and I love him. He gave me the nickname A*M*Y. He is the son of Mike and Anne and the brother of Isabel, Nate, and Tommy.

Isabel—Now a grown woman, at the time of these letters, Isabel was a child. But more than that, she was my teammate who

---

6 Scone Palace is a real place that has little to do with scones. Scone Cabin will be all about actual scones

consistently showed me she cared about me. I love her. She is the daughter of Mike and Anne and the sister of Gabe, Nate, and Tommy.

James—Sichaun College of Education has a relationship with a small Christian Liberal Arts College in the US. Visiting scholars came two springs and exchange students came one fall. James was a six-month foreign exchange student who lived in the same hallway I did at the Sichuan College of Education.

Jason—Jason is the English name of Mark's Chinese friend who wanted to practice English. When Mark returned to the US, he became our friend.

Joann—Joann is my teammate and coworker in Beijing. Our friendship continues and you can read about some of our adventures in her book The Bells Are Not Silent: Stories of Church Bells in China.

JoDee—JoDee is the friend of my friend Kim. JoDee, Kim, and Natalie visited me when I lived in Chengdu.

John and Barb White—The Whites were in my parent's Bible study when I was a child and remain family friends. Mr. White (aka John) had clients that brought him to China often enough that he got to see where I lived in both Chengdu and Beijing.

Katy—Katy is my second niece. I did not get to meet her in person until she was ten months old. Watching videos of her as a baby helped to bridge the distance. Katy helped me to see that her sister wasn't a fluke . . . it turns out all nieces are amazing.

Kim—Kim and I met in the hallowed halls of the University of Kansas and have been life-long friends ever since. I have been on more continents with Kim than any other person I know. Not everyone has friends who will visit them multiple times on foreign soil. I am blessed!

Lan-lan—Lan-lan is Shen Yang's granddaughter. She lived on an off with her grandma who lived in the same floor we did at Sichuan College of Education.

Laura—My sister, friend, and cheerleader, Laura (and Elizabeth) came to visit me a year after I nearly died. Their visit brought several special memories that have added to our "sister vocabulary." Red Panda anyone?

Liesl—Liesl was my teammate for two years in Beijing. If you have a Liesl in your life you are blessed. Her energy and enthusiasm breathe life into any situation.

Lisa—A fellow coworker in Beijing who has turned into a life long friend, Lisa enriched my time in Beijing. Though we now live miles apart, God has kept us on similar life paths. I am grateful for the ways Lisa loved my shenanigans and me!

Mark—Mark taught at Sichuan College of Education the year before Erin and I were assigned to teach at SCE. Our first year in China, he studied Sichuan Opera[7] and then returned to the US to get married.

Marsha Young—Or as I call, Marsha Young, Mom.

Mike—Mike is my teammate and coworker in Beijing. Working with Mike, Joann, and others was one of the most positive ministry and leadership experiences of my life. Because of that season I know that life, ministry, and leadership can be positive and rewarding; Mike is the husband of Anne and father of Isabel, Gabe, Nate, and Tommy.

Natalie—Natalie is the friend of my friend Kim. JoDee, Kim, and Natalie visited me when I lived in Chengdu.

Nate—Now nearing adulthood, at the time of these letters, Nate was born and a young child. But more than that, he was my teammate and I love him. He is the son of Mike and Anne and the brother of Isabel, Gabe, and Tommy.

Paul—Sichaun College of Education has a relationship with a small Christian Liberal Arts College in the US. Visiting scholars came two springs and exchange students came one fall. Paul was a visiting art scholar and I still smile to think of Xiao Feng having to translate for Paul's class when he had the students draw "nudies."

---

7 Chinese opera comes in hundreds of forms, you might have heard for Beijing Opera (or Peking Opera). Many regions have their own style. Sichuan Opera was known for having clowns and Mark has been a clown in a circus in America

Peter—Peter is the English name for one of my Chinese students at Sichuan College of Education. He became a dear friend and I cannot thank him enough for helping me to see the world through Chinese eyes on certain political topics. He also helped me understand how trapped in their lives many of his generation felt.

Robbie—Robbie is the English name for one of my Chinese students at Sichuan College of Education. Like Peter, I owe much to Robbie for his friendship and willingness to answer questions as I learned how very similar and different Chinese and American culture are. One semester he taught me tai chi.

Shelley—Shelley and I were teammates for three years in Chengdu. Shelley shared a love of watching movies, one of the few entertainment options in the era before DVD's or live streaming.

Shen Yang—Shen Yang is my Chinese mama. I did not know you could love someone this deeply when vocabulary was lacking on both sides. We have lost touch due to China's changing insurance laws and Sichuan College of Education needing to let her go. But even as I type this, my heart is swelling a bit. I miss her dearly.

Simie—Sichaun College of Education has a relationship with a small Christian Liberal Arts College in the US. Visiting scholars came two springs and exchange students came one fall. Simie was a six-month foreign exchange student who lived in the same hallway I did at the Sichuan College of Education.

Steve—Steve studied Chinese in Chengdu and we worshipped together in the small foreign fellowship that met in our apartments at Sichuan College of Education.

Sue—Sue is the best sister-in-law in the world.

Tom Young—Or as I call Tom Young, Dad.

Tommy—Now nearing adulthood, at the time of these letters, Tommy was born and a young child. But more than that, he was my teammate and I love him. He is the son of Mike and Anne and the brother of Isabel, Gabe, and Nate.

Varland Family—Sichaun College of Education has a relationship with a small Christian Liberal Arts College in the US. Visiting scholars came two springs and exchange students came one fall. Roger was a visiting art scholar and brought his wife Deb and their two kids.

Wendy—Wendy is the English name for one of my Chinese students at Sichuan College of Education. After she graduated, she lived near SCE and we were able to continue our friendship. I visited her father's school several times as a guest lecture.

Xiao Feng[8]—Xiao Feng worked in the *waiban* (the Foreign Affairs Office) all five years I was at SCE.

Xiao Luo—Xiao Luo worked in the *waiban* (the Foreign Affairs Office) for four of the five years I was at SCE.

Xiao Yang—Xiao Yang worked in the *waiban* (the Foreign Affairs Office) my last year at SCE.

---

8   *Xiao* means "Miss" or "Mister" and is used with someone who is younger than you

Acknowledgements

When I get a book, I love to read the acknowledgements before I start reading (hello to you who are reading this first!). Often an author will leave breadcrumbs about the project, their process, and share a bit about their relational context. *Love, Amy* unofficially started many years ago with my first newsletter. At that time I had no idea the letters would turn into a book or that I would still be writing newsletter more than two decades later. Officially it came to be after *Looming Transitions* was born into the world and caught me off-guard.

First, after having been told that it was not worth the commercial risk, I hoped God would help *Looming Transitions* get into a few hands that needed her. He did and I am grateful. But much to my surprise, after nearly twenty years *on the field,* almost overnight I became more known for helping people transition *off the field.* I thought of myself as one who *stayed* rooted for the long haul. I wanted to help people not only come and go well, but stay well too. In considering what had been one of the greatest frustrations I heard from fellow workers over the years, writing newsletters, I thought: I can help.

This book would never have been possible if these letters had not been read in relative obscurity for years. To my family, friends, supporters, and churches that sent me, supported me, loved me, and never wearied of hearing from me, thank you.

To my TIC family who did life with me, I was reminded as I reread and edited these letters how unbelievably dull my life would be without you. Thank you.

To my Chinese students and friends I am humbled how you took in a loved a young foreign woman who came in knowing almost nothing about your culture and history and made more mistakes than one person is often allotted for an entire lifetime. Thank you.

To the TIC communication department who faithfully formatted, printed, and mailed these newsletters, quietly serving both the writer and the reader. You are undervalued and overlooked. Thank you.

Too often the writer's life is isolated and lonely. Thankfully, I am the exception! To my writer groups, you each play a special role in rooting me in community, cheering me on, and answering questions. KB Mastermind, you held me to my goals, you are the midwives of this book. The Inkwell, you answered grammar questions, supported me through several life curveballs, and help me stay in love with this writing life. Writers on the Rock, because you are local, you actually hear me laugh out loud, share your writing journeys at our monthly meetings, and dream about Denver being the Nashville of the writing world. Thank you.

To The Messy Middle and Velvet Ashes communities: thank you for being drawn to throwing your lot in with others for the long haul too. Thank you being my kind of people and letting me be yours.

To those who helped with this particular project—Davita Freeman, Vanessa Mendozzi, Deb Hall, Tanya Marlow, Amy Boucher Pye, Cecily Willard, Britta Lafont, and Andy Bruner—thank you.

I thank my God every time I remember you.
Philippians 1:3

About the Author

Amy Young is a writer, speaker, and advocate for embracing the messy middle of your one glorious life. Author of *Looming Transitions, Twenty Two Activities for Families in Transition,* and *The Looming Transitions Workbook,* she also created the blog The Messy Middle (http://www.messymiddle.com), has been a part of Velvet Ashes from the beginning, and contributes regularly to A Life Overseas. Amy enjoys nothing more than being with her people, wherever they are in the world. She can be found cheering on the Denver Broncos and Kansas Jayhawks. Currently she lives in Denver, and much to her surprise, enjoys gardening.

Coming soon: A short ten lesson newsletter writing course. To be notified of its release, you will first receive 14 Tools for Navigating the Messy Middle (http://bit.ly/2nWSEkB) for free.

To help this book find its way into other hands, please leave a review of *Love, Amy* on Amazon.

Endnotes

1. Many organizations in creative access countries will have correspondence guidelines to help friends and family know what can be communicated. In essence, it is not illegal to be a Christian, so it is okay to ask about a person's own spiritual walk or to offer to pray for them. However, any form of criticizing the government or speaking openly about any "missionary" activity would not be okay. Instead, people could speak creatively about aspects of sharing their faith such as "knee time" or "we are thinking about you."

2. Teaching at a College of Education meant that our students were junior and senior middle school teachers. Junior middle school would be similar to seventh to ninth grade in the US and senior middle school covers tenth to twelfth grades. They had received a two-year certificate before and had been given the chance for two more years of education. Even though many were married and had a child, the chance for more education was worth being away from their family.

3. November's newsletter had a number of pictures with descriptions from daily life, thus I will only include the beginning and ending of the letter.

4. My editor asked me what had made it a bad day. I honestly don't recall why that day had been bad. Maybe it was the cold weather that seeped into our bones. Maybe it was problems with the post office. Maybe we were given some frustrating information from the school and felt helpless. Maybe it was all of the above!

5. I cringe a tiny bit at how sappily I wrote at times.

6. Proverbs 25:25

7. Isaiah 40: 28-31

8. My editor wrote, "Why would the doctor say that? This is unclear to me." Me too. It seemed very out of place. I tried to comment and Erin gave me the look that said, "Amy, please don't. This is very stressful and we do not have to engage nonsense."

9. James 3:1

10. C. S. Lewis, *The Screwtape Letters* (New York: Collier, 1982), 155.

11. Luke 9:62

12. I know it would make more sense if she called and asked if she could bring me. The student, however, was the take-charge kind of person. She didn't ask him, she told him I would attend. ☺

13. This was the first time the government shuffled "days off." It has now, as of the printing of this book, become so common that my notion has shifted with China's, showing that notions can flex. ☺

14. Romans 12:15

15. Luke 11:11–13

16. Psalm 100: 4–5

17. This quiz may not reflect current norms or values as culture is somewhat fluid, but overall it gives you a sense of the culture.

18. John 3:16

19. Richard J. Foster, *Celebration of Discipline: The Path to Spiritual Growth* (San Francisco: Harper & Row, 1988), 101.

20. Ken Gire, *Intense Moments with the Savior: Learning to Feel* (Grand Rapids, MI: Zondervan, 1994), 113.

21. C. S. Lewis, *Mere Christianity* (New York: HarperCollins, 2015), 154.

22. Psalm 40:11 TBL

23. Hee-hee, to get students to class on time each class I began with a vocabulary quiz, and if they were not there on time, they earned a zero.

24. It has been years since I taught this course. I no longer have a copy of the article and couldn't find it on the Internet.

25. Psalm 15:1, NIV, http://bibles.org/NIV/Ps/15. Accessed March 11, 2017.

26. Jane Kathryn Vella, Learning to Listen, Learning to Teach: The Power of Dialogue in Educating Adults (San Francisco: Jossey-Bass, 1994), 176.

27. I have since changed my theology a bit on this statement. We can be given more than we can handle; however, what is promised in the Bible is that God will be with us and others will help us bear it.

28. Bruce Wilkinson, *Secrets of the Vine: Breaking through to Abundance* (Sisters, OR: Multnomah, 2001), 96.

29. I have searched the Internet for the additional publication data, but failed. If you know the author or the publication please contact me allowing me to properly cite this source.

30. C. S. Lewis, *The Pilgrim's Regress; an Allegorical Apology for Christianity, Reason, and Romanticism* (Grand Rapids: Eerdmans, 1959), 198.

31. Amy Young, "5 Tips for Newsletter Writing {The Grove: Author Interview}," *Velvet Ashes.* http://velvetashes.com/5-tips-for-newsletter-writing-the-grove-author-interview/. Accessed March 17, 2017.

37741034R00152

Made in the USA
Columbia, SC
01 December 2018